My
STORIES
and
REFLECTIONS
of
COMMUNISM
and
CAPITALISM

ION GRUMEZA

Conclusive Books

Cover conceived by Ion Grumeza; created by Sarah Smith

Interior by Rachel L. Hall, Writely Divided Editing & More

Photos of Ion Grumeza in "A Note to the Reader" and on the back cover, while lecturing, are from the author's personal collection.

ISBN: 979-8-9863323-6-9 (Paperback)

ISBN: 979-8-9863323-7-6 (eBook)

My Stories and Reflections of Communism and Capitalism / Ion Grumeza — 1st ed., 1st printing.

CONTENTS

PART II

PART III

A NOTE TO THE READER

D EAR READER,

I was born in Romania. I wrote my first short story in 1967 based on dialogues and stories I'd overheard and amusing happenings I'd witnessed while commuting to work by train. Another source of inspiration for future stories came from retired people who lived during the Romanian monarchic reign before 1948 and afterward under the Communist regime. They rested on the benches in Cismigiu, the central park in Bucharest, where I often took my three-year-old son to play. I listened intently as the surprisingly genuine and humorous old-timers reminisced about the old and new social orders.

A steady source of inspiration was my own experience of living in a Communist society for 29 years. I observed people trying to cheat the tyrannical system or coping with it with defiant laughter.

> *A Romanian joke states that in Capitalism, there is the exploitation of men by other men, but thank God, in Communism, it is exactly the opposite.*

My stories are not intended to be political but to open windows for readers to view the realities for starving Romanians living under a dictatorial Communist regime. Their leaders were determined to apply Marxist-Leninist ideology to create a new Romanian Socialist society.

Most of my stories are satirical, but they reflect a grim reality. Life in Romania consisted of ever-increasing inflation, standing in line for hours in front of empty food stores, and constantly facing shortages of all vital necessities. People had no hope. I was one of them.

I wrote some 200 short stories. My stories were rejected by the state publishing houses. I was an outcast for not being a member of the Communist Party. Therefore, I defected to Austria, where I finished writing Part I of this book, "From the East... Communism."

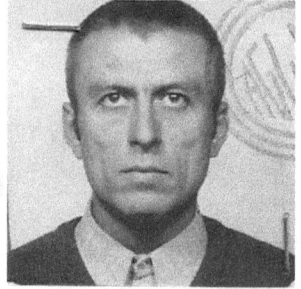

Ion Grumeza, 1972

After Part I, I include a brief collection titled "Essays and Reflections" about how historically and always surprisingly, the Communist and Capitalist empires were created under opposite social systems which affected cultural, economic, military, and political life. Under these very different systems, the circumstances which took place affected the lives of billions of people. It is impossible for me as a writer, who experienced both for decades, not to find humor in them and write about many of those events under those systems.

Even though the Communist empire fell in 1991, liberal, democratic and socialist parties of many countries wished to continue following Marxist-Leninist slogans of international brotherhood without capitalistic "exploitation." They intend to create a newly non-competitive socialist society based on principles diversity, equity and inclusion. But for many years, countries like England, France and Germany have tried unsuccessfully to make this type of utopian society work.

After I was approved by the American Consulate in Vienna in 1973, I left the refugee camp in Austria, legally immigrated to the United States and became a naturalized American citizen in 1978. Life took me to many surprising destinations. I again began writing short stories about comical situations that happened to me and about others' amusing experiences. These stories are found in Part III, "From the West… Capitalism." A topic I frequently address is how some

Ion Grumeza, 1977

self-entitled "smart" refugees try to achieve the American dream by shortcutting the time and effort necessary to achieve it.

In many short stories, it is essentially me who is the main hero. I know firsthand what happened and why the situations are comical because I lived them. I never intend for any of my stories to slander others or to be critical. I have always written as an observer who wants to expose what is absurd and laughable. Yet, humor or satire pushed too far can be harmful and litigious.

The capitalistic system is "Not perfect, but the best there is," as I narrate in one story, and I conclude, "God Bless America!"

Dear reader, I have lived in two worlds, both with antagonistic regimes. My experiences have provided me with many anecdotes, to which I add comical twists. I hope that you find valuable information and hidden messages to appreciate in these stories, and I hope you find them enjoyable and memorable.

Thank you, observant reader,

Ion Grumeza Ph.D.
Metaphysical Sciences

My
STORIES
and
REFLECTIONS
of
COMMUNISM
and
CAPITALISM

PART I

FROM THE EAST...
COMMUNISM

1. EVOCATION

The college gym was packed with Social Studies students. They were waiting to listen to a veteran who had been a member of the illegal Romanian Communist Party since 1936. He was going to lecture about how the communists fought to achieve what has become a happy reality for the Romanian people. The improvised podium was decorated with artificial flowers, a Romanian tricolor flag with the socialist emblem in the middle, the red Communist flag with the yellow sickle and hammer in the middle, crowned with laurel and "PCR" (for the Romanian Communist Party) on the top, and between the two flags was a large white banner with red letters exclaiming, "LONG LIVE THE WISEST LEADER OF THE ROMANIAN COMMUNIST PARTY, NICOLAE CEAUSESCU!"

With polite applause from the young audience, a small old man, his feet shuffling, went to the podium. He looked uncomfortable in his blue tie and blue suit given by the Communist Party, which was too large and heavy for him. He stepped up on a high platform to be seen above the microphone. In a sure but weak voice, without any introduction, he began relating his heroic memoir, which he repeated many times in front of the public.

"Dear young comrades, on that big day for me in 1936, a Communist came to our loading dock and said, 'Let's get rid of the tyrannical monarchy and the exploiting bourgeoisie and claim democracy.' In the beginning, I did not know what he meant, but after our Communist Party grabbed their rifles, destroyed the heinous German Army and welcomed the liberating Soviet divisions, we saw that happiness comes from Moscow. We kicked the traitorous young king out of Romania and installed the democratic regime of our trusted Romanian Communist Party under the leadership of comrade Ceausescu. He was a personal friend of mine since we fought together. At that time, I walked barefoot and didn't go to school because I didn't have any money. That was the situation before our beloved Communist Party took over, and now you benefit greatly from free schooling."

The students listened in silence, imagining how the small man and the little Ceausescu, along with other members of the Communist Party, had overthrown the monarchy, defeated the German army of 13,600,000 soldiers, and they did all this with only 740 Communist members, half of them being informers of the old police regime.

━★━

2. AN ORAL HISTORY

While commuting by train, I met many people and heard their stories. I distinctly remember an old man and his story. I leave it for the reader to decide why.

He was small, hunchbacked, and hardly able to walk even with the aid of his cane. His hair was uncombed and he was unshaven. He was dressed in a tattered coat and pants—in two words, he was pitiful looking. He carried a saddle bag made of burlap with nothing in it. He looked at me with his penetrating black eyes, and I looked at him with compassion. I asked how far he would travel.

The old man struck a match, lit a cigarette, spit on the match flame and inhaled deeply, releasing a long trail of smoke upwards towards the ceiling. His eyes followed it. Then, crossing his legs with an elegant move, despite his broken boots, he lowered his eyes on me. I repeated the question, and he answered, "I will go very far." He then elegantly tapped the cigarette ashes into his small, shaking palm.

"Will you see your children and grandchildren?" I asked.

"I do not have either because I was never married."

He released another comet of smoke and continued, "See, my young man, before you were born, I was once young. It was during the turbulent times of the radical transformations. Many revolutionary events took place, and I helped create heroic social change in Romania when we moved from capitalism to socialism. You younger generations know nothing about that except the lies they teach you in school or Ceausescu's version from his public speeches."

I began to worry and looked at the other passengers in my compartment: two were sleeping, a mother was feeding a child and was worried about the falling crumbs, one looked out the window, and two older women whispered to each other. None were paying attention to the cocky old man. I was interested to hear more about how much he had suffered and to learn why his experiences left him looking so poor and sick. I encouraged him to keep speaking. "Go ahead, grandpa!"

His smile revealed he had no teeth. He shook the ashes from the cigarette and gave me a patronizing look. "Do not judge me by how I look today. At one time, people fainted or had a heart attack when they saw me. Yes, sirree! I was small, but I had the power of life and death in my hands."

"Really?! How?"

"I'll tell you how: I was needed. After I was a corporal fighting with the Germans at Stalingrad, and after I was taken prisoner by the Soviets and sent to the gulag with many other prisoners to die there, I chose to volunteer to fight against the Germans. I was recruited in the newly formed Romanian anti-Fascist Division 'Tudor Vladimirescu' and became a member of the Communist Party in Russia in 1943.

"After I entered Bucharest on a Red Army tank at the end of August 1944, I was kept in the NKVD, Soviet Security Police, with the rank of major to help the Russian occupation of Romania. At that time, I could arrest Ceausescu and anyone in Romania, for I was backed up by many Red divisions stationed to assist with revolutionary changes, like forced collectivization."

The train whistled loudly, covering his next words. The old

man lit another cigarette.

"You smoke too much!" I said.

He nodded his head and explained that his bad habit started with smoking makhorka, the cheap, toxic Russian tobacco. It ruined his teeth but kept him awake many nights when he had to interrogate the "enemies of the people." One night in October 1951, 80 former highly-ranked politicians of the old bourgeoisie regime were arrested, and thousands of other suspected anti-communists were incarcerated in the cells of Securitate, the Romanian version of the NKVD. "I could order the arrest, interrogation, imprisonment or deportation of anyone in Romania, even of Ceausescu, who was the butler, the chief servant and a gofer for the Communist leader Gheorghiu-Dej."

After meditating for a few seconds, he continued. "You'd be amazed how the cold steel of a pistol barrel pushed into the back of a neck can make anyone sign any statement of self-incrimination. Or, in the case of the much-acclaimed success of collectivization, it forced the *chiaburi*, the wealthy farmers, to surrender their vast lands to the state *kolkhoz*, Soviet-type collective farming. I was small, including my rank, but I caused an immense fear with my Communist activity."

Tickled by fond memories, the feeble old man continued: "I could leave my military hat with the Securitate insignia on it in the middle of an intersection, and three days later, nobody dared to touch it. Was Napoleon, Hitler or Stalin able to do that?"

Elegantly puffing another cigarette but still looking like a beggar, he concluded: "In my young years, I did not have time to have a family. I was too busy working to expel the king and destroy the monarchy in Romania, nationalize all the institutions, make the collective and…"

I interrupted. "You did all those things?"

After spitting on a smoking cigarette butt he dropped on the floor, he proudly confessed: "You should have seen me taking diamonds and gold coins from the rich and famous, even gold teeth from their mouths, all to enrich the Communist regime… Each time I showed my Securitate ID, I could have them all licking my high boots!"

"Wait! Then what's happened to you?"

The triumphant but pitiful-looking old man explained, "Now, I am retired as a shoemaker, my original job before the war. It is how I met Ceausescu. He was an apprentice in the same repair shop in Bucharest. That is why I always called him by his first name, Nicolae, as his parents baptized him. That is why I look like this now—I was never intimidated by the fifty political titles he assumed. His semi-illiterate wife Elena, who flunked the fourth or sixth grade, was a girl who liked the company of German soldiers, and she is now a doctor docent, PhD in chemistry, an academician, and the Deputy Prime Minister of Romania."

He spit in disgust. "After they took power in Romania, they demoted me in private, stripped me of my rank of colonel, and accused me of pocketing diamonds and gold from my victims. They made me responsible for the mistakes of the Romanian Communist Party—after all I had done to help it!"

—★—

3. A LIVE RADIO REPORT

"How about you, comrade? What can you tell us about…" The worker being interviewed interrupted the reporter's question. He complained that in the factory washing room, there was no running water for the long line of faucets and no running water for the bathrooms. His co-workers elbowed each other, laughing with their mouths closed, while the complainer continued undisturbed. "Each time I stand up in a meeting and ask for repairs, everyone makes fun of me, and those at the podium ask me to sit down with the bathroom problem since there are more serious topics to consider."

"I am sure your problem will be resolved soon," concluded the reporter, but the worker had not finished.

"I go home dirty and fight with my wife for water because, to save water, they turn it off in our building."

This time, the other workers added their vocal assent. "They also turn off our electricity except for one hour in the morning and two hours in the evening." Others hollered, "Same with the heat in our apartments!" More shouted, "All for us to pay the billions of dollars of debt Ceausescu borrowed from Western banks for industrialization—like for our new factory!"

The reporter had already turned off the microphone and was fishing to find the right worker who would say something flattering about the great Communist Party anniversary event. He moved the big microphone under the nose of a worker who seemed to be a good bet: "How about you, comrade? What do you think about our great Party event…"

But he was cut off as the man being interviewed interjected, "Our main problem is the lack of food in any state market and in the grocery stores where our loved ones stand in line for hours for food that often never arrives. In the winter cold and rain, they get sick, standing, waiting. We are hungry all the time, left holding worthless ration coupons that expire, and all the while inflation keeps increasing."

A chorus of workers agreed and demanded to know where their promised factory lunch cafeteria was. It still remained a distant promise.

The reporter tried to redirect the interview in a different direction. He asked if the workers were informed about the Great Anniversary Event of the Romanian Communist Party scheduled to happen soon, and he finally received a favorable answer from one.

"Yes, we had to buy brochures about the glorious event."

The reporter insisted, "Did you read them?"

The unwanted answer: "Read them? After working 12 hours overtime to fulfill production quotas, we go home and collapse. I gave them to my high schooler, who had to buy the same brochures. Nobody reads them."

The reporter did not listen because a comrade dressed in a blue suit and blue tie stepped in front of the workers and asked, "Are you the comrade reporter from the radio?" He received an affirmative answer and apologized for being late. After coughing into his fist to clear his throat, he began reading from a piece of paper: "Regarding the Great Anniversary Event of the Romanian Communist Party that will happen soon, our factory workers are unanimously committed to exceeding the assigned production by 20 percent and will succeed in saving 16 million leis (Romanian money). The Five Year Plan for industry production will be achieved in only four years and three months or less. Thus, our workers happily join in the general enthusiasm that vibrates in our hearts, along with the entire Romanian people, to prove our desire to honor the wisdom of our Communist Party under the superior guidance provided personally by our most esteemed comrade, Nicolae Ceausescu. Therefore, we are looking forward to the glorious and Great Anniversary Event of the Romanian Communist Party, which will boast of even more achievements..."

The happy reporter interrupted the enthusiasm of the well-dressed man: "One moment, please. Would you tell our listeners your name?"

"David Ionescu!"

"Do you work in this factory?"

"I sure do. I am the Secretary of the factory based on the Romanian Communist Party and..."

"So, dear listeners, you just heard a factory man relaying the justifiable pride and attachment felt by the workers of this new socialist factory to the efforts of our forward-thinking leader, Nicolae Ceausescu. Please, continue your well-founded announcement!" said the reporter as David Ionescu looked at his notes.

The workers, stunned, listened with open mouths as the factory secretary further elaborated on points of support for the Communist organization.

— ★ —

4. THE OFFICIAL TELEGRAM

An agitated, heavily perspiring CEO spoke at the factory's board of directors meeting.

"Comrades, I assure you that I understand the main problem about our workers being late or leaving early because they have to wait in long lines for hours to use their ration cards to buy food for their families. I understand most of them commute long distances to come to work, and the trains are late, so they are late as well. The fact that our workers still do not have apartments for their families means they do not have access to soup kitchens for lunch or showers at the end of their shifts. I understand our specialized technicians do not know how to use the newly imported machines because nobody has trained them. And nobody knows how to repair the old, broken machines. The fact that high school students are not transported here one day a week to learn the trade is because there are no buses to bring them. And after three years of vocational school, new young workers haven't had experienced teachers train them, or they've never seen our magnificent new factory, and now they do janitorial jobs."

The director stopped to wipe his perspiration, drink a glass of water, and then continued. He pointed to a large, disarming production graphic displayed on the conference room wall. He was obviously aggravated.

Loudly emphasizing each syllable to clarify his point, he bellowed, "The main problem is that we did-not-ac-com-plish-our-pro-duc-tion-pledge-for-this semester! We did not honor our clients with their expected products because we did not bring the needed supplies on time. We have two large sections of the factory that are still empty. And worst of all, we do not even have a production plan for this year, never mind that it is already June."

The boss, a former mechanical engineer and an old member of the Communist Party, walked the room. Participants shifted in their seats uncomfortably, some gulping glasses of water, some thumbing through their production files pretending to check the numbers, and almost all lit cigarettes to calm their nerves.

Their proposals, solutions, and corrections, which had worked for years in other factories (without producing any improvements), were worthless at this time when they were faced with frightening low production reports. No proposed solution to rectify so many problems seemed it would work until the secretary of the local Communist Party, a former agitator and veteran member who could hardly sign his own name, stood up and firmly stated:

"Comrades, as our wise leader Comrade Nicolae Ceausescu once said, 'Only those who do not work do not make mistakes.' In that spirit of admission, we do not have to wonder why we made so many mistakes—it's because we worked too hard. So, no wonder we failed in so many ways.

"What we need to do is what all others in our situation do: send a telegram to our beloved visionary Nicolae Ceausescu, true chairman of the Supreme Council for Economic and Social Development, president of the National Council of Working People and chairman of the Socialist Democracy and Unity Front. In the telegram, we will express our commitment and devotion to continuing our fight, inspired by our glorious Communist Party, to eliminate mistakes and make sure that in the future, we will increase production and trust in our factory."

Everybody in the conference room was relieved and applauded loudly. Later, the telegram was sent personally to Nicolae Ceausescu.

According to a popular anecdote at the time, after Nicolae Ceausescu became the Communist leader of Romania, he ordered the reforestation of previously existing forests that had been harvested during the Soviet occupation. The massive tree planting project was entrusted to army conscripts and high school and college students as volunteer work each Sunday. After one year, local Communist leaders reported double the number of trees planted. At the county, regional, and then state levels, they doubled the surface area planted. In the end, the reported surface area planted, before submitting the results to Ceausescu, had tripled. The Communist leaders in charge of the reforestation were decorated and rewarded at all levels. Later on, it was calculated that entire surface of Romania and the Black Sea had been reforested.

In reality, Ceausescu's acceptance of this "multiplication policy" and the communist chieftains' inflated reports of local production efforts and food abundance did immense damage. The local communist chieftains flattered the leadership of the Romanian Communist Party for its role in creating fictional food excess. This caused Ceausescu to export the reported excess, leaving an insufficient food supply for the hungry Romanians. The same thing happened with the "five-year plans" for the rest of the economy: these, too, were only on paper and produced a shortage of vital goods for the suffering people. Showing how much the workers believed in and loved Ceausescu and his government was great for Communist propaganda but not for the hungry people.

5. EXISTENTIALISM

The redactor-in-chief threw a bulky package of typed papers in front of a young writer and asked angrily: "What is this, comrade?!"

"This is the package with my short stories I brought to you," answered the writer, who felt a bit scared after hearing the chief's tone.

"Short stories, yes—I am not an idiot. But I am asking you, what *kind* of short stories?"

"I believe they are the humorous kind…"

"You may believe you wrote humor, but publishing these would be a self-inflicted crime for you and me. Take them back! Throw these in the fire, in the garbage, and do anything you like to destroy them, but do not leave this incriminating evidence with me. I have a family to feed, unlike you, a freeloader who *believes* he writes funny stuff! Got it?"

He threw the package at me, and I caught it mid-air. Confused, I asked, "Did something happen?"

"Nothing has happened yet because I have been a member of the Romanian Communist Party since 1947, and lucky for you, I am the only one who read your manuscript. Now, listen to my advice. I have a son your age, and I can see you are young and talented, so write something different, my son."

"What do you mean, *different*? Like what?"

"Like what?! Like what all these mother-faker literary mercenaries publish today: write about class struggle and show the Communists as victorious; how the young generation like yours continues the fight of our beloved Communist Party to build a new and happy socialist society; how if we all follow the directives of our genius leader, comrade Nicolae Ceausescu, we will overcome the old, bourgeois reactionary mentality; how to work better and faster to achieve more production for the good of our working people..."

"I am a humorist. I write satirical stories about the same things, but I'm inclined to show how things can go wrong following Communist Party instructions..."

"To hell with your inclinations. Write humorous personal stories—they won't send us both to the re-education prison. I see how smart you are. I recommend you explore psychoanalysis, investigate funny types of personalities, and explain how wrong the old interpretation of existentialism is. Nobody knows anything about that, but it sounds like a smart, apolitical subject.

The writer was unable to reply with anything more than a quizzical "What?!"

"I see your puzzlement, so here is an example. I just published an author of a successful book on the subject. In the book, a man loves his fiancée, but he does not love *her*. Ok, so far? But his consciousness will not let him lose her, so he marries her to learn how to love her simply because she is a valuable member of our socialist society. Each day, he falls more and more in love with her. I am asking you, my young and confused but talented writer, how hard could it be for you to write about existentialism in our socialist society that fights under the wise direction of our devoted Communist Party to create a new type of perfect citizen?!"

"I understand, but..."

"No 'but!' Who do you think you are? I've talked enough.

Come back to me with a manuscript package in line with the Romanian Communist Party line under the best leadership of our brilliant leader Nicolae Ceausescu and mention his name so you can make a good living as a writer. Try to improve your mind and talent, or go easy on yourself and give up writing and do something else. Like, try becoming a good electrician, which is useful for our advanced socialist society. I am so glad to help. Good luck to you!"

The young and talented writer left the publishing house with his worthless manuscript under his arm. He gazed at the falling leaves. Winter was on its way.

6. ANOTHER FAILED LECTURE

The Secretary of the Romanian Communist Party in charge of educating the young generation in Bucharest had his elbows propped on the desk and his head in his palms. He kept looking at the young man with a bushy beard and long hair down to his shoulders sitting in front of him. After studying him for a while, the secretary took a deep breath and said in a low voice:

"Young man, I keep looking at you to figure out why you refuse to be part of our revolutionary Communist movement regarding the discipline of our young generation. Do you think you are different? Maybe better? You think you have something special to offer and must fit a special look?"

The young man gave a short answer: "I do not think so."

"Then what is going on with your shaggy, decadent look? It makes you an eyesore in our socialist society."

"Nothing is going on. I like the way I look. Girls like it."

"You think the fathers of the girls like you?"

"Maybe not."

"Then why don't you shave that ridiculous beard and cut your hair short so that you don't look like a terrorist?"

"I will, but I need to grow it a little more first to take a picture for my future grandchildren," joked the young man.

"To see you looking like a long-haired monkey? Like a wild, uneducated, sleazy youngster? Or are you trying to look like a woman with long hair? Are you an abnormal woman or a degenerate man?" The angry secretary hit the desk with his fist. "Huh? Answer me."

"What do you think?"

"I think you must shave that horrible beard and trim your hair like mine. See?" The party chief turned to show the back of his head and neck, exposing his perfect trim. "I do not want to look like a parasite on our advanced socialist society, like a beggar, like a loser and someone looking for a handout. No sir! The young generation should not blindly imitate the decadent fashion of the confused young Americans who burn their own national flags because they have beards and long hair and do not know what to do with themselves.

"Look at me." The still young-looking Communist secretary was dressed in a blue suit and tie to match, freshly shaved with an expensive haircut. He wanted to prove his point. He began to walk back and forth in front of the youngster, who was bored to death. "What would you say if you saw me looking like you—as if I'd just escaped from a mental institution, totally insane and dangerous? Huh?"

"I would say that you look just like those two with bushy beards and long hair from the framed pictures hanging on the wall behind your desk—Marx and Engels, the greatest Communist teachers of mankind!" laughed the young man.

But the last laugh was on him. Later, when the young man came out of the Communist Party building, his beard was shaved, and his hair was cut to the skin.

━ ☆ ━

7. MISTER STELIAN

The political prisoners—over twenty of them crowded in a cell with eight metal beds with metallic grids instead of mattresses and shoes instead of pillows—learned the name of a small, gray-haired older newcomer. Dressed in overalls, he had rolled-up sleeves and wore the dirty, muddy boots of a worker. He entered the cell carrying a large wooden toolbox.

Curiously observing the "enemies of the people" before him, as all arrested anti-communists were officially named, he did not utter a word and sat down on his toolbox facing the door. Paying no attention to what the other occupants, all dressed in long striped shirts and pants, did or talked about, his eyes were on the door. He waited unmoving, elbows on his knees, face in his palms.

There were no windows in the overcrowded room, a single electric bulb hung by a wire from the ceiling, and nobody had a watch. It was late afternoon because the "prisoners of conscience," as the inmates liked to be called, were waiting for what was called dinner.

When the old man fell asleep on his toolbox, the group's unofficial spokesman approached him and politely asked if he wanted to lay on a bed.

The man jumped to his feet with an agility none could have guessed he had. He shouted, "I am not staying here, and I do not need a bed. I believe that my son already talked to the warden, and at any moment, I will be out of here. Is that clear?"

The benevolent man who'd offered the bed mumbled, "As

you wish, Pappy," and returned to the others.

The old man sat again on his box, in the same position, eyes on the door.

Nobody bothered him anymore until the door opened with a long screech. A prison guard held a metal bucket full of watery polenta with a large wooden spoon in it.

The old man jumped up again and almost shouted, "Tell the warden I am ready to leave at any moment. Did you hear me? Huh?"

The guard pushed him aside, saying, "Take it easy, old-timer!" and locked the heavy door from outside.

The cellmates divided the diluted polenta among themselves and began drinking it from their aluminum canteens. There was an extra portion left in the bucket. The compassionate fellow offered the anxious elderly man a canteen. "Why not eat something until the warden comes to get you?"

The rest of the men burst into friendly laughter, knowing too well the impossibility.

The man ignored their laughter and responded, "See, I do not want to ruin my appetite. My wife has cooked baby back ribs with mashed potatoes and pickles for supper. So, you understand…"

A noisy chorus of *Ha, ha, has* of belly laughter covered his last words. One asked, "Pappy, aren't you afraid that your meal will be cold?" Additional waves of laughter followed.

The old man's reply surprised them: "I do not worry about my meal. I worry about the floral designs I left unfinished…"

Almost all uttered at once, "What is that?!"

The elderly man answered, "*That* is about my floral designs, which, without me, nobody can master. I am Mr. Stelian, the best landscaper in the entire city…"

Again, he was interrupted: "Well, that changes *everything* if you are *Mr. Stelian*," the voice dripped with irony.

Undisturbed, Mr. Stelian continued. "See, for 45 years, my helpers have not been able to draw a proper floral line without me, and my new assignment needs me badly."

The men played along. Faking concern, they asked, "So, what can they do without you? We cannot imagine."

Mr. Stelian agreed: "That is my point; you understand it. They cannot lay out a simple star, never mind the complicated lyre I left unfinished…"

Ignoring the old gardener's concerns, the men urged him to eat the polenta. "Of course you are right, but in the meantime, eat something because the night is long," smiled an older cellmate.

Mr. Stelian remained convinced he would dine at home and argued, "If I eat this, my wife will be very upset. Is that clear?"

One prisoner understood and asked to eat the disputed polenta portion, to which Mr. Stelian replied, "Please, I insist— eat it since I am saving my appetite for my home-cooked dinner."

The rest of the evening belonged to Mr. Stelian. Still sitting half-turned on the toolbox to keep an eye on the door since he expected he'd be allowed to leave at any moment, he described his passion for designing gardens and parks. He'd won many awards and, as he explained, had also won the latest competition to landscape the garden in front of the opera house, where he worked before his arrest. Obviously, it was an identity mistake. He had never been involved in politics, and after all, it was the Communist leaders of the city who'd awarded him the complicated garden project.

When the electric bulb turned off, indicating bedtime, Mr.

Stelian refused to sleep on the beds pushed together by the cell occupants, explaining that he must be ready to leave at any moment without waking up the rest. But the common advice was, "Mr. Stelian, rest your body; otherwise, you'll be too tired to finish your lyre tomorrow."

"I'll sleep at home: don't worry, because I need to finish the floral lyre I designed for so many years in front of the Opera House."

He continued saying something that the cellmates could hardly believe. They could not sleep after what Mr. Stelian disclosed: "Can you imagine the Communist Party leaders asking me to design a floral hammer crossing the sickle, their bloody symbol? I refused to do it because I knew better, and everybody I told agreed. In past years, I always designed the opera house's traditional large, beautiful lyre—the symbol of the arts and music.

"Well, today, a few fat Communist chiefs in charge of my project got out of their limousine and came to see how I was doing. They froze when they saw the beautiful unfinished lyre and avoided talking to me. Half an hour later, a black windowless van brought me here—for no reason! I believe they arrested the wrong person, so I expect to be freed as soon as possible to finish my lyre!"

The entire cell went silent except for a few muffled sobs.

***

In the morning, the electric bulb was lit. Everybody woke up to go to the bathroom in a large wooden bucket, except Mr. Stelian, who was still curled up on his toolbox, sound asleep. When he stirred because of the noise, someone asked him, "Still here?"

He answered, "Still here, and I am supposed to be at the opera house before the sun is high or the nursery flowers will dry out from the sun."

The door opened with its characteristic long screech, and a new guard held out the bucket filled with the same watery, colorless polenta. This time, Mr. Stelian did not say a word to the guard, who asked two prisoners to carry out and empty the large latrine bucket.

"Mr. Stelian, would you like a portion of our polenta? It will not hurt you."

His almost whispered answer was, "I think it is a good idea because if I go to my lyre, I may not have time to eat breakfast." He drank the polenta without breathing. At lunch, he ate a piece of black bread. At dinner, he ate polenta again.

When the electric bulb went out, he was asked to come and sleep on the collective bed again. A joker added, "So in the morning, you are strong enough to finish your lyre…"

A few choked-back laughs did not deter the old gardener from agreeing. "You are right, but I will sleep dressed and ready to go, just in case…"

His words attracted a welcome consolation: "That is the spirit, in case you must finish your lyre."

Mr. Stelian continued unabated: "I hope to be there before sunset to plant the flowers because…"

He was interrupted. "In the meantime, do what we do, and you will do well. Good night, old-timer. God bless you!"

The exhausted Mr. Stelian immediately fell asleep and dreamt what had become a floral fantasy.

8. A TRUE COMMUNIST

Once Romania became a People's Republic in 1948, the massive old prison founded by Empress Maria Theresa in Aiud in the middle of Transylvania became a death prison for former anti-Communists—officers, war criminals, intellectuals, priests, well-to-do landlords, and most of all, pro-German politicians. In 1950, the prison, which had been designed to hold 800 inmates in 312 cells, held some 4,000 "enemies of the people." They had been sentenced by Communist courts and were subject to extremely punishing treatments, mental and physical torture and a food ration of not more than 700 calories a day. Eight or more prisoners lived in cells measuring only 2x4 meters or 6x12 feet.

This story is not about the inhumane conditions meant to degrade and eventually kill former members of the cream of Romanian society before the Red armies occupied Romania, but about one young man.

One day, he was pushed into one of the overcrowded cells at the old prison. He did not introduce himself. Through his first four days, he didn't say a word. His cellmates respected his silence. Some believed he was an informer placed there to spy on them.

Since he was the youngest, he slept on the floor next to the door. If it needed to be opened, he was forced to stand up. He always seemed sleepy, and he tried not to make anyone uncomfortable. The watery polenta served from a communal bowl was meant to be divided among all the cellmates. Often, the newcomer did not receive any, yet he never protested. As he was still strong, he went to sleep every night hungry. His eyes were closed most of the time, and he seemed to reflect an angelic aura of goodness. His brown beard grew quickly, and so did his hair. As he lost weight, he looked almost saintly. Sometimes, he smiled during a very funny situation or a long, comical dialog.

A few weeks had passed when he was removed from the cell. It was clear to his cellmates that he must be a spy, placed in their miserable, small enclosure to report on what they said and did. When he returned the next day, he collapsed. They put him in one of the two bunk beds, gave him water and food and placed a small wet cloth on his feverish forehead. He healed quickly, thanks to his youth. He thanked everyone and again resumed his same silent attitude.

This time, a former police officer asked him what was going on outside the cell.

He answered, "Nothing you do not know; I was just told five more years were added to my sentence."

The rest of the men raised their eyebrows. One remarked that was unusual.

When he was asked the reason, he explained, "As a former member of the Romanian Communist Party, I betrayed its cause. I tried to organize a reactionary group of friends to enlist in my party."

Total silence dominated the cell, where the men were squeezed together like sardines in a can. After a while, one asked, "You seem to be such a decent man… What did you do before being arrested?"

The man smiled and explained, "I was a student in law school."

Silence fell over the cell, eventually interrupted by another question. "Were you forced to become a member of the Communist Party?"

His answer confused everyone: "Not at all. I believed it was my duty to become a communist!"

Almost all declared together in one voice, "You believed *what?!*"

After the shock had settled, a former mayor shook his head and declared, "This is the difference between you, the young generation willing to betray our country and its people, and us, the older generation who loved both. We would rather suffer here than ever join Stalin's party!"

It seemed as if everyone approved of the former mayor's statement.

The young man, though, was not impressed by their patriotism and stated: "You older generation should be the first to become communist and fill all the leading positions in the Republic of Romania, now held by Gypsies, foreign criminals who change their names to Romanian names, and charlatans who plunder the wealth of the country."

The mayor spoke again. "We are here suffering until the Anglo-Americans can liberate Romania. Then, we will be ready to fill those leading governmental positions. Mark my words!"

All approved.

However, the law student took a deep breath and said sadly, "Gentlemen, if Anglo-American troops were coming to free us by wheelbarrow transportation, they would have been here a long time ago. Yet, at the Yalta Conference, eight months before the war was over, Romania was already occupied by the Red Army— and it still is. The only way to defeat Stalin's communists is for true Romanians to turn communist and block their access to the leadership positions of the country. But true patriots like you choose to die in these cells in Aiud, the prison of all prisons in Romania. I tried to outsmart the foreigners whose pictures line the walls, but as the Romanian proverb says, 'With one flower, springtime is yet too far.'"

For the rest of the day, the cell was silent.

9. THE LAW IS THE LAW

One of the most crowded places in Bucharest is the largest train station in Romania, Gara de Nord, the North Railway Station. It's like a smaller version of Paris' main station. Its many tracks and platforms are filled with people from all over the country. Most are confused by the garbled announcements from the two loudspeakers marking the arrival and departure of each train. Many coming off the trains wander about, searching for the exit to the street where they'll next take an electric cable tramway to their final destination. Others have to cross the tracks to change trains. Some fall between the tracks under the weight of their luggage. Mainly, these are visitors carrying food to their starving relatives and friends in the capital of Romania.

Everybody shouts at each other to be heard over the loud-speakers, which are so distorted that nobody can understand the announcements. In the meantime, trains come and go, signaling their presence with scary, piercing whistles and puffs of hot steam, which help accelerate the trains' departures or stop those incoming. Travelers, scared nearly to death and wet from the steam, come running in and out from the engines' prolific steam clouds. Some people run desperately to catch their departing trains, and some, utterly confused, just hurry about, trying to find the correct platforms.

Children cry aloud, peasant women in beautiful national folk costumes cry silently, and others cry, too. Those who come to greet arriving guests scream out when others get off the train. With buttons missing on their coats from their struggles, they fight to advance through the busy platforms between trains, eager to find loved ones waiting for them, holding flowers and wiping tears on their handkerchiefs. Finally, all join in screams of happiness, like good sentimental Romanians, unaware (or not caring) that their group hugs and handshakes block the traffic of those in such a hurry to advance on the platforms. Trying to find shortcuts, they stumble over benches where some lie sleeping, and believing they've been robbed, the wakened sleepers scream for help.

Among the hubbub of disoriented country folks, the station employees are the only ones who are calm and sure of themselves. Distinctively dressed in blue uniforms, white shirts, red ties and a large military-like blue hat emblazoned with the letters CFR (*Caile Ferate Romane*, the Romanian State Railway), they make up the second uniformed civilian army of the Socialist Republic of Romania. From the most minor of ranks up to the railroad station chief, they are the final authority to ensure the normal flow of the trains pulled by monstrous locomotives all over the country, some of which go to Moscow, Vienna, and even Paris.

In Gara de Nord, its uniformed employees have no doubts regarding their superior status, except perhaps at the entrance and exit of this colossal train station. Travelers must respect the strictly separated in and out flow, as with any two-way traffic. Yet, conflicts sometimes arise.

***

One day, a young man hurrying to catch his train entered through the exit gate. A uniformed CFR traffic employee promptly detected him and shouted in a commanding voice: "Hey, hey, hey, hey! You, with the rolled sleeves, eating the loaf of bread, move back and use the legal entranceway!"

The man, undisturbed and undeterred, simply kept walking inside Gara de Nord, so the employee blew his metallic whistle to sound a sharp alert. The trespasser ignored it. The employee ran after him and stopped the undisciplined man who was carrying a large bundle of loaves of bread.

The stubborn bread-consumer shouted, "Take your filthy paws off me, or I'll belt you!"

"Oh, yes? Then you will pay the legal fee for infringing upon the CFR law and illegally gaining access to the train station." The traffic supervisor pulled out a small pad from his pocket.

The man shook his head and said, "I ain't paying any fake fee!" He tried to walk away but was stopped by the employee who demanded 25 leis. "Why should I pay you if I am already inside the train station?" asked the man.

"You pay because you broke the law and used the exit to enter the train station!" the official clarified.

As expected, the usual traffic stopped. The crowd was curious to witness this heated debate. The train station chief joined the crowd for the same reason. As the man who'd made his illegal entrance continued walking, the employee and the crowd followed, the chief along with them. The supervisor tried to negotiate, saying, "Listen, my man, go back, reenter through the entrance gate, and everything will be in order."

In the meantime, a militia sergeant with a pistol holstered on his belt joined the crowd, curious to see what the commotion was. The train station chief stepped forward to back up his subordinate, who had lost control of the rebellious man. The chief ordered: "Young man, you went too far with your defiant attitude, so I have to arrest you for breaking the safety laws of the CFR."

The man put his bundle of bread on his head and made to run away, only stopping when the sergeant reached for his pistol.

Suddenly, the troublemaker dropped to his knees, begged to pay the 25 lei fine and go back and reenter through the correct gate like all the other law-abiding people had done. He began to sob over the heavy bundle he had dropped in front of him.

***

One hour later, the man (who at this point had long since missed his train) sat on the platform bench, tormented, his elbows on his knees, holding his head, looking blankly at the bundle of bread before him.

From his left, the traffic employee explained, "Hey buddy, I am sorry I fined you, but my boss was in the crowd. I had no choice."

The man put his arm up to signal that he was not bothered, and the employee left.

Minutes later, the chief came and sat next to the upset man and said, "I hate to see what happened to you, but you saw the sergeant spying on us. I had to do my duty. If you want, I'll give you your 25 leis back." He held out the money, but the man waved his arm as he had to the traffic employee, indicating he wanted to be left alone.

After a while, the sergeant sat on the same bench, took off his hat, which was full of perspiration, and wiped its interior with a wrinkled handkerchief. He explained he regretted his action: "I must enforce the law, especially in front of the two CFR employees and the entire crowd, to show them that the law is the law."

Like the man, the sergeant put his elbows on his knees and rested his head in his palms.

Both closed their eyes. Neither wanted to see any more details of what was happening all around the noisy central railroad station.

10. PROFICIENCY IN ACTION

In the Socialist era, the Communist Party was fully committed to excellence at all levels. The Romanian people had to be given the best of all things, whether in the workplace or in life. Newspapers—whether printed in Bucharest (reflecting the Central Communist Party's achievements domestically and internationally) or locally (concerning daily activities under the regional party's instructions and supervision)—were essential. In that spirit of competent dedication, newspapers were committed to translating Party tasks to explain how they were achieving a better life for the golden socialist future of the country.

This all happened in a distant city fully transformed from the old, evil, defunct monarchy to the present freedom, equality, and happiness of the working class. A new editor-in-chief had been sent by the party to improve the local newspaper's quality. His arrival was a notable event. The first prime secretary of the regional Communist Party introduced himself as also being the president and councilman of the city. He also introduced all of the local communist leaders, who threw a banquet in the newcomer's honor. The next day, the newspaper reporters announced that comrade Hartea would be taking over the paper.

On the first day, the new chief editor, an old and trusted member of the Communist Party, met with his staff of seven newsmen reporters and their female secretaries. He spoke in high terms about the journalist's duty to report on new socialist achievements and said, "I do not know how you operated previously, but my expectations of you are very high and strict."

From time to time, the red-faced, middle-aged, overweight chief coughed in his fist and pressed his belly where the middle button of his coat was, showing some discomfort. He said, "It is our professional duty, as our beloved Communist Party orders, to renounce the old way of journalism. We must not say, 'Let's see the reverse of the problem.' After all, we do not want to encourage the sabotage of our Socialist society." Thus he concluded the inspirational speech.

Afterward, he announced there would be a test of the quality of their writing in describing the role of the Communist Party in building a new socialist society in Romania. He gave them one week to write a sample article, no longer than two pages. Obviously, this was to check their reporting abilities. All applauded and thanked their new chief for the trust he was investing in them. A few stepped forward, expressing their desire to follow the party line even closer, to the last dot, in their journalistic duties.

Because the chief was away participating in a communist meeting, the next few days at the newspaper office saw no real changes. As usual, the journalists visited each other's desks while holding their small yogurt containers for lunch. They were all trying to save enough money to buy a Trabant, the two-stroke engine East German mini car made of Duroplast (a resin made partially from recycled cotton fibers), which had no fuel pump, headlights, or turn signals. It took ten years on a good salary to save enough and another ten years to wait on a list to become the owner of the most polluting car in the world. But driving a Trabant was proof that one had made it big in socialist Romania. Nobody said a word about the assigned report, but in general, they had a good feeling about the new chief, who obviously had some sort of stomach problem.

When the chief returned, he held another meeting announcing new instructions he had received from the important meetings he'd attended while away from the office. He read his notes aloud, stressing keywords and phrases such as *fact-checking, "no" to ambiguity, duality, formalism, impartiality, lack of vigilance, superficiality, stereotypical, right-wing influence* and most of all, *showing incompetence*. He reminded everyone about the two-page essay due in just a few days.

On deadline day, his secretary presented him with a folder with two-page articles inside, each stapled together with the author's name written on the back of the second page. The chief invited his female secretary to sit next to his desk to read the articles and briefly scribe his comments above each title. He held a paper from the important meeting to help him recall the instructions for making his evaluations. He glanced at it from time to time while she loudly read out each article.

After the first reading ended, the chief stated, "He understands little of our Party line." The secretary wrote the chief's words above the article title. The second got the comment, "Lacks a journalistic view of our Communist movement." The third, "No personal involvement to be convincing about our Party's role." The fourth was noted: "Boring and superficial knowledge of our Party's contributions." The fifth journalist's article was qualified as "Almost a deviationist from our Party line." The sixth was "confused about the victory of Socialism in the world," and the seventh, "not up to the latest recommendations of the Romanian Communist Party."

The last article the secretary read was full of grammatical errors and misspellings. And while it had an abundance of Communist slogans, it was obviously plagiarized from political books. The chief exploded hearing so many unconnected quotes used to try to explain the role of the Communist Party in building a new socialist society in Romania. He shouted, "Who is this imbecilic, fake journalist who can barely write?"

The secretary turned the second page and froze.

"Well, come on, what is the last name?"

The secretary handed him the paper and mumbled, "You, comrade editor-in-chief, also submitted this article for evaluation…"

—★—

11. TOO MUCH

To be perfectly honest, I was surprised to learn that my Communist boss wanted me, in the middle of the winter, a non-member of the Communist Party, to be part of his group for an important industrial conference in Bucharest. I was impressed with the meeting by the experts in the chemical industry who studied in France, and even I learned a lot from them. The meeting was held in a spacious, well-heated ballroom decorated with the flags of Socialist Romania, the Romanian Communist Party, and the Soviet Union. There was a prominent podium, and large pictures of influential Romanian communist leaders hung from the wall. Under them was a large white banner, and written on it in red was a bold proclamation: "Proletarians of the world, united under the Communist flag." I noticed that all the leaders seemed to look straight at me. I was likely the only non-communist member in attendance.

The uncomfortable feelings I had were quickly overcome after the meeting. Those of us attending the conference were treated to an expensive dinner. Most Romanian people stood in line for a half-day or longer to buy a loaf of bread—if the truck happened to deliver it. The lavish dinner was the highlight of my trip. Imagine being in front of a buffet with dozens of different cold cuts, salads with all types of vegetables and dressings (some of which I'd never seen), many different kinds of cheeses, tasteful hot entrees, various sausages, including an expensive one made in Sibiu city, beef steaks, baby back pork ribs with an array of sauces, fried fish, pickles, and colorful cakes and cookies of all kinds. Everything was stocked in abundance, and the servers kept bringing more and more food as some one hundred meeting participants consumed it. Wine, beer and real coffee (not the kind we could buy made of roasted oats) were poured without limit by uniformed valets, and one could eat as much ice cream as one wanted, served from special machines with on and off handles. I must say, the Communist Party seemed too good for people like me, and I felt guilty for my previous ignorance.

***

The hotel suite we had offered another splendid experience. We were pampered with the best beds and linens, puffy towels, and perfumed soaps. The bathrooms had running hot water available at all times. Most people in Bucharest received hot water just one day per week, and their electricity only functioned for one hour in the morning and two hours at night. Such rationing saved energy for export, which served as payment for the party that borrowed billions of dollars from the West.

My boss had chosen me to share his suite along with two other co-workers. And suddenly, here I was, flooded by light from tall, fancy electric lamps and sparkling chandeliers, and I had the ability to take a hot bath anytime I desired. I was shocked, and pleasantly so, because I was the only one to take a shower.

Well, my comrade friends, there was only one problem with this experience of glorious abundance: my boss, or more specifically, his odorous feet as they cast the smell of dead animals left to rot putridly in the sun. All was fine until bedtime when we undressed to go to sleep. Suddenly, when he removed his shoes, my boss' unwashed socks let off an explosion of an unbearable stench, which didn't seem to bother my other two roommates because their feet smelled the same way. As for the boss, he sat in his bed with three pillows behind his back. He was covered by a colorful quilt, except for his feet, which hung out at the end of the bed, now with no socks. He happily wiggled his exposed, damp, soiled toes, releasing poisonous odors into the room while contentedly watching the large television set.

I pretended to read a newspaper while using it as a buffer against the unbearable smell. It did not work.

My bed was next to the balcony door. I opened it to air out the room, but the cold air bothered my two colleagues. They frowned and asked me if I had to open the door. Was I too hot?

After reluctantly closing the balcony door, I went into the bathroom and washed my feet again. I dried them with a towel in front of my boss, hoping he would get the hint. He smiled and said, "In the army, soldiers are allowed to take a shower twice a month," hinting that I was so spoiled that I washed my feet after I had already enjoyed a long shower.

Wanting to win the battle of being able to breathe, I began to cough. Excusing myself, I went out on the balcony for fresh air, where my teeth chattered and I really began to cough, so I ran inside before catching pneumonia. I decided to announce that our boots and socks must be put out on the balcony, and after I did so, I promptly took mine to the balcony.

When I returned, everyone laughed at my demonstration, and my boss grinned: "Once, I had a friend whose feet smelled so bad that I asked him to leave his shoes and socks outside the door. You remind me of him. What are the odds? Ha?! You tell me!"

But by then, I was in the fancy bathroom, vomiting all the

good food I had eaten for the first and what would be the only time in my life to enjoy a Communist Party treat.

—☆—

12. THE APPROVAL

A richly mustached clerk, losing his patience, coughed in his fist, rearranged his glasses on his nose, and, trying to be calm, explained again:

"Dear comrade, I told you to write a request report regarding what you want to be resolved, and we will study your case…" (coughing again in his fist) "…to see what your problem is, and in two months, we…" (coughing again) "…will send you a letter with our decision." He coughed again.

"I understand your procedure, but my case is urgent. Look, I have all the papers you need, including the report. Here, take them and solve my urgent case. Pleeeease!"

The clerk coughed again, looked through the papers, returned them to the client and firmly said, "Comrade, we are very busy here. Send all papers you have to the City Hall office and a commissioner of ours…"

"But I am right here in your office now!"

"Yes, but you do not have proof of work from your boss, so…"

"I mailed it to this office with all the required certificates a month ago!"

"The term to examine your case is *two* months. Please make room for the next person. Your boss could call me, too…"

"Please, allow me to call my boss right now on your telephone so you can talk to him?"

The clerk coughed in his fist, wiped his glasses while looking at his stubborn client, and asked in a low tone, "Do I remember you said you work for the main telephone office? Maybe you can help me with an urgent problem. Dial, and I will talk to your boss." He handed the telephone through the small window in the wall that separated the waiting room from the office space.

The client dialed the phone. Assuming which of his colleagues would answer, the client gave his greeting and request: "Hello, comrade Dimitrie. May I talk to my boss? It is urgent."

From the other end, a laughing voice replied, "You, my buddy, this is Nick, your friend. You dialed *me*, not your office."

The client continued, "Please excuse me, comrade vice minister." (His friend Nick happened to have the same name as the vice minister of labor, and he sometimes jokingly called him by that title.) "I dialed you by mistake." And he handed the telephone back to the clerk to hang up.

Surprised, the clerk asked: "Did you dial the wrong number? It happens to me, too. Dial it again." He returned the telephone to the now-embarrassed client.

He explained, "I am sorry. I dialed the phone number of my very good friend, Nick Nastase."

The clerk almost jumped through the little window and whispered, "You know the vice minister of labor?"

Calmly, the client sensed an opportunity and answered, "Do I know him?! He has been my best friend for years."

"And is he your friend?" insisted the clerk with eyes lit beyond his spectacles.

"Didn't you hear me talking to him? He knows I am here to solve my case."

"Hand me your papers again!" The clerk rushed to grab the papers and chose the claiming report.

He returned to his desk with it, grabbed a large stamp,

applied "APPROVED," and signed the client's report. He wrote something on a piece of paper and handed everything back to the client, whispering, "I wrote down my name. Please tell your friend that I will be calling him regarding an urgent matter. I hope you will remember me in a good way, and please come back anytime with any grievance you have!"

"Thank *you*, my friend!" The client shook the clerk's hand through the small window.

━★━

13. ACCORDING TO INSTRUCTIONS

If a socialist society is distinctly different from any other society in history, it is in the care it provides for each individual, especially if they are sick. Medical care is free of charge.

I was waiting in a medical clinic hallway for a friend of mine to come down by lift after they finished having some needed lab tests done. The small elevator in the two-story building went up and down all day, making it easy for patients to get to their medical appointments upstairs.

A nurse dressed in a white hospital uniform had just escorted a few patients down. They looked sicker than the sick people going up. Friends and relatives stood around the hallway, balancing their tired bodies on one foot and then the other as they waited for the patients to return from their appointments.

Evidently, the nurse determines who goes up to see the doctors or is going to have labs done. She asks for their referrals, appointment times, doctors' names, and the last time the person was there to be seen, and she records all the information on her pad. The medical procedure protocols and the instructions coming from superiors make everything clear and allow for quick admissions. At the time, everyone seemed to be at ease with the system.

In some cases, like with a very shaky old man I saw bent over a walking stick or the very pregnant woman who I saw come in, patients are admitted very quickly without any questions from the nurse into the small elevator.

But a third individual came along—a healthy young man. He was daring and impatient, and the nurse promptly stopped him from entering the elevator.

"Stop! Where is your referral, comrade?"

And thus began a rapid dialog between the nurse and the man.

"I do not need one!"

"When is your appointment?"

"I do not need one!"

"Who is your doctor?"

"I do not need one!"

"Why are you here? What do you need?" The nurse was losing all her patience. The other patients clearly needed to get to their appointments. The pregnant woman was ready to vomit. Their relatives were jumping in to try to help them.

The nurse was determined to win the debate with the young man. "You need a referral and an appointment to go up to see a doctor."

"I do not need any freaking referral because I do not need a doctor!"

"Then, comrade, what do you need?"

"I need an injection in my arm."

"You need *what*?" The bossy nurse was nearly yelling at this point.

"What is the matter with you? You never heard of the word *injection*?" the man almost shouted, and he looked around with an accusatory smile to try to garner the onlookers' approval.

Undisturbed, the nurse continued, "We do not administer injections in the arm here." She hoped to cut the discussion short.

"Then do it in my ass!" laughed the young punk, looking to collect laughter and win a popularity contest from the audience.

Meanwhile, other frail, sick people waiting to use the elevator had seen the commotion and were now trying to use the stairs to reach the upper floor. Because of the lack of handrails, some were falling down, one on top of another, all screaming and cursing, as only Romanians know how to express themselves. Handbags, canes, shoes, and glasses tumbled down to the bottom of the stairs. Screaming, friends and relatives ran to rescue their loved ones, who piled up on the unwashed, dangerously slippery steps.

The nurse continued unabated with her instructions: "No injections here. Comrade, leave at once and let me do my duty."

The defiant comrade held the elevator door and said in contempt, "What do you medical people do here, sell eggs and potatoes? Isn't this a socialist clinic to take care of working people like me? Huh?"

The nurse pushed his hand away from the elevator door. "Go away and make room for a legitimate patient."

The agitated man declared, "I will not go anywhere unless I get my injection because that is why and what we pay your salary for."

"Comrade, this is a clinic, not an emergency room or a hospital. Here, we diagnose, prescribe medications, and treat sick people. If you want an injection, go to your district medical cabinet."

"Listen: I work across the street. My medical cabinet is one hour away by tramway, and my lunchtime is only half an hour!"

"I do not care about your problems. I am here to make sure only registered patients ride the elevator; otherwise, people like you would abuse the system." The nurse allowed another person inside, closed the door, and the elevator disappeared.

The man did not accept defeat, and jumping over the fallen patients, he ran up the stairs.

I continued waiting for my friend, passing the time by reading the wall posters about killing lice, washing dirty hands before eating, avoiding typhoid fever and the importance of vitamins in daily nutrition, which was probably needed after all the hungry people stood in line in front of the empty food stores, waiting for a truck to deliver something to eat. (Usually, all that was unloaded were frozen chicken claws and necks with heads attached, imported from China, or frozen pig hooves covered with hair.)

My friend finally came out. He whispered in my ear, "The doctor saw my money bundle, which I'd wrapped in a hundred-leis banknote. I stuck it in his pocket to bribe him, and he cleaned my ear infection. I shouldn't tip the doorman so much next time."

As we left, we passed the information desk where the outraged man had reappeared. He was repeating in a loud voice for everyone to hear, "You mean that I can only come here at night from my faraway apartment to get the shot? According to the legal instructions, this clinic runs the emergency room from only six o'clock in the evening until six in the morning?!"

━★━

14. THE CHIMNEY SWEEP

According to the official party reports on the television news, people's lives continued to improve in the Socialist Republic of Romania. Yet, in spite of those reports, everything was rationed. Each individual received monthly coupons specifying the exact number of eggs and how much bread, meat, sugar, and other vital products they could purchase from the state grocery shop. Beginning as early as three o'clock in the morning, long lines of sweaty or freezing buyers (depending on the weather) would wait for supplies to be delivered to the otherwise empty state-run stores. Even the quantity of wood and coal one could obtain to heat one's home was rationed, and those households with small children received priority.

However, because Romanian science was very advanced under the instruction of the Communist Party, the chunks of coal were eventually replaced with little black egg-shaped briquettes made of coal dust pressed together with a flammable lubricant. Besides the black dust and heavy sulfuric smell it emitted while burning, the new briquettes produced a cloud of heavy smoke that darkened the surrounding areas, changing white linens hanging to dry on the clotheslines outside to black.

The same dense smoke quickly added layers of creosote that coated the cinder blocks and set the chimneys afire, endangering the houses they warmed. For that reason, by November, the most in-demand handyman in Bucharest is the chimney sweep. The Communist Party did not provide such a specialist.

Fortunately, the familiar figure of an older gypsy always makes an appearance on street corners. The creosote covering him makes his outfit black and darkens his white hair and already darkened face—indeed, all about him is dark except for his two eyes and white teeth. On one shoulder, he carries a long coiled-up cable with a mini black, heavy wrecking ball hanging at one end, which he uses to break up crystallized creosote inside chimneys. On the other shoulder is another thick coil of black cable. This one ends with a dark wire brush he uses to clean the cracked creosote from the inside wall of the chimney.

His walk is noisy from the clanging of the long metallic hooks and spoons of different sizes, hammers, scrapers and small masons' tools hanging from his belt since he also repairs chimney cracks. Sometimes, he carries a long ladder. The chimney sweep is a one-man ambulant repair shop that commands respect, trust and popularity—enough to match any famous character.

But, instead of admirers asking for his autograph, the old sweep, Matei, finds himself surrounded by solicitors. They are mostly women who are there vainly looking to buy food. By good fortune, they've run into the only chimney sweep they know—the busiest man in Bucharest. Because of his skill, he plays an important, protective role for each household that uses briquette-burning stoves. He is a unique and irreplaceable craftsman.

Without exception, he is assaulted by demanding former clients. Each asks him to come to their house first. Typically, the dialog sounds like this: "Old Matei, you did not come last week as you promised me. Maybe you will come this week?" To which he responds, "Dear ma'am, do you know how heavily I am booked till Christmas? I will come; rest assured." Or, he might hear someone say, "You left a pile of sand and cement on my porch to fix and clean my chimney. Are you still coming?" Every time, Matei sincerely answers: "I am one guy with 200 clients. I can't split myself to serve everyone at the same time... D'you understand?" A lady offers to pay double, but Matei, who already has plans to serve another customer, is not swayed by the high bid. As he tries to cross the street, the group of unhappy customers moves with him, pulling him in all directions.

Finally reaching the opposite street corner, the noisy group stops before a short, fat man whose reddened neck skinfolds flow over his shirt collar. His dirty necktie is undone halfway down between the open lapels of his coat, which does not cover his prominent belly. With a toothpick between his front teeth, he sucks air in. Poking old Matei in the chest, he says, "You! I need you to clean my chimney today. Come at four when I am home. Got it?" He sucks air in through his teeth again and walks through the parted crowd into the street.

The chimney sweep bows his body forward and, lifting his black hat, shouts, "Yes, comrade boss, I will be waiting for you. Yes, sir!"

Without turning around, the short, fat general inspector for food distribution over the entire city of Bucharest waves his arm and continues walking across the street.

The now happy old Matei keeps bowing and shouting, "Thank you, chief, it is my honor to serve you! Yes, sir, like always!"

The women hold their hands over their mouths, mute with amazement. They silently watch old Matei walk on his way, proudly now, chimney sweep tools jingling.

━ ★ ━

15. HIGH UP

One of the most efficient ways ever found to offer culture to the masses was through television, and beginning in 1957, it was the primary means used, thanks to the educational efforts of the Romanian Communist Party. I was determined not to remain behind the rest of the population's knowledge, and I was eager to be well-educated on many topics at all levels. To be able to talk with others about subjects featured on television programs, I bought a TV set made in Romania under a French license. To watch programs, I needed to install an aerial antenna. A specialist showed up one November morning with a package so large and heavy he could hardly carry it from his van to my door.

"You, comrade, are lucky to have hired me for this job." He could barely breathe out the words as he signaled to me to help him carry the voluminous box. He continued, "You could have ended up with one of those schooled technicians good for nothing except to do a monkey's job and take your money. Now, let's do a good job before I freeze to death. Where is your roof?" He blew into his hands to warm them.

I pointed to my sharp-steeped roof, and the expert installer nearly choked. Looking straight up into the sky and shaking his head, he said, "I am afraid of such steep heights, but you look athletic enough to climb up to the chimney where the antenna must be attached. I will hand you all the pieces from the box to be assembled there. Do not worry because I know what I am doing. *Capisce?*"

Carrying the heavy box between us, we walked inside the

house. As my wife looked on skeptically, we made our way to the attic, where I opened a trap door to the roof. The cold air hit our faces, and a colder wind nearly pushed us back into the attic. But we bravely continued our mission.

Before I knew it, the specialist had tied a rope around my belly. After placing another coil of thick rope around my neck, he pointed to the chimney. My entire body shook. Ignoring my wife's screams of protest, I began my way up the nearly vertical path to the chimney. I crawled on all fours across the crest of the roof. Relieved I'd finally made my way without incident, I embraced the brick chimney and tied myself to it.

From below, the specialist approvingly announced, "You did very well, comrade! Now, throw the end of the rope that's around your neck down to me so I can send up the antenna parts."

One by one, he took some thirty metallic pieces plus a long steel post out of the box. The expert tied each item to the rope so that I could pull them up. I carefully stacked each part around the chimney. At the end of this process, the fat antenna man, sporting a heavy tool belt around his waist, held onto the second rope and signaled me to pull him upwards. This was not executed according to the highly developed specifications of the worldwide-recognized industry, at least not according to what I'd read in party newspapers. But inch by inch, he reached the chimney. Cursing and breathing heavily as perspiration ran down his face, it was clear he was no longer freezing.

To make a long story short, he quickly assembled all the parts. The antenna looked like an airplane with many rods instead of wings. He screwed it onto the long post I'd pulled up to the roof and braced it to the chimney. The TV transmitter was in

Bucharest, so he aimed the antenna in that direction. "There is the TV tower," he said, pointing to the northeast horizon. He shouted over the noise of the increasingly strong wind, "Remember it!"

From the top of my roof, Bucharest looked unfamiliar, like a sea of buildings separated by winding streets ending in straight boulevards. Quickly, I pointed where I spotted a tall, steepled church in the northeast. The expert nodded in confirmation.

I left both ropes secured to the chimney. The wind was howling now. Holding each other and the second rope for dear life, we began sliding and dangling our way downwards towards the roof trap. We had to stop numerous times for me to steady his slippery feet and direct his steps in the right direction. With careful determination and a lot of luck, we reached the trap door. I tied both rope ends to the trap door handle, just in case, and we successfully lowered ourselves into the warm attic. With dripping noses and red cheeks and ears, we both rubbed our hands together to regain feeling and mobility in our frozen fingers.

Back down in the house, he showed me how to turn the television set on and off, how to change buttons to tune in the only channel, and how to dial it in for a better picture. He regretted it was not night. If it had been, he could have connected my set to the TV tower's signal. "You can do that later by adjusting the antenna to the northeast till the picture is clear. Remember, to the northeast," he repeatedly advised me.

He refused the shot of tzuica (a strong drink made of distilled prunes) my wife offered. Politely, he intimated that it was only one o'clock in the afternoon. He had two more antenna jobs to do—hopefully on flat roofs. He took the money and rushed to his van, leaving my wife and I exchanging puzzled looks.

Anxiously, we waited for the eight o'clock television program that night. When we finally turned the set on, a loud buzzing emitted from the speaker, and lines scrambled in all directions across the screen. Under a disapproving glare from my wife, I adjusted the dial, but I succeeded only in having snow fly across the screen. She left the room and slammed the door.

I headed up to the roof trap and adventured into the darkness of the night. Holding the ends of the two ropes I had left there, I pulled myself up to the chimney. The fact that Bucharest had only a few illuminated streets (to save electricity for export) did not help my attempt to spot the tall church steeple toward which I needed to adjust the antenna. So, I redirected the cold antenna just a little to the left. Full of enthusiasm and hope, I have no idea how I ended up back in front of my convex television screen, which now showed parallel lines running downwards. The loud whistling emanating from the speaker hurt my ears.

Climbing like an alpinist, I made my way back to the top of our steep roof. Rather out of breath, I redirected the antenna a little to the right. I rushed like an acrobat to the roof trap and then downstairs to the screen, which now showed four heads with eight eyes like in a horror movie. The speaker thundered out banging noises. In vain, I adjusted the dial back and forth, trying to get the image to come in clearly. Suddenly, the entire image disappeared. I frantically rotated the dial back until the heads reappeared.

I erupted in a scream of triumph, and my wife rushed in. When she saw the distorted heads, she screamed for the opposite reason. She ran out of the room crying. Determined to improve the reception, I ran upstairs to the still-open roof trap. By now, snow had begun to cover the roof in white. Suddenly, I faced a new challenge I had not anticipated. I felt like a climber stranded on the slopes of Mount Everest.

Under snowy conditions, reaching the chimney now seemed a nearly impossible task. My wet, freezing hands slid on the ropes, and I could not get solid footing on the roof with the shoes I had on. But where there is a will, there is a way. I rushed back into the house, got heavy gloves and changed into rubber-soled sneakers. Now wearing a warm coat with a hood, I returned to the roof with a small round flashlight. Holding the flashlight in my mouth, I coiled the ropes around my shoulders and armpits. Very slowly, slipping a bit every time I made a move, I carefully pulled myself upwards, mainly using my biceps. When I finally reached the chimney, I was sweating profoundly.

Hurriedly, I stood up on the sharp roof. Holding the antenna, I tried to move it to the right, but the metal post joints froze. I put all my strength into pushing it, only to slip and fall on the almost vertical roof. I yelled out with fear. Thankfully, my fall was broken by the ropes coiled under my armpits, and I found myself suddenly stopped with my back against the roof. Facing the darkness of Bucharest, hanging there with my arms apart, I felt like our Lord Jesus on the cross. I screamed, "God save me!" as my flashlight rolled down the roof to the pavement. Pushing myself from one side, I regained my crawling position. In total desperation, I reached and embraced the chimney, which puffed billows of smoke out into the falling snow.

I never felt more attached to and secured by anything else in my life than that chimney, my only steady help in the universe. Of course, thanks to God's help, I am still alive. I sometimes wonder if I dreamed the entire commotion, too brutal and dangerous to be real—me, dangling by two ropes, 30 feet above the cement pavement.

Indeed, it is incredible how the primitive human brain reacts to deadly situations, pumping out the extra muscle power needed to save a life. I felt numb for a little while but was relieved to hug the smoking chimney as I was slowly convinced that I was still alive and that life went on below the roof. Despite all that was happening, I felt that I had won against gravity, the geometry of the roof and the snowstorm.

I have no memory of how I ended up back inside my house looking at my television screen. It now showed just two heads and four eyes and sounded like an echo of a cow's *moo* between two mountains. I was happy with the improvement because a doubled head is better than a gray screen with lines.

However, hearing the snowstorm's howling winds continue outside, I decided to close the roof trap rather than venture out again. I resigned myself to watching my television screen that night in its state of imperfect reception. Unfortunately, when I returned from the attic, programming had ended. An unidentifiable flag waved in duplicate and something that sounded remotely like the Romanian anthem was playing. I was convinced that with one more gentle nudge of the aerial antenna toward the northeast, I would have perfect reception on my screen. But I would have to accomplish that another time since I had challenged my luck on the snowy roof more than I should have already.

Thus, in my effort to keep up with the cultural and political doctrine of the Romanian Communist Party, I had my first and hopefully my last episode of an out-of-body experience hanging on a snow-white roof while hearing the angelic music of a snowstorm.

I am sure no religious miracle was ever mentioned in the teachings of Marx and Lenin.

Maybe that was one of the reasons I did not become a member of the Communist Party. I went to church instead of communist meetings. And to that, I say, Amen!

━★━

16. REFLECTOR

With only 21 transmissions a month, most television airtime in Romania was reserved for the news, which showcased how the Communist Party improved the lives of Romanians by building factories and apartment buildings all across the country. Nearly the entire programmed time was filled with speeches delivered by important party leaders. A few good news segments featuring Socialist accomplishments internally and abroad were also thrown in. Everything reported about happenings in Western capitalistic societies was bad. Coverage of domestic sports events (mainly the most beloved, soccer) and entertainment programs with folk singers and dancers, comedy sketches and even circus acts made it worth paying the state television fees.

The most popular show was *Reflector*. On it, reporters investigated local Communist leaders' disturbing acts of corruption, bribes and negligence, covering their punishments and detailing how the Communist Party rectified problems. To the general public, it was clear that the entire Socialist system was full of holes made by profiteers, thieves, incompetents and idiots. All those with power were members of the Romanian Communist Party, who illegally enriched themselves by plundering state-owned institutions, farms and factories.

In an indignant voice, a *Reflector* reporter would describe abysmal scenes from an institution they'd investigated. To conclude, he would make a strong appeal: "We hope that the neglect and irresponsibility of comrade Mocanu will radically change into an exemplary display of professional leadership when the

Reflector revisits his worksite. Otherwise, he must be held directly responsible for the financial damage caused by his dereliction of duty." The stern reporter would almost shout, "Did you hear me, comrade Mocanu?"

On another evening, another determined reporter from *Reflector*, looking straight at the camera, addressed the viewers in a resounding voice:

"Now, comrade Mocanu is asked to carefully look at what we will show from images filmed at the warehouse complex where he is in charge. He must rectify all the wrongdoings and the horrific irregularities we saw as we re-inspected his worksite." One after another, the television screen showed scenes of walls ready to collapse and ceilings leaking on products stocked inside. Outside the buildings, the camera crew had shot footage of big new rolls of wire sinking in the mud and expensive imported tool-making machines rusting because the tarps meant to keep them from being exposed to rain had been blown off by winds. All kinds of hard-to-obtain industrial utensils, appliances, and materials were shown carelessly left in big piles, rotting between the falling buildings. No maintenance workers could be found on site to take care of the costly mess. Why? Well, they were too busy stealing from their workplace and were off hiding the high-cost items they'd looted that had never been inventoried in the first place. Therefore, the goods they stole had never even existed—at least not officially.

A few million Romanian viewers saw the appalling situation and heard the reporters' stern messages, but not comrade Mocanu. Though he was sitting in bed in front of his television screen as the program aired, he was asleep, still holding a bottle of beer. Four empty bottles lay scattered on the floor.

Despite the damning news report, he had nothing to fear. The party chief of the entire region was his brother-in-law, a big shot, and it was he who had put Mocanu in charge of the warehouse industrial complex.

Life was good and easy for comrade Mocanu, a veteran member of the Romanian Communist Party.

━ ★ ━

17. THE TELEPHONE MESSAGE

Stefan was a good electric company office worker and the only one who had completed a few years of technical college. He acted sure of himself when bossing everybody around. He even confronted his superiors. He was not a bad guy, but no one liked him because of his air of superiority and self-confidence. He needed an attitude adjustment, and his co-workers found one that fit his personality and taught him a lesson in humility.

Stefan had been inside the local militia building earlier in the morning and opened the door with the number six on it. He was welcomed with an annoyed "What do you want?" from the militia officer on duty, whose breakfast was being interrupted.

"I was asked to go to room number six."

"What did you do? What is the problem?"

"I do not know. My co-workers said I had a telephone message from the militia office to be here at 7:30 AM."

"Well, come back later. It is only seven o'clock." The officer continued eating his breakfast sandwich and told Stefan to leave and close the door behind him.

A punctual man himself, Stefan did just that and waited. At 7:30 sharp, he knocked on the door again and entered the same room, number 6.

"You again?! Go upstairs to number 8 and ask why you've been directed to come here."

Jumping two stairs at a time, Stefan arrived at number 8 and knocked on the door, but from behind, he heard, "Stay in line, young man, like we all do."

Stefan apologized, and with his heart fluttering fast, he sat down to relax on a long wooden bench. Finally, his turn came, and he entered the room.

An officer resting his elbow on the desk asked, "Are you here about the stolen bicycle, or did you steal it?"

Stefan explained that he had been called by phone to come to room number 6 that morning.

"Well, go downstairs, second door on the left."

"I just went there and was told to come to this room."

The officer asked his name, then looked at a long list and said, "I understand the mistake. Go to room 7; they may be waiting for you there."

Nobody was inside room 7, and Stefan waited outside until an officer with muddy boots and a dirty uniform entered the room. After a while, Stefan knocked on the door, and the officer lifted his head from his palms, as he had already fallen asleep on the desk. He asked Stefan, "Who are you looking for?"

"I do not know. I was told to come here, and…"

"Show me the letter that was sent to you telling you to come here."

"My workers told me you called for me to come to the militia building this morning. I have a pass from my boss to return to work before 10 o'clock."

The officer shook his head and said, "Go to room 6, and they will tell you why they want to see you. What did you do?"

"Nothing wrong!"

"No one comes here if they did nothing wrong. We'll interrogate you and find out about you; do not worry. Today, everybody is guilty of something. You will be amazed at what a good beating will do for your confession." He signaled for Stefan to leave the room.

By now, Stefan, once so sure of himself, had begun sweating, wheezing, and feeling afraid. He ran out into the courtyard and approached a group of four civilians to ask them the time.

Before getting an answer, an officer came to the group. "Follow me. You, too," he directed, pointing at Stefan.

As they were close to the street gate, he ran toward it, shouting to the guard that he would be back. Stefan cowardly vanished onto the next street.

As the Romanians used to say: "Fuga este rusinous, dar sanatoasa" ("Running from danger is shameful but healthy")!

Arriving at his office, hardly breathing, his co-workers cheered upon seeing him. Confused, Stefan, still shaken from the scary morning, asked them about the telephone message directing him to the militia building.

He was told, "There was no telephone call. It is April first— the fool's day to remember who you really are."

Stefan had to swallow his pride. As a rule, nobody escaped from militia offices. Well, this time at least, a frightened but still self-confident Stefan did. After all, he realized that a strong attitude can sometimes be a lifesaver.

18. A NIGHT REBEL

On the night express train from the city of Pitesti to the capital of Bucharest, no passengers were in the corridors because, frankly speaking, the train was almost empty. I was alone inside a compartment meant to hold eight travelers. Lost in my thoughts, I looked out the window, noticing how the old-fashioned, loudly whistling steam locomotive released traces of sparks into the darkness. The telephone poles appeared to run fast behind the train, and the electric bulbs flickered from bright white to yellow.

Suddenly, the cabin door was forcefully pulled open. A middle-aged man, his hair disheveled by the strong air currents in the long and narrow corridor, addressed me.

"Hi there!" He spoke with a twisted tongue and offered me the bottle he held in his hand. "I hate to drink alone, so drink with me!"

"Thank you, but I don't drink at 11 o'clock at night."

"God, not again… Another paper-pusher who avoids me."

"I don't know you."

"Then drink with me!" He swung the bottle in my face.

"No, thank you. I am on medication and not allowed to drink alcohol."

"Well, then, you are not with those clerks from the offices who push papers around their desks. Correct?" He hiccupped a few times between words and almost fell into my compartment. I helped him sit on the bench. He managed to say, "I appreciate…" and gulped down two big swigs from the bottle. Moving his head around, he pointed at me and asked, "Are you sure you're not with those manicured clerks? Because I see you wear a tie."

"You see me, don't you? I am alone." I started becoming defensive.

"Correct!"

He closed his eyes and dropped his head in an affirmative way. I thought he was going to sleep it off because he began to snore. But his head snapped back up. He took a few sips from the bottle, and with a jolt, he tried to regroup himself. After some apparent deep thinking and heavy breathing, he continued: "We both fight against those… What do you call them? *Be… burr… ocrates…* Correct?" He then whispered with his index finger in front of his lips, "Those lousy bums take our money and call themselves communists." The drunkard succeeded in speaking all the words clearly. He again put his index finger in front of his lips and lowered his voice. "None of them ever did an honest day's work, and now they tell us how to work and what to do. Right?" He seemed happy to deliver all his revolting thoughts in one non-interrupted sentence. He looked at me to say something more.

I emphasized again I was alone and whispered, "I do not mind them too much because they have bosses who tell them what to do and make their lives miserable."

"You *are* a communist, aren't you?" The man jumped up. Opening the door, he shouted, "Go, go to them… Jump off the train and join them against those of us who work hard in basements with boilers and elevator engines… Go!" He collapsed on the bench, dropping the now-empty bottle on the floor.

I closed the door and cracked the window to get him some fresh air. I put his legs up and laid his body on the opposite bench.

For a while, he lay unmoving. But he eventually got up and pointed at me, asking, "Are you with me and against them, our enemies from the offices?"

I said, "Yes."

It was a mistake because the rebel went into the corridor and shouted, "I got my workers behind me, you lousy louse!" He returned to my compartment and asked, "Are you still with me? Now, I will show those who fired me what they deserve."

How he snapped out of being drunk and now looked like a communard from the French Revolution was beside me. I heard him in the corridor, challenging someone to come out and fight, but nobody came.

The man did not give up and continued shouting, "You, the one who said I was drunk, you lousy bastard, did I drink your money? Huh? Did I need to come to your office to ask permission to drink? Boo, mother faker!" (Only he said the actual curse word.) "Come out and fight a real worker, not a pencil sharpener! You stinky leech. Boo!"

Nobody came to confront the worked-up, defiant man. Satisfied by the challenge he'd voiced, he returned to my compartment, looking almost normal. For a while, he sat with his eyes closed and kept silent.

Then, he confessed why he was so upset: he had been fired and had been to Pitesti to find a job at a new factory. While there, he was told to bring back references from his old job. So, he had to return to the bureaucratic office he hated and ask his former boss, who'd fired him, for a recommendation. When he got on the train and was in the first compartment, he'd started to drink. A passenger with a tie told him to stop drinking, which triggered the commotion when he entered my compartment.

To console him, I said, "My man, this is the system today in Romania."

He replied, "It is a communist system to punish good workers like me. I even slept overnight in the basement to make sure the old boilers did not explode from too much pressure; I worked unpaid overtime and never had a vacation." He picked up the empty bottle, opened the window and threw it out. Taking a deep breath of the fresh air, he commented, "If I were a member of the Communist Party, I would be promoted. But I am not. So I drink."

I asked, "Are you married?"

He waved his hands and answered with a smirk on his face, "Yes, but she was an office employee, and I bet my boss slept with her. Who needs that? I think that is why I was fired… And that is why I drink." Sobbing, he looked out into the darkness.

"Listen, why don't you go back to your compartment and…"

"Next to the paper-pusher wearing a tie? Never!"

"But I know him. He works in a smelting factory, where iron and steel are melted. He faces fire and explosions every day. He's only wearing a tie because he's going to a wedding," I lied.

"In that case, I will go and apologize."

The rebel never came back.

— ★ —

19. WITHOUT RIGHTS?

"From what you told me, I understand it cannot be done, but I feel deprived of my rights," sobbed the helpless man in front of the city hall clerk, who was waiting for a bribe to solve the written complaint.

"There is no way I can approve your complaint," repeated the bureaucrat.

The worker took a deep breath and rose off the chair, feeling like a victim. With his hand on the door handle, he looked back again at the city hall clerk with his gold-framed glasses and bitterly asked, "Do I have no rights in this socialist country of ours?"

The fat middle-aged functionary jumped onto his feet and threateningly said, "What did you say?! Come back so I can explain something. Sit down."

The man turned around and said, "I've had enough of your cheap advice and talk about nothing, and I am not afraid to ask, what are my rights?"

The clerk picked up a red pencil. Blowing the air from his cheeks in an effort to be more clear, he officially stated, "Comrade citizen, let me tell you about your rights in case you do not know: you have the right to become a member of the Romanian Communist Party, the right to vote and the right to be elected, the right to speak about improving our social life, the right to work, and the right to improve your own and the collective production."

Seeing the citizen listen intently, his mouth open because he'd never thought about having so many rights, the clerk continued to enumerate those rights: "You have a right to be sick and be treated for free; to buy a car; to take a vacation and go any place—but only in Romania; to send your children to school; to save money in the state bank; to have a place to live and be part of the tenant association; and the right to claim your other rights…"

To which the citizen added, "Like getting a rental apartment 16 years from now because I am not a member of the Communist Party, but I live with three children, my wife and my mother-in-law in a two-room apartment?"

20. A QUESTION OF GLOBAL PEACE

"Village citizens and comrades, since the Gypsy band and singer have not arrived yet, and our distinctive guest from the regional Communist Party is here and has his lecture ready, he will take the floor to talk about..." The announcer leaned toward his helper who whispered the subject in his ear, which he then repeated to the audience, "To talk about the role of the laser in maintaining global peace."

A murmur arose among the 80-some peasants from a distant mountain dressed in shepherds' clothes present inside the village hall. They had come to hear the Gypsy musicians. They had never heard of or cared about lasers.

The facilitator, who was the only one present wearing a tie, held his arms out to the crowd and tried to silence them. "The Communist Party is here to inform our people of all there is that is new in science, so let's have the professor explain the miracle of the laser."

With well-ironed pants and a jacket buttoned to his neck like a Chinese tunic, the professor, in a shaky voice, began to read from his notes about the great discovery of the laser, which can cut through any object. In scientific terms, he explained how the laser's contribution to developing industries would be very import-ant in their socialist society, detailing how the laser's special light can make precision cuts and can even help perform complicated surgeries. Of course, in the capitalistic world, the laser is used to make space weapons that can destroy everything they touch. In contrast, socialist societies will use lasers for humanitarian reasons and to maintain global peace.

In half an hour, he finished his lecture. He asked if there were any questions from the audience, who so far had listened in disbelief with their mouths open.

Apparently, nobody knew what to ask except for Old Grigore, who stood up and asked, "What does it look like?"

"What does what look like?" asked the professor.

"This thing to maintain global peace..."

"Aah... the laser? Well, it is an emission of stimulated atoms and molecules that emit concentrated beams of light that have an incredible penetrating frequency. Its name comes from the description, '*light amplification* by *stimulating* the *emission* of *radiation*,' which is self-explanatory and describes how the laser works. Any other questions?" asked the professor of his unmoved audience of shepherds, many of whom were leaning with their hands on top of their thick staffs, chins on their hands, unblinking eyes looking at the professor. No questions immediately followed the professor's inquiry.

But Old Grigore finally asked, "Is it like a fired bullet?"

The professor answered that a laser could penetrate just like a bullet, but its beam was strong enough to run through its target, reach the moon, and return to the source that launched it.

"Does it go through the source as well?"

"No, because it is redirected through powerful mirrors and then can go further again..." answered the professor, somewhat uncertainly.

"Can it go through a soldier?" asked an elderly man.

"Easily. The laser can go through a hundred soldiers!" confirmed the professor, smiling.

Old Grigore, who had fought in both world wars, shook his head. Disappointed, he asked, "How can this thing of yours maintain global peace if it kills more than a bomb? Fighting so much for peace, not a stone will be left on another stone...'" Disapproving of the invention of the century, he turned and left the village hall. He knew all too well that in the name of so-called humanity and peace, one-third of the global population—mostly innocent civilians—had died, even before lasers.

In the meantime, the Gypsies came on stage. They played familiar tunes on violins, accordion and a portable hammered cimbalon (dulcimer). The village audience, immersed in the community and camaraderie of tradition and music, forgot all about using lasers for the good of mankind.

21. ON RUNNING

It was summer, and since my athletic competition season was over, I decided to take a break from the stress and spend two weeks at my grandmother's house in the pristine Muscel region. Unlike Bucharest, which is under a continuous cloud of smog, Muscel enjoys crystal-clean, breathable air. I decided I'd take my training runs in the village pasture, which was surrounded by a dense forest that produced plenty of oxygen to counterbalance the manure left by some 200 cows. Each morning before sunrise, I ran around the large green *islaz,* as they call the area, breathing in the ionized air. It penetrated my lungs, purifying my city-air polluted body. Wearing sneakers, shorts, and a tank top, I felt so good that I ignored the sneering looks from the two local cowboys who tended the cows in the communal pasture. Once in a while, they ran, cracking their long whips to direct stray cows back to the herd.

After a few days, one approached me with his whip on his shoulder and politely asked why I was running.

"I'm in training," I answered and continued my run.

He waited patiently for me to pass by him again and asked, "Where is your cow?"

"I do not have a cow."

I circled the pasture again at a steady pace.

His next question was, "So, why do you run?"

"To keep myself in shape."

After another tour of the pasture, he asked if I wanted to run after their cows when the horse flies made them wild. I stopped running, and I explained again that I run to build stamina.

His questioning became repetitive. "But you say you do not have a cow?"

"No, I do not have a cow."

The cowboy was dressed in the ancient Dacian folk style with long white trousers, moccasins made of pig skin, and a flowered stitched shirt with long, large sleeves, and a small round hat. He stopped me again as I circled around, only to question, "If you do not have a cow to run after, why run so much? If we did not have these damn cows, we would rest, not sweat as we do now, running after these wild animals. You should stop running after nothing. It ain't smart to get tired for nothing!"

He turned around and walked away, realizing he was wasting his time with me, who had no cow but kept on running aimlessly.

—★—

22. FUTURE PROJECTS

On a short leave, the future son-in-law, dressed as a conscript in a soldier's uniform, pushed on the floorboard. It sank, making him think aloud: "I must change the floors in the entire house." Looking around carefully, he added, "I have to repair the whole house, inside and out. First, I must install electricity because I cannot stand kerosene lamps. I must have an indoor bathroom. Of course, I'll wait to install it till after I replace the old windows with double-paned ones. There is a need for a man who is a real doer on this property."

Taken aback, the future wife and her mother covered their mouths and said not one word. They followed the soldier as he stepped out to survey the rest of the residence. He stopped in the middle of the front yard, placed his hands on his hips and let out a few long whistles. He looked up and said, "I need to change the roof and replace the rafters and gutters. On second thought, it will be easier to simply tear down this old house and build a new one."

"Do *what*?!" screamed the women.

"You heard me right. What else is to be done? A new house cannot be properly built on the same old foundation."

Nervously, the future mother-in-law dared to ask, "Where would you build a new house?"

"My house has to have a lot of sunlight all day, so it will be built there." The soldier pointed to the spot.

The future wife asked, "There? Where the barn stands?"

"Exactly, because I will move the barn over there," he said, pointing where the old house stood, "so you can throw the hay right from the street into the barn."

With a prolonged, meditative "Hmm…" and seeing his sound reasoning, the two women seemed to agree.

"By the way, the entire fence around the property must be made new. Its wide gate must have a roof, and it must be open to the street. We'll need a cement bridge placed over the wet trench. And—why not?—for the cows I will purchase, I will put in a fountain with two long troughs for them to drink water from. You'll see me in action because nothing can stop me from doing it." The soldier firmly made his pronouncement and sealed his future project plans with a loud spit.

With tears in her eyes, the old woman crossed her heart and said, "God will help you!" She silently wiped her tears of joy with the corner of her scarf. The daughter placed her hands on her belly, and with her eyes closed, she seemed to pray.

"He must help me: do not worry!" the future son-in-law assured his future mother-in-law. "Let her have the baby. I need just three years to complete my time in the army and to find a job somewhere around here. Maybe I will go to night school to study further, and then, all these projects will be in place. First, I have to become a member of the Communist Party to make it big, like others I know have done. After all, I am dirt poor. But having nothing and without a single black spot on my past, I will be accepted."

That afternoon, the soldier returned to his distant army camp.

That night, the old woman dreamed of a beautiful house to replace the barn, a new barn by the street fence, two cows drinking at a trough in front of a tall, sculpted covered gate, and a little grandchild playing in the front yard.

Yet the pregnant daughter did not have any such dreams after she put out the single kerosene lamp that barely lit the room. She knew her man too well.

———★———

23. AN UNLIKELY SOLIDARITY

I have noticed that older people are quick to condemn the actions of younger generations. The same condescending attitude probably existed in the Roman Empire and was likely present in ancient tribal cultures because old people live a steady lifestyle, while younger generations are restless: they move frequently, make noise, and act rebelliously to find their way in the world.

Anyway, on electric tramway number 3, which crosses almost the entire city of Bucharest, a group of students from a particular college occupied the space between the back wall of the vehicle and the desk of the tramway cashier who collected money and issued travel tickets. While most travelers immediately paid the cashier and stepped forward holding their tickets, the youthful group failed to follow that protocol. They took up room, spoke loudly and laughed, the girls pushing away the cocky, hormonally-charged boys who, as yet, needed to shave just once a week.

The cashier, an old woman from the suburbs with limited formal education, felt intimidated by the college-aged youngsters. She waited for someone from the group to pay for the tickets, but this did not happen. The tramway doors opened at each stop, and many new passengers hopped in and bought their tickets, but not the students. They never acknowledged the cashier, who continued waiting for their payment from her seat inside the raised, round, wooden partition.

Disturbed by the fraudulent situation, the cashier firmly addressed the youngsters from the back tramway platform,

"Attention! Those who forgot to purchase their tickets must come to buy them immediately."

None of the students paid any attention to the cashier.

She stood up and yelled: "You, on the platform, pay for your tickets, or I will throw you off the tramway."

The group turned toward her and drowned out her warning with a distractingly loud version of the song "Happy Birthday to You." When they finished their singing and applause, happy shouts came from other passengers, apparently duped into believing it was the cashier's birthday by the students' calculated, deceptive maneuver.

The humiliated cashier was beside herself now. In a hoarse voice, she cursed the students in the worst way, as only suburbanites of Bucharest can enunciate in such a filthy manner.

A tall student turned around and said, "We will get off at the first tramway stop. We do not need tickets."

The cashier exploded, "That is it! I will stop the tramway and call the police to arrest you." She pulled the emergency signal rope, and the tramway came to a stop with a long, awful screech. Each standing traveler took two steps forward and one backward as they desperately looked for something to hang onto to steady themselves.

The old tramway driver came to see what the fuss was all about. He shouted, "You vagabonds! If you do not have money for tickets, walk! You cannot ride the state tramway for free."

The cashier shouted, "Those books you study in school teach you nothing. You waste people's money with your worthless education. I'll go get the policeman. He will teach you something!" She moved the shiny handle to the *Open* position. The driver went back to his seat in the front, and the cashier stepped down to the street. A student, seeing the opportunity, moved the same shiny handle to the *Close* position, locking the cashier out. The cashier, furious, yelled at the driver not to move the car. He opened the front door for the cashier. Her face was full of perspiration. She raced to the student group to demand the money for their fares. It was turmoil inside the tramway car as travelers shouted their pros for and cons against the students' position.

Suddenly, the tramway stopped, and a middle-aged man in a supervisor's uniform entered the tramway car. After the cashier briefed him, he went straight to the noisy group, ready to fine them. The supervisor addressed the students in a commanding tone: "Buy the tickets."

They answered, "We have no money!"

The supervisor pulled out a fee book. Opening it, he said, "Then you will pay the legal fee. Let me have your names."

One student replied, "If we do not have the money for tickets, we do not have the money for a fine, either."

As things turned ugly, a smart student stepped forward and, with an almost begging tone, flattered the supervisor: "Comrade chief, don't you remember when you were a university student, and sometimes…"

The chief cut him short: "When I was a university student…"

A burst of ironic laughter came from the student group.

The insulted tramway chief was red with anger: "Oh, yes?! According to the law, you must be arrested for committing fraud against our socialist republic property. As a member of our beloved Communist party, I must enforce transportation law."

A sudden silence fell inside the tramway car.

A much older lady stepped between the furious supervisor and the panicking students. She was dressed as if it were still the 1920s, and she wore a black hat with multi-colored peacock feathers. Calmly and sweetly, she addressed him: "Comrade chief, please do not hurt these foolish, penniless youngsters. Think about their good but needy parents. You probably do not have enough pocket money to give to your children to buy movie tickets or books, so please let them go. You already taught them a lesson to remember."

Everyone in the tramway clapped at once, chanting, "Please, pretty please…"

The supervisor's face, now pleased by the ovations he received, turned red again. Now in a better mood, he agreed to overlook the infraction on the grounds that the youngsters needed to take the tramway but could not pay. He got off at the next stop.

At the second stop, the students helped the fancily-dressed old lady get off at the station with them. They thanked her for standing up for them.

After a small ceremony of gratitude, she smiled, winked an eye, and confessed, "I did it for all of us. I did not purchase a tramway ticket either."

The students were left in stitches with admiring laughter at her admission. As the old-fashioned lady walked away, they sang the celebratory song, *"Multi ani traiasca, multi ani traiasca/Long live many years to you…"* In English, they might have sung, "For she's a jolly good fellow…." She truly deserved the accolades.

━★━

24. THE GODMOTHER AND HER GODSON

Old Elizabeta's family used to be the richest in their mountain village. As a good Christian, and as tradition demanded, Elizabeta was named the godmother of many babies from the village's poor families. As they reached adulthood, she would help them with wedding expenses and starting new lives. She would become their children's godmother; thus, she was famous and much respected in that forgotten part of the country.

Nothing had changed with that way of life until the Communists took over in Romania. "In the name of the people," they confiscated her inherited lands, hundreds of sheep, horses, donkeys, and the multipurpose water mill built on her property by the fast-flowing mountain stream. Overnight, she became poor, though she still lived in the biggest house around. It was currently in need of repairs to its river stone foundation. At 80 years old, she needed charity for the first time. One godson brought a pile of gravel to her front yard, and another, a mason, volunteered to fix the damaged foundation. But the gravel had to be sifted for the mason to have the fine sand he needed for the repairs.

On a summer morning, she was negotiating with Manuel, a dark-skinned godson of hers. As others like him did, he lived in a hovel lodged halfway in the ground in the hamlet by the stream, not far from the water mill. He had been born poor and was still a poor handyman 50 years later. Better put, he was a beggar, always looking for a handout. He preferred living in humble misfortune to working. He was impoverished largely from having to support the 14 children he'd fathered from a few different women he never bothered to marry.

On this early morning, Manuel found himself in a position of power. "For God's sake, you want me to work for free?" Upset by the initial low offer he'd received, he complained as he moved his large, dirty bag onto his other shoulder. Playing the strict businessman, he stated in a firm voice: "God-ma, I ask very little. For 10 leis and two meals, I will sift that big pile of gravel to make sand for your repair."

Old Elizabeta tried to set her rules nicely. She said, "Look, Mani, my dear, I need the sand sifted by this evening. Can you do it?"

Manuel agreed with three conditions: "I'll do it if you pay me now and let me have a good meal before I go home to get my shovel and then another meal after I return."

Taken aback, Elizabeta wondered aloud, "Why would you walk for hours both ways when we can borrow a shovel from the next-door neighbor?"

"Why?! Because I am a professional who needs my own tools to do a good job. That is why!"

It was hard to argue with that logic, so the godmother handed 10 leis to her godson and got him a good meal. He ate like a wolf and drank a glass of tzuica, a 50-proof homemade plum brandy. After he finished, he opened his large shoulder bag. With a guilty smile, he made a plea. "Maybe you have some extra dry food, like smoked sausages, bacon, ham or cheese, some bread or fruit that I may take to those hungry children of mine… At least to the ones you, their god-sent grand lady, baptized? Pretty please?" implored the concerned father.

The good-hearted godmother fully obliged.

He left in a hurry with his dirty bag full of good food.

***

He returned at noon for the second meal, which he again wolfed down while telling the godmother how happy she made some of his children. But, he said, it was not enough food for all of them. Drinking another full glass of the strong tzuica, he inquired, "Maybe you have some more food to give them? Now, though, I will get to work."

"Mani, did you forget the shovel?" wondered old Elizabeta.

"Me?! No way; I have it."

"I do not see it. Where is it?"

"Right here, in my bag. Where else?" The man pulled out a rusty shovel head full of dried clay. "See?" He proudly waved it.

"Where is the rest of it?"

"You mean the long handle? I told you: I am a professional. I'll go to those trees in the back of your garden and cut a branch to fit the shovel head. Wait to see me at work. And don't forget the food for my children." Whistling and in a good mood, Manuel walked slowly to the garden. When he returned, he sheepishly said, "God-ma, I need an ax to make the shovel handle."

Together, they went inside the wooden barn and looked for an ax, which seemed to be missing. Elizabeta rushed over to the neighbor's house and came back with a good, sharp ax. Her godson put it on his shoulder, and after reaching the trees, he came back again, wobbling a bit. Laughing, he explained, "I wonder where my head is today: I forgot the shovel again. Ah! Here it is—I'd put it back in my bag. I will leave the bag with you for my children's food."

By this time, old Elizabeta had enough of her godson's antics. She reminded him the sand needed to be ready the next morning for the mason to work on her foundation.

Acting deeply hurt, Mani reproached her: "Ma'am, is this how you think of me after so long, as good-for-nothing? Honestly, I am shocked!" Balancing the ax and the shovel in each hand and walking straight to the garden, he vanished beyond the trees.

***

By now, it was three o'clock in the afternoon. The sunbeams shone above the mountains which enclosed the village.

Hearing no sound of cutting wood, Elizabeta walked to the trees to look for her godson. She followed a loud snore and found him lying in the grass, recovering from having drunk two full glasses of strong tzuica. She looked around, and she did not see the ax or shovel. Alarmed, she began to shake and scream at Mani, who could barely wake up.

Finally, after rubbing his eyes, he recognized his agitated godmother and asked where she put the ax and the shovel. The godmother let out an exasperated sigh. They looked around together and found both at a distance from where he'd fallen asleep. Mani found a branch in the grass with dry leaves and cut the end, after which he tried desperately to fit it in the opening of the shovel.

Old Elizabeta glared at him. She was angry that he had no fine sand ready for the mason. She lamented aloud, "Can you do the sifting this evening and tonight?"

Finishing shaving the end of the branch to fit the shovel, Manuel stopped with his mouth open and, approaching the gravel pile, asked: "How many carriage loads are in this pile? Three?!"

He continued, trying to stay calm, "Now, god-ma, listen to me, this is a heavy job, not one for 10 leis, but for 100!"

The old woman began to cry. She explained through her tears that she had held him in her arms before his baptism. She ended with the accusation: "You charge me more than a stranger!"

The godson wanted to negotiate: "You old woman. I will keep 10 leis from this morning's work, and now you must pay me an extra 50 leis for this half day of more work, or I am gone for good."

"What did you do to earn 10 leis?"

"I went home to get the shovel!"

"What did you do for 50 more leis?"

"I put the long handle on the shovel to sieve your sand."

"You have not even gotten close to the gravel pile," complained the godmother.

"If you had not hired me, I would not have needed to go home to get the shovel or to work on putting a long handle on it. Because of you, I lost nearly an entire day when I could have been productive elsewhere."

Elizabeta was stunned. She asked for her 10 leis back; otherwise, she said she would call the neighbors, who would make him pay her back. She added, "You listen to me: you pay me for the two meals, the two glasses of tzuica and the bag full of food you took to your children. Do you hear me, you snake in the grass?"

But Mani knew how to reply since he and others like him from the hamlet had been trained by a Communist agitator. "The old days of you exploiting poor people like me are long over. Now we, the working class, are protected by our glorious Romanian Communist Party. Soon, I will be a member of it. I already applied. You'll see—all who you tried to rip off in the past will become rich."

Now, old Elizabeta began to shout for help, and her close neighbors, hearing her, walked to her house.

Manuel quickly assessed the threat. Placing the shovel in his shoulder bag, he threw the 10 leis in the grass and ran for his life towards the garden, disappearing behind the trees.

The neighbors listened to Elizabeta's saga. Then, bringing their shovels, they began to sift the gravel to have the fine sand ready the next morning for the mason.

━★━

25. OLD MARIA

Before 1948, when King Mihai I left Romania and the Communists took over the government, which was protected by Soviet troops stationed there after the war, Lady Maria was the most respected person in Muscel county. Her husband was the town mayor a number of times. Her family had the best house, owned a large farm that extended into the forested mountain, had the only running water mill and had hundreds of sheep. At church, even after her husband died, she had her own pew and was the first to receive communion since she was the biggest donor and supporter of the congregation. Her charity extended beyond the church as she was godmother to many babies from poor families, including the Gypsies. Everybody, including the priest, the teacher, and the mayor, kissed her hand as a respectful greeting.

By the year 1950, everything changed in Lady Maria's life when the Communists, who declared her an "exploiter of the people," took over her wealth "in the name of the people." Still living in her big house, she was now called "Old Maria." In retaliation against the Communists, she kept the large, framed portrait of King Mihai I on her living room wall and listened to the monarchic national anthem on her gramophone each morning after getting up and each evening before going to bed. She refused to go to church when she heard the priest (a former member of the Iron Guard) bless the Communist leaders during each mass. He hoped not to be arrested like most anti-Communists from the much-blamed and accused fascist movement were.

Yet, the unpredictable changes of time caught up with Old Maria. The former town hall was renamed *Sfatul Popular* (loosely translated as "The Place of Wisdom"). A red communist flag and a new Romanian tricolor flag with the Communist coat of arms in the middle hung above the entrance.

***

One day, the sounds of a trumpet and a drum came from a group of young people. They held the same two flags high and carried portraits of the Communist leaders. They had a few white posters with red slogans:

ETERNAL GLORY TO THE ROMANIAN
COMMUNIST PARTY,
STALIN AND THE SOVIET PEOPLE MADE
ROMANIA FREE,
and
DEATH TO AMERICAN IMPERIALISM.

Neither the drummer nor the trumpeter knew how to play their instruments, but they compensated by making loud sounds with no musical affiliation. Because of that, the entire group of some 30 men and women tried hard to march in lockstep but they bumped into each other frequently, pushing and pulling against one another as they tried to keep walking straight. Once in a while, when the two players stopped their infernal noise, the entire group would chant, "WE WANT PEACE AND WE FIGHT FOR IT! PROLETARIANS UNITE UNDER THE COMMUNIST FLAG! THE IMMORTAL STALIN IS OUR SAVIOUR!"

After each slogan, they shouted a long "Hurray-hurray-

hurray!" and waved the flags, banners and portraits affixed to the tops of thick sticks. It was early morning, and the cold air and clouds of dust made by the energetic marchers caused them to sneeze and cough, adding some comic relief to the enthusiastic Communist manifestation.

When they walked by Old Maria, since most of them had been baptized by her, they stopped. She asked, "Where are you stupid kids going?"

The answer was yelled back: "We are going to the city to celebrate International Workers' Day. Come along with us!"

"What is that—a losers' meeting?" laughed the old woman.

"We are Communists, the future of Romania!" shouted one of them.

"You never went to school or work. Go back home. Do your parents know what you are doing? Come on, turn around and stop fooling yourselves."

"We are going to parade with other Communist comrades who fight for peace in the world!" shouted the drummer, punctuating his proud announcement with a loud drum roll.

At this point, old Maria stepped out onto the road and addressed the group (half of whom were barefoot) in a warm voice: "Listen, my children: I held many of you in my arms as you were baptized in the church. So I tell you, go back home and don't do this again, understood? Let me see you walking back. Hurry up!" she said, clapping her hands.

The tallest, a dark-skinned male, stepped out from the group. Holding the communist flag as a lance, he spoke out for everyone: "Listen, old witch exploiter, now is our time to live a good life, as our city agitator and his comrades told us to parade for our rights. Now, it is our turn to become Communists and live well. You belong to the dark history of the past!"

The group moved forward to the excruciating sounds of the drum and trumpet, shouting slogans to mobilize the former shepherds and farmers to join their group and celebrate the International Workers' holiday. No townspeople joined the noisy group.

Old Maria remained in the middle of the road, crossing her heart and trying to remember the name of the leader with the red flag. She'd held him while he was being baptized. Sobbing a few times, she went back to her house to listen to the royal marches and remember the good old days when she was somebody and had done so much good for so many people.

***

Hours later, a strong wind from the mountains pushed the dark clouds to cover the clear blue sky, and after a short display of lightning and thunder, heavy rain and hailstones made all the poultry run into their chicken coop. Dogs howled frightened dialogs to one another. Old Maria closed all the windows and put some logs in the stove to bake a loaf of sponge cake. Just as quickly as the storm came, an hour later, it was over, but the rain still fell densely.

From outside, she heard a noise at the gate and a trembling voice calling, "Godmother, please let me in before I get sick…" She went to the front porch and saw the leader of the earlier group wrapped in the Communist red flag to try to stay dry from the rain, while others, holding framed portraits and banners above their heads, tried to go around the water-filled potholes in the road. They were shaking in the cold, coughing and blowing their noses. Men were cursing, and women were crying. Unmoved, Old Maria did not unlock the front gate for her dark-skinned godson to walk in.

Curious, she asked, "What happened to you, the future of the country and your international parade?"

"What parade? Everybody ran for cover, and the Communist agitators left without feeding us as they had promised. Please, Lady Maria, let me in where it smells of something baking." Assuming his godmother wanted to charge him something, the leader unwrapped his red flag and, holding it above his head to protect himself from the rain, offered her a bargain: "Here is our beloved Romanian Communist Party flag for which our Communist heroes fought to win our freedom. I'll give it to you for some of what you are baking. Pleeease, godmother…"

Maria's motherly instinct was to help the young man. He was still shaking and turning blue in the cold wind that had begun blowing again. But she held fast and asked, "So, my godson, when will you go to another Communist parade?"

He answered, crossing his heart, "Never, I swear!" He dropped his flag in the mud and ran down the street.

Old Maria closed the door and enjoyed some of her baked sponge loaf to the sounds of her gramophone.

━★━

26. THE PICTURE

One may believe that in an advanced Socialist society like Romania, the entire population is highly educated and maintains the best cultural standards of elite European nations. Well, consider the case of a large man with many golden rings on his fingers and many gold teeth. One evening, with his imposing stature, loud voice, and stories, he was dominating the conversation with his male friends around a restaurant table. One story went like this:

***

The dentist went to his little office in the countryside twice a month, where he also took pictures of the villagers who needed to obtain IDs. Most were illiterate, and they paid him only with food. This is why he had meat, cheese, fruits, honey, drinks, and everything else a person could want at any time in his house—products one could never find in the state markets.

Well, one day, he was driving back to Bucharest in his Trabant. His car was filled with all the food he needed for the next two weeks. On the road inside the canyon, three shepherds with conical lambskin hats, wearing long sheepskins with the wool outside and holding long and thick staffs, jumped in front of his car and asked him to take their pictures for ID cards they needed.

The dentist told them he did not have his camera with him and tried to drive away. But they waved their sticks, shouting, "You give us the pictures, or we'll throw you and your car in the river." Indeed, a fast brook ran between the high stone spurs and the road. So he tried to convince them that he would take their pictures at his office in two weeks.

"Aren't you the city dentist?"

"Why? Does your tooth hurt?"

"No! We want to go buy corn from the Danube farms."

"I cannot drive you to the train station because I am loaded down with produce my patients have used to pay me."

"Just get out of your car and take our pictures! Aren't you the one who took pictures at the Manole wedding?"

"Yes, but... "

"No *buts*, or we'll crash the windows with our shepherd's staffs."

"My good men! Believe me, if I had the camera with me..."

"Didn't you come with the same car to the Manole's wedding?"

"Yes, but I knew before the wedding to bring my tripod, my big camera, enough film..." He couldn't finish his explanation because two of the shepherds grabbed him by the collar and shook him, nearly choking him. He finally screamed, "I'll do it!"

The dentist lined the three peasants up at a distance from each other in front of his car, got inside it and began to instruct them through the open window. "Pull your hats back so I can see your foreheads. Now, chins up and smile. Wait—throw your staffs aside. They are not needed in the picture. Good... very good... Now, do not move till I tell you. Do not blink and hold your breath. Perfect!"

He started the car, turned the lights on and off a few times, and honked the horn. Then, he said, waving to them: "I'll bring your pictures in two weeks. I need to develop the film and..."

The shepherds had enough. They picked up and shook their

long staffs like weapons and charged at the car, shouting, "We need the pictures tomorrow morning for train passes!"

The dentist, fearing a bloody beating, quickly found an envelope in the glove compartment and waved it at the furious assailants. "Fine, fine. You can have the pictures. Come get them." He quickly pulled out three pictures of other people who slightly resembled the three shepherds and handed them out the window one by one.

Each man held his picture with pride and amazement. One said, a bit perplexed, "In my picture, my staff is not showing by my feet." Another stated: "My mustache seems short, one eye is bigger than the other, and I seem to be missing two teeth." The third said, "How come the city dentist made me wear a tie and a city-style hat instead of my fur hat?!"

The Trabant, its driver afraid and shaking, was already driving away.

━★━

27. IMPROVEMENT NEEDED

It is a verifiable fact that two qualities are necessary to advance in any field: education and experience. A young philosophy teacher knew that all too well. It was night. He was next to his childhood friend Daniel, lying underneath a large wet hedge in front of a wall topped with three rows of barbed wire. He was deficient in this kind of experience, which was why he was so nervous. An armed watchman patrolled the perimeter of the fence, walking only yards away from their cover. If caught, the teacher's career would be ruined, plus he would spend years in prison. However, Daniel's confidence (Daniel never went beyond the seventh grade but had proven experience) made the teacher believe that together, they would pass the two requirements for success in their mission.

Yet, the way the guard looked around the hedges made the teacher believe he knew the two were there, hidden on their bellies. Maybe he was waiting to catch them during their infraction and shoot them. He stepped steadily away from them. Daniel whispered that there was no danger, reassuring him that he had done this successfully at least twice a week and had made a lot of money doing it. As there is no replacement for experience, the teacher rested his head on his palms to calm his nerves. He was already guilty of fraudulent misconduct.

Suddenly, at midnight, Daniel elbowed him, pointing to the wall some 20 yards away. A head appeared between the barbed wires, quickly looking to the left and right to make sure the watchman was not near. The head disappeared, and the two conspirators heard a muffled sound behind the hedge. The head again appeared, carefully watching to see where something fell in the tall grass. Knowing where to come the next day and pick up his package, the head disappeared for good. Or maybe the watchman would pick it up for him?

Daniel slowly stood up and got a glimpse of the watchman at the far end of the wall. He helped the teacher, who was shaking, out from under the hedge. Together, they crawled to the rolling object. Daniel picked it up—six pounds of meat wrapped in waxed butchers' paper, tied with a crisscrossed string. He handed the package to the teacher. "This is yours. Now, let's go get mine."

They walked to the next large hedge, where the teacher lay on the wet grass, waiting until Daniel returned with his package of meat, which was the same size and weight. This one had been thrown by another butcher beyond the wall.

They waited for the watchman to walk back to the other end of the wall, crawled behind another row of hedges, and ran to their hidden bikes. Quickly putting their packages inside rucksacks, they peddled away from the meat packing plant toward the lights of the city. They hid the bikes again for the next time, took the first public transportation tramway, and changed to another to get closer to their apartments.

The two friends walked home with something that was a dream for most people: fresh meat! No waiting for ten hours in the rain and freezing snow for a food truck that rarely came, only to buy a half pound of frozen bones. The philosophy teacher felt better now that he had experience. Besides, stealing from thieves who work in the meat industry is not real theft.

Perhaps that is why there was such a meat shortage in socialist

Romania—stealing from state factories or farms was considered a necessary skill to provide for one's family because the government could not provide enough food.

━☆━

28. THE BIG SHOT

Sofia was an old widow who inherited an apartment with one room for rent to supplement the small pension left by her late husband. She lived there since the apartment block was built for workers like her husband in a factory nearby, and both were constructed by the orders of the Romanian Communist Party at the edge of Bucharest. A few hundred feet from the building, a cornfield extended to the horizon line. The nosey Sofia knew everything about everybody living in the district. However, she knew nothing about her new tenant, George, a nearly middle-aged man who had just moved in. He told her he was on vacation, he needed fresh air and quiet, and he did not want to see anybody. Though he agreed to rent the room, he complained the rent was too high. Because he had many books, she let everybody know that her new tenant was a lonely, poor poet.

What she did not know was that George was an unemployable loser. He lived off the money his grandmother gave him. She'd once been rich but now illegally sold collectibles like stamp albums, Lalique trinkets, expensive jewelry and famous paintings to her wealthy, trusty clients. As an eternal student (thus the book collection), George had never worked nor gained any respect in the old neighborhood where he grew up. Money had become tight, so he had to move into the blue-collar district.

Everything went on as usual in Sofia's neighborhood until one morning, a well-dressed man shouted outside the building, "Comrade Director, comrade Director, you must come with me to the Ministry of Culture building to look into its archives.

Comrade Director, they need you. It is very, very urgent! The minister's limo is waiting for you around the corner! Hurry up, I am waiting for you!"

George opened the window and yelled, "Daniel, are you crazy? What are you screaming about?" Daniel had been George's childhood friend.

By now, everyone's apartment windows had been opened, and Sofia, like the other tenants, was all ears to find out what the fuss was about. Daniel kept yelling for George to come to the important meeting at the Romanian Ministry of Culture.

George got dressed in an old double-breasted suit from the roaring twenties and put on the piano key patterned tie his grand-mother gave him for his birthday. He rushed out of the building and went around the corner to meet Daniel. "How did you know I had moved here?"

Ushering George into a taxi, which was waiting on them, Daniel explained he had gotten the address from George's grandmother.

"Where are we going?" asked George.

"Nowhere, really. But you better not return to your room till after midnight… you know, the archives of Romanian culture take a lot of time to search…," laughed Daniel. They went to Daniel's to watch TV until midnight, when they took another taxicab back to George's rented room in the workers' apartment building.

In the meantime, the entire gossiping community of older women came to Sofia to inquire about her tenant. He seemed to be important—they assumed he must have a distinctive job to be called to the Ministry of Culture. Many hoped he could use his influence to asphalt over their dirt country road, install a better sewer system, telephone lines, and streetlights and build a grocery store… All assumed he must be very well-paid since he was obviously a high-ranking employee of the Communist Party.

***

Days later, dressed the same, George met Daniel at the three-leis menu bodega, where George asked to borrow 10 leis. The joking response he received from his childhood friend was not funny to him at all.

"Comrade Director of Romanian Culture, with your high government wages, why would you borrow money to pay for three sausages and French fries?"

George, his eyes bulging with fury, whispered, "Listen, my mother-faker friend, all I've had to eat over the last two days is a single can of beans, and thanks to your idiotic joke, Sofia tripled my rent!"

Daniel laughed until he hiccupped and said, "Well, George, you've finally gotten the respect you've always wanted—no price is too high for that!"

—★—

29. A MINOR CONFESSION

My sister and brother-in-law trusted me to take care of their seven-year-old son, Andrei, while they went on a one-week summer vacation. They brought him from the city to my country house. He was very good and well-behaved, except for his afternoon nap. He would just stare at the ceiling, wrapped in his own thoughts. I tried to make it easier for him and asked why he did not sleep. I thought that he missed his parents. To my surprise, the little boy said he was thinking about his grandfather, and he told me a story that deserves to be known by many others.

He began: "Do you realize that my grandpa will retire from the Army in five years? I am seven, and adding another five years is 12 years, which is a lifetime. My grandpa said if that 'Dry Prune' retires one day earlier or his pension is one penny bigger, my grandpa will refuse his pension. How about that?"

I asked who the "Dry Prune" was and what the problem was.

With a big sob, Andrei explained, "'Dry Prune' knows nothing about the Army repair shop he is in charge of, even though he has the same rank as my grandpa. But he is a member of the Romanian Communist Party. Imagine that! A technical sergeant who does nothing but read the party newspaper to the mechanics, telling them nonsense about the heroic sacrifices he made to win the war against the beastly Nazis. The true fact is that he and my grandpa joined the Army on the same day after the war was over, only the Dry Prune enlisted in the Romanian Communist Party, but not my grandpa. Is it possible to lie like that?!"

"That is the reason you cannot take a nap?" I tried to put his problem to rest.

"Wait, there is more about the Dry Prune, who is stupid and looks like one. He is so fat that he had to have a special order placed for his Army belt—he should not even be in the army. He has holes in his socks, and one can imagine what a cow his neglectful wife is not to mend them, yet he pulls rank on my grandpa! To tell you that he has only one apple or one pear for lunch because his lazy cow of a wife does not even cook—and he orders my grandpa around? Can you take that? Even more, the cow never says 'Hello' to my grandma, even though they used to be classmates. But now she believes she is a lady because her Dry Prune is a big communist boss in the Army. Doesn't that make you feel like dying?"

He had more to say, so I continued to listen.

"But hold on: the cow looks like a cow, and she is so overweight that she broke a few chairs in her office. Because of her Dry Prune political connections, she does not do any accounting work, and she complains that their daughter—who looks like a fat scarecrow—cannot enter college because the examiners are former fascists and communist haters. Buy that, I urge you!

"But my grandma knows better why the scary-looking daughter fails one entry exam after another. It does not matter how much money they spend on expensive tutors. Why? Because she was born stupid like her parents. My mother, who passed the entry exam on her first try, is a very capable nurse practitioner now and is well-appreciated. And that is a true fact!"

Little Andrei sobbed with a thoughtful sound. He checked on me to see if I understood how one problem generated more problems, and, satisfied with my approving look, he continued: "Did you ever think how they bought a Trabant car when even his army colonel or my grandparents who do honest work could not? Because the fat Dry Prune steals at least one new expensive auto piece from the Army depot each day and takes it out in his large Army bag to sell on the black market. Did you know that?!

"And how can they afford to buy gasoline so the cow and their stupid daughter can use the Trabant as a taxi each day? How about that nobody in Dry Prune's family ever stands in a food line for hours day and night but they keep gaining weight? How come they have parties each Sunday for Dry Prune's communist friends? Is that fair for our family, who takes turns standing in food lines? I forgot that the cow fell in the office and now wants to retire early with a permanent work accident disability because Dry Prune has communist friends at the workmen's compensation office. Say something about that scam!" the little boy challenged me.

Unable to alleviate his problems, I appealed to the highest problem solver. Piously, I said, "God the merciful will take care of all of us. Now, take a nap because we need to roll the cut hay over in the garden."

But he jumped up, saying, "I forgot to tell you the best of all. The cow goes to the church to pray to marry off her scary daughter and to have a nephew as smart as me. Is she all gone mentally? My grandpa said that if that happens, he will get drunk for the first time ever. Imagine how depressed he is! And grandma said she will move elsewhere since there is no room for her and the cow in the same city. I do not blame her!"

The smell of the fresh-cut hay wafted through the open

window. Relieved after pouring out all his problems, little Andrei turned over with his face to the wall and fell asleep.

30. THE FATHER AND SON

I t was summertime. The park of Cismigiu in the middle of Bucharest had countless colorful flower beds of all shapes, protected by small signs reading "DO NOT TOUCH THE FLOWERS" or "DO NOT STEP ON THE GRASS," which made them extra appealing to admiring visitors. Among them was a young father holding the little hand of his perceptive four-year-old son. The boy noticed other children eating white ice cream from small, pinkish-colored ice cream cones. Slowly but surely, he pulled his skinny, tired-looking father toward where a private vendor had colorful butterflies painted on his carriage. A small bell sounded every so often to attract customers who happily stood in line to buy their treats. The son knew the sound because the last time he heard the bell, his father took him for a walk in the opposite direction to see the row boats on the lake.

Holding his father's hand, the son began to jump and skip. "My friend Nick gets a sore throat each time he eats ice cream, but I do not have that problem!" He went on to explain that, to the contrary, when he had his tonsils out, the doctor recommended ice cream for faster healing, and ever since then, he has wanted ice cream, which is very hard to find in the state *Bomboniera* with its delicious sweets.

The father listened in silence. He had no money to buy the ice cream for his talkative son.

"Do you know what?" asked the little one, and without losing a beat, he continued, "I do not mind standing in line with all the other people for bread and vegetables early in the morning. Daddy, you and Mommy can sleep more before you go to work when Grandma comes to stay with me. You know, she never brings ice cream or candies for me…"

They kept walking and the son continued: "If I stay in line for food, I will pay less because I am little and do not eat much, so then you can pay on time for the furniture and electric stove. Too bad I am not old enough to work and help you with money…"

The father picked the boy up and kissed him on both cheeks, saying, "You will work all your life. Now is the time to be a kid and play. Let's go see what the swans and their babies are doing!"

"Do they stay in line for food?"

"No, they do not. They eat fish," laughed the father.

"How do they open the cans with fish?"

"They do not because they catch the fish from the lake."

"Is that better fish than the very salty and smelly ones we eat?"

The father nodded and let the son run ahead to see the graceful white swans.

But he came right back, excitedly lifted his index finger, and said, "Do you hear that?"

Indeed, from far away, music that sounded like a military band with distinct drumbeats was in the air.

"Quick, Daddy, quick: let's ride the carousel! Grandmother took me there last week."

He pulled his father away from the lake. The father stopped, saying, "Next time, we will go for a ride."

The child looked down and gently said, "My mommy said that I am a good boy and I do not dirty my clothes or rip them… do you know why? Because I do not have a tricycle or a bicycle to fall off in the dirt like the other kids do."

But the father insisted on going to the lake: "Son, those swans may fly away at any time, and we will not get to see them. Do you want them to be mad at us?"

The little boy agreed, and they walked down the alley, going to the lake, when the son stopped again. "Do you have your ID with you?"

The father asked why.

"So you can rent a little boat and we can row to see the swans closer."

The father looked in his pockets but could not find his picture ID.

"You don't need an ID to buy ice cream, so let's go and get one."

The father took a deep breath and said, "I have money to buy bread…"

The child replied that they could stand in line for many hours for the bread truck that might never come as they had done before, but the ice cream vendor was there now, and the bell was ringing.

They continued walking. They came across an older boy loading sand into his large toy truck.

"Daddy, forget the ice cream, the bicycle, and the carousel. Just buy me a truck like that!" He pointed to the other boy and his truck.

The father swallowed to clear the lump in his throat, blinked back tears, and patted his son's hair, promising, "As soon as I am paid, I will buy you one!"

"Is that payment on Thursday, as always?"

The father nodded his head.

The son understood the problem and said, "I will help you with what I have saved in my piggy bank."

━☆━

31. THE SENTRY

Any army, since ancient times of warfare, believes that a sentry (an armed soldier patrolling back and forth a certain distance to secure an important or secret objective) is a necessary military position. Indeed, having a sentry at an important entry point to a military, political or industrial institution is an obvious need, as his presence ensures only those authorized can access it. Yet I have doubts about such militaristic, macho, so-called *wisdom* since the defenseless sentry is a visible, vulnerable and predictably moving target for an enemy.

Here is my first point, which is connected to the security of the Military Museum in Bucharest. It was almost dark. I was waiting for a friend when the sentry on duty, with his white gloves, a shiny rifle on his shoulder, and an equally shiny dagger on his white belt, made one-two-three noisy steps and stopped next to me. I saw he had a whistle, like a coach's, hanging around his neck.

He said in the most civilian way, "It feels good not to be so hot today."

Surprised by his casual statement, I agreed, and I asked if he was not afraid to sentry such a large building and the enclosed area with its wall around it.

"Not at all. Do you think a thief wants to steal a bygone, rusted tank without an engine or a cannon on wood blocks with cement poured inside its barrel? Let's be serious. Our people steal from factories, state farms and warehouses."

I asked, "Have you visited inside the museum?"

"Come on, man, I am in the military. I have only two months left, and I will go home. I have had enough of the army and soldiery. I want to see my mother, not what is inside the museum. Man, does she know how to cook—that is when she has anything to cook with."

The sentry, his back to the museum, began to tell me that he was a mason. He had been going to night school when he was conscripted. He complained about how hard boot camp was with the drill sergeant always after him. "I'll tell you what the only good thing in the army is: the sour soups with potatoes, carrots, chopped cabbage, sauerkraut and big marrow bones boiled for hours in a cauldron. That is the only thing I will miss when my military duty is over."

Anyone could have gone over the wall and entered the museum while the talkative sentry was faced away from it.

I asked, "Are you not afraid to stand sentry during the night?"

He laughed: "Afraid of what? On my left is a civilian night watchman for the electric company building. Behind the museum is a college dormitory with lights on all the time, and to the right is a street with a long line of people there all night, waiting for the food truck to deliver something to the empty grocery store. You see, the museum and I are watched all the time. This is a good thing in our socialist society: everybody is watched all the time. However, if I am told, 'Look for the one between the two poplars ready to jump the wall to steal from the museum,' I'll shoot him dead, regardless of whether he is a spy from America, England or Germany. Yes, my comrade, I will do my duty."

"Don't you think that in the past half-hour, somebody might have jumped over the wall?"

The sentry panicked, "How come?"

"Because you've been talking to me the entire time with your back to the museum wall."

"Is it your buddy who jumped? Let me whistle for alarm." He grabbed the whistle.

It just so happened that my friend was walking very quickly toward us, and I stopped the vigilant sentry from blowing the whistle.

Relieved, he said, "Man, you nearly scared the pants off me. Thank God: I will see my mother in two months, not the drill sergeant."

— ★ —

32. AN EXEMPLARY GENERAL

In the Socialist Republic of Romania, it is rare to see an Army general on the street. Even soldiers seldom see one unless they are marching in a parade, and they happen to look at generals observing from their reviewing stand. Therefore, it was quite unusual when an Army-uniformed driver, his covered truck stuck, almost floating, in a large pool of mud, saw a long limousine with a triangular red flag and two yellow stars on its bumper stop, its door open, and a general come out and run over to the messy spot he was in. The general shouted to his driver to wait inside the limousine, and he asked the truck driver, "Hey, soldier, you need help?" The two-star general took off his coat with the golden epaulets and chest full of medals.

The poor sergeant jumped from the cabin right into the middle of the mud pool, snapped to attention, saluted, and reported, "Comrade General, thank you for offering to help, but I already asked my camp for help. They will arrive at any moment. I am Sergeant Vasile…"

The general stopped him with a flick of his hand and looked around. "Sergeant, in our socialist republic, we have the people's army of citizen soldiers, a new army—all soldiers who serve equally regarding rank. We help each other, so I offer myself as an example." The general laughed, rolled his sleeves up and stepped in the mud with his high, shiny boots to examine the situation. "Do you have an ax and a shovel?"

The driver went to the side of his truck and came back with tools. Signaling for the soldier to follow him, the general went toward the roadside forest. "I will cut down some strong branches, and you lay them down in front of the wheels, pressing them under with your shovel. Clear?"

The soldier snapped to attention and shouted, "Yes, comrade General!"

For the next hour, the captain who chauffeured the limousine watched in shock as the general showed amazing stamina and skill, chopping down not just limbs but even small trees to salvage the sinking, tarp-covered truck. The sergeant was eager to contribute and did a good job at making a long track from the green wood in the mud in front of the wheels. When the improvised ramp was ready, the general ordered the sergeant to drive the truck slowly, but the wheels rotated in place, and it did not move.

"Let me push the truck from behind, and you drive even slower," said the general. He first pushed the large branches more firmly under the wheels with his shovel. Then he ran behind the truck to find a good position in the mud to shoulder the vehicle. "Now, sergeant, very easy. One, two, threee…" he commanded as he pushed with all his strength on the middle of the back of the truck. The truck began to move slowly, gripping the branches. Suddenly, it jolted forward, throwing the general into the mud.

The truck was back on firm road. The general, fully covered in mud, stepped out of the pothole, which was now full of muddy branches. Oily fuel shined on top of the mud.

The sergeant quickly grabbed a large green blanket and ran to wipe the mud from the general's head, face, and the rest of his body.

Breathing hard, the general was in a victorious mood and in the same tone of voice, said: "See sergeant, in our Socialist army, under the leadership of the Romanian Communist Party led by our illustrious comrade Nicolae Ceausescu, we soldiers, regardless of any rank, can cooperate and accomplish anything together. By the way, what are you transporting in the truck we saved?"

"Thirty-three new recruits, comrade General," reported the sergeant as he happily saluted.

"Private, you are no longer a sergeant!" the general yelled back.

33. FEELING GOOD

It was close to midnight on a freezing night. I was going home after standing in line for hours. I'd hoped to buy a bottle of cooking oil, one of many of my wishes that had not materialized. From tramway number 20, I got off at the stop at Major Ene. I quickly made the first left on my narrow street, Militari, in old Bucharest. Both sides of the street were lined with country-style houses with ancient stoves heated with wood and chunks of coal. There were small gardens in front of the little houses with barking dogs inside. All were kept in check by country fences leaning in all directions. The snow drifts had melted, and a blanket of slippery ice covered everything from fence to fence. The two yellowish electric lights hanging from a wooden post barely lit the scene. The white moon came out from behind the clouds. At a distance, I saw a tall man with a cane, advancing one step at a time after first carefully checking the ice in front of him.

I hurried to approach the old gentleman whom I knew.

"Hello, colonel, sir! Slippery, huh? Let me hold your arm so we can fall together!" I joked.

The colonel had retired in 1948 when the Communists took over the Romanian Army. He rewarded me with laughter, saying, "After I had an evening like this in the good old days, I didn't care if I took a fall. As you know, I was in the special regiment of the engineer corps. While fixing bridges during the winter, we slid and fell like it was a normal way of doing things."

"Well, colonel, you sound good and look good, but why are

you on the street at this late hour? Aren't you freezing without a long coat?"

He stopped to fix his old torn muffler. He spoke in a manner revealing his excellent mood: "Late, you said? Add to that that I am also very tipsy and not cold at all!"

"Really? It doesn't show." I flattered him, catching him in my arms so he wouldn't completely lose his balance.

"Of course it does not show, because, my young friend, in the past, before communism, I lived a really good life. I was so strong and healthy, like a bull, that I could drink a small barrel of wine at night, and the next day, I was ready for war games in the snow-covered mountains, pulverized by the high winds. That was the Romanian officer, not like they are now, only reading Marx and Engels in the library and passing their political exams to keep their commissions. Hours ago, I had the time of my life! And I am happy to have had it."

"Good for you, *mon colonel*. But what happened to you?"

"Well, dear, today was the regiment reunion of us boys who are still alive and are mainly from Bucharest. We were in the coffee shop talking when our academician entered. He looked at us and how poor we are and said, 'Come on boys—come with me to The House of Scientists and we will celebrate.' We got scared because that place is the most expensive lounge in Bucharest, and with our 700-leis a month pensions, we can hardly pay for coffee and a piece of cake. 'Don't worry about money: it is on me,' he said, and all nine of us followed him into the most elegant Art Deco place. I've only seen anything similar in Paris when I studied military engineering. There were crystal chandeliers and mirrors all over, leather sofas and armchairs,

Persian carpets and real silver silverware, crystal glasses, waiters in black and white uniforms, a big band with a beautiful lady singer, champagne and caviar, steaks larger than our plates… All of it was wonderful."

"Colonel, sir, who was the academician?"

The old timer shook his head and said, "He was just a first lieutenant in 1944 when Russian troops invaded Romania, and the communist agitators came to our barracks for us to sign forms to become members of the Romanian Communist Party. All of us officers refused to do it because, at that time, the Romanian officer was for the country, not for any political party. Only one of us—later we nicknamed him 'the academician'—signed up, and by 1950, he was a general, while those of us who were anti-politics were forced to retire or were fired like the losers we were. He was the only one of us admitted into the Romanian Academy of Science. So, my friend, we ate and drank, honoring those no longer with us. We sang with the band and danced because, after all, the military profession is both the science and the art of war. Did I tell you that the lady singer spoke French and sat on my knees? What do you think about that, *mon ami*?" The colonel laughed as we arrived at his house.

"I am so happy for you, colonel." I shook his frozen hand and led him up the slippery steps to his front door.

"Me too, and I cannot wait to rest my head on my pillow… Ach, by the way, can you bring me some wood and coal so I can have a fire in my freezing room? I paid for my wood and coal in September. Still, those Communist thieves have not delivered it, and I never hear anything from them. Please understand I will return all I owe you…"

"Come on, colonel sir, we are neighbors. I will be right back." I waited until he unlocked the front door, whistling French chansons. I watched as he entered his house, all his windows frozen shut.

━★━

34. DO YOU UNDERSTAND, COMRADE?

"Do you see how the waiter gives me a dirty look? He knows I do not have money. Well, my young comrade, an officer like me would have left him a 100-lei tip before the war. Was that too much for him? Not at all! But for me now, that would be a fortune compared to my current Army salary. It is the price of two kilograms of meat, two of sugar and two liters of cooking oil. And I wonder, what do you think about me? I have been a major for 15 years and am a war veteran. Huh?!"

"Comrade major, can't you see that nobody has money? Look at me, after all..." I tried to calm him, but the major burst out again, hitting the table with his fist, nearly breaking the glasses that bounced from the vibration.

"I know, I know, but Romanian officers always had plenty of money and were elegantly dressed, unlike me now... Do you know what my salary was when I was first lieutenant? Of course you don't—you were not born yet. Well, it was enough. Plus, we had such elegant uniforms that even the Germans envied us, and... Damn them for their war! Not even the finicky French were dressed better than we were. If my orderly did not see me back by 11:00 at night, he would jump in a taxi and look for me in all the restaurants. How about that? Huh?" He laughed, amused by his own history.

I asked him, "Would he know what restaurant you were in?"

"Well, my young friend, there were only five expensive restaurants in Bucharest then, and I could have been in any of them. You call this bodega a restaurant? Let's be serious. Back then, a Romanian officer was a real officer who had respect. Not like now—I am pushed and pulled at in buses and tramways, my boots get stepped on, and grocery bags are put on my head. Eh-hey, in my time, if people did not make room for an officer to stroll on the sidewalk, he would charge them with his sword. See? He always carried a side sword or at least a dress dagger."

He gazed into his empty glass and continued: "Do not get me wrong... An officer was highly respected *because* he was an officer. Do you *un-der-stand, co-ma-rade*?" He heavily emphasized his question with those last two words. "Nobody saw him waiting in line for hours with civilian misfits or carrying onions and potatoes from the market, or even worse, freezing in a bus station waiting to be taken to the terminal and from there, walking to the garrison like a loser... Worst of all, waking up at four in the morning like I do to take the train to an army post near the Danube River. If I miss the five o'clock train, I will be fired and lose my pension... Do you *un-der-stand, co-ma-rade*? Huh?" Again, he almost broke the glasses, hitting the table with his fist. By now, the restaurant was almost empty, and the few patrons remaining could clearly hear every one of his words. As any of them could have been secret communist spies, I began to fear for myself. Determined to calm him down, I nearly whispered, "I surely understand..."

"I tell you, you do not understand *anything*, comrade. Before all these dirty rats calling themselves communists took over Romania, an officer was punished if he carried a handbag or a package. He was only allowed to hold his leather gloves in his hands and nothing else, got it? In fact, by law, he was not allowed to marry a girl who did not have a dowry because he had to have two bedrooms, one guest room, a dining room, a family room, at least one indoor bathroom and a large kitchen. Of course, rooms for children were not like what mine have now. My children all sleep in the same room with me and my wife, who cooks in the bathroom. What do you say to that? Huh?" The glasses clattered with a *zing* again, jumping on the table.

Timidly, I dared to say, "But comrade major, we know you officers have the best apartments…"

He almost shouted, "Of course, if I move my family to the miserable town near my army post by the Danube, I will get at least a five-room apartment. But my two children attend school here in Bucharest to get the best education, and my wife works in an office—she doesn't harvest grains for the state farm. I am ready to sacrifice myself, to ruin my health—but not to destroy the future of my children nor to see my wife barefoot in the farm fields. Yes, I can endure the horrible train commute, the false alarms and war games, take exams in Marxism-Leninism and criticize myself in front of my officer corps, go to re-education courses and do volunteer work, but my two children and my wife are my sacred family!"

The conversation felt dangerous at this point. I tried to excuse myself and leave, especially after I saw the waiter look at his watch. Nobody else remained in the restaurant now. I said, "Comrade major, I really must go since I…"

The major hit the table again and shouted, "I understand your fear because I am also afraid. But I do not run away. I never miss a political lecture or a parade, and I make my commute six days a week. Because I never wanted to become a member of the Communist Party, I will retire as a major while my communist classmates become admirals and generals. But there are so many like me commuting and standing in long lines just to carry food home. But one day, we will carry something else in our hands." The major choked back tears of regret, anger, and fear while raising a glass in his hand—an empty glass—toasted, "To the good old times!"

Author's Note: In 1989, the Army executed Romanian dictator Nicolae Ceaușescu and his wife. The Communist regime ended.

35. TWO UNFULFILLED WISHES

Stalin was in full power as the Communist dictator of the Soviet Union. He invited his mother, Ekaterine, to Moscow. She came from a peasant family, and her occupation was as a seamstress in Gori, Georgia. She was a devoted religious woman belonging to the Georgian Orthodox Church. Her youngest son, Joseb Jughashvili (the future Stalin), was raised in a strict Orthodox religious spirit. His father (a cobbler and the village drunkard) abandoned his family.

Ekaterine, who knew how to read and write only in the Georgian language and never spoke Russian, had only one ambition in life, which was to have her son Joseb become a priest. For that reason, she worked hard, even doing laundry and cleaning, to put him through the Tbilisi Theological Academy and Seminary, a prestigious school. There, he learned to speak and write in Russian in order to become an Orthodox priest. Due to his Marxist revolutionary activities, including robbing banks, in 1899, Joseb was expelled from the seminary. He took the new name of Joseph Stalin ("strong as steel") to impress his comrades as they fought for the Russian Revolution, which landed him as an exile in Siberia.

For the next 10 years, Ekaterine attended church faithfully, never heard any updates about her son, yet all the while, she piously prayed for him. Eventually, she learned from the papers about Joseph Stalin, who was now a leader of the newly formed Soviet Union. Stalin remembered his mother and gave her an apartment in the former palace of the Viceroy of the Caucasus.

He assigned secret agents to watch over her when she was going out to the market.

Legend says that his mother finally visited him in the Kremlin, and when she saw its expensive, luxurious, palatial interiors, she realized her son was incredibly powerful and famous. She asked him who he was, exactly. Stalin answered, using his hidden humor, "Mother, I am much bigger than our tzar!" To which the disappointed mother replied, "But you could have made such a good priest…"

Another version of the story purports that Ekaterine fell ill in 1935, and Stalin went to Gori to visit her. A doctor present with them is said to have written down the famous dialog when Stalin said, "Mama, do you remember our tzar? Well, I'm something like a tzar." The mother pitied him, saying, "You'd have done better to become a priest." When Stalin asked why, she explained that priests work little, live well, and are highly respected. Besides, he once said, she "… would be proud that I was a priest's mother. But I confess, even about that, I was wrong."

Ekaterine died in Gori two years later at the age of 78 or 81, but Stalin could not come to her funeral since he was too busy with a massive purge of the army and political leaders. Instead, Lavrenti Beria, his henchman who built a marble temple over the small house where Stalin was born, came with a wreath inscribed in Georgian and Russian: "To [my] dear and beloved mother, from your son Joseph Jughashvili (Stalin)."

At Beria's orders, Stalin's mother was lowered into her grave in Tbilisi not with the blessings of a priest, as she would have wished, but with the army band playing the Communist hymn

"Internationala." And thus, a second of Ekaterine's wishes was left unfulfilled, the last one, post-mortem.

═ ☆ ═

PART II

Essays and Reflections

I. THE MAKING OF EMPIRES

This may seem to be a misplaced title in a volume of short stories, but for me, who refused to live in a communist empire and chose to live in the capitalistic empire of the United States, it makes sense to briefly review how history reached this complex division of two opposite worlds. Since ancient times, the rise and fall of empires that were believed would last forever reached immense geographical extensions inhabited by millions of people who were divided by religion, race, skin color, nationality, culture and economic levels. The Assyrian, Egyptian, Babylonian, Persian, Greek and Roman empires were all economic and military superpowers, which eventually succumbed to internal revolts or were replaced by the next empire claiming its global role. Imperial changes generated tsunami migrations of ethnic populations, displacing other populations as they looked for better places to inhabit. Thus, today, we have people with genetic variations living thousands of miles from where their ancestors originated.

After WWI, four mighty empires considered invincible disappeared, and after WWII, the Third Reich, the Empire of Japan, the colonial system and seven countries took their names off the world map. This required old borders to change their lines, populations to live in different countries and two huge empires to claim world supremacy, the Soviet Union and the United States. For obvious reasons, not many immigrants are known to enter the Communist Empire, but tens of millions of people from all over the world chose to make America their new home.

Today, economic empires translate as world monopolies on economic, financial, and industrial titans, which were helped by the hegemony of the internet and established other new empires. The United States of America stands as the only current global power, and the rest of the world perceives its military strikes as imperialistic expansion. With 50 states united by one flag and one language, the U.S. is the only empire in history to rule based on principles of freedom, justice and democracy. Its armies occupied aggressive Germany and Japan and forced them to write peaceful constitutions. Its GIs gallantly fought in Indochina to stop the spread of the Communist empire. Thus, America survived the Cold War and emerged more powerful than ever. Like any global power at any time in history, the U.S. found itself in the unenviable position of policing the world, ironically including former Communist countries.

A significant problem is that in the name of fighting international terrorism, American influence in Arab nations caused the Shah of Iran to be exiled during the Iranian Revolution in 1979 since people refused to change their secular ways of life. In spite of well-intentioned economic and humanitarian help, those nations that happen to be Muslim feel pushed into a modern colonial system, with occupation troops ready to fire at any provocation. The American "imperial package" misses one important ingredient: an emperor replaced by the Capitol in Washington, built to resemble imperial Rome in the first four centuries of our era. Unlike other imperial powers, the U.S. is the only one to lose and not to gain money with its military conquests. This demonstrates its financial and economic power as a backup for its military might.

***

The building of an empire originates with the personal ambition of a megalomaniac leader, his need to solve a financial crisis by plundering other nations, or the vital control of peace in adversarial foreign lands. Both ancient and modern empires functioned by means of a strictly enforced hierarchy to provide an orderly life to diverse skin colors, races, religions, and caste systems. Subdivided into provinces, colonies, dominions, and states, an empire must be skillfully governed to hold everything together.

The ancient empires, as well as other global powers, were built at the expense of many tribes and nations, which were held by force of arms or economic necessity into imperial submission. This complex geo-political action generated the word *imperious* and its meaning of a domineering, commanding, or arrogant attitude. Its later sister term, *imperialism*, describes nearly the same qualities: the domination and extension of powers of one country over others.

Long-lasting empires, such as the Chinese and British, functioned on solid military, economic and social principles, unlike short-lived empires hastily put together by meteoric leaders. Alexander the Great, who founded some 70 cities in Asia alone, Attila, Genghis Khan, and Hitler conquered vast foreign lands and built empires that ended with their deaths.

One of the longest-lived empires was the Ottoman Empire, which was blamed for almost everything that went wrong in the Middle Ages and in the modern European era. Yet, its secrets to longevity deserve disclosure. Its religion, Islam, was tolerant of others. Even expelled Jews from other countries found safe and prosperous shelter inside the Ottoman Empire. The wisdom of the Porte, the sultan's government, protected capable and useful foreigners who administered its vast territories. In fact, the sultans were half-foreigners, for their mothers—beautiful harem girls— were not Turkish. Moreover, the sultans' Praetorian Guard was formed by the Janissaries, foreign boys raised in fanatical devotion to their masters. Their military power took down the Byzantine Empire and penetrated Southern Europe.

Most importantly, the conquering Ottoman soldiers, like the Roman legionnaires, rarely mingled with local religions or joined the social lives of the natives. Their punitive actions focused on quiet revolts, showing the flag, installing the highest bidder on a provincial throne, and collecting taxes. Adopting the Koran's teachings was a tempting option for the servile kings and their opportunistic functionaries, allowing them to advance up the Turkish administrative ladder.

The British learned many lessons from the Ottomans and creatively applied them to their colonies, which covered one-fifth of the globe. Each time the arrogant officers, clerks, and even Christian missionaries tried to impose their way of life on the natives, the rebellious nations slaughtered them. The Spanish Empire, where the sun never set because it was over 13 million square kilometers, collapsed as its distant colonies revolted over three continents,

To their historical credit and contrary to their many faults, imperial eras produced past civilizations that still astonish us with their imposing pyramids, temples, lasting roads and cities, and art masterpieces. After failing in his imperial mission to unite Europe under French rule, Napoleon bitterly concluded, "Empires are built only to be destroyed." But the history of making empires went on.

The Soviet Empire was the effect of the ruinous Imperial Russia, which lost its power in World War I, and of a new Marxist-Leninist "religion" imposed by the self-declared demi-gods from the Kremlin topped by the Communist red star of ruby glass. After World War II, the victorious Red Empire engulfed the eastern European nations and became a Communist empire held together by terror, bribery, and impenetrable, guarded borders. It collapsed under its imperialistic ambition to extend beyond its economic and military capacity.

Third-millennium imperialism may be masked by different names and performed with different rules. A new Communist empire, China, officially named the People's Republic of China, is rising to continue its imperial tradition, trying to dominate Asia and the South China Sea.

Still, any kind of empire is built on the same principles of dividing and conquering, crushing revolts and forcing its subjects to give adulation to the emperor. In the absence of an emperor, the adulation of the imperial economy and culture suits the empire just as well. Hopefully, the American Empire of 50 states has enough wealth and military power to maintain the New World Order and has learned from the many valuable lessons of history, particularly what made empires happy, prosperous, strong, and long-lasting.

Why did I write this short history of empires? Because the United States of America is the only empire built by immigrants!

II. THE RISK OF BEING A SUPERPOWER

From military and economic points of view, only a global superpower can ensure a safe and orderly world. The ancient Persians, the Greeks, and the Romans almost achieved that status. In the Middle Ages, the Spanish and the British built colonial empires, and Napoleon and Hitler had ambitions to create their empires in Europe. Across the ocean, the United States of America kept adding more stars to its striped flag and built a successful, modern, capitalistic empire.

Hitler took a big goose step and envisioned his Third Reich ruling the entire world for a thousand (peaceful) years. But just like Genghis Kahn and Timur the Lame, who built their equestrian empires, Hitler failed in his conquering mission because he spread his divisions too thin and too wide on too many continents. However, unlike most empires, which were destroyed by revolts from within, his Third Reich, which lasted almost 12 years, was destroyed from the outside by forces of international coalitions.

The arms race for world supremacy between the Americans and the Soviets ended after more than 70 years when the Red superpower collapsed under its own military weight. Fighting too long in Afghanistan added to its economic decline, and rising social unrest in a Communist society marked by rampant bribery and corruption finally caused its collapse.

With its market-oriented approach and backed by its military might, the USA felt entitled to be the arbitrator of a world in perpetual turmoil after WWII and the collapse of the Communist empire. It supported its ambition by providing more humanitarian aid to underprivileged countries than any other nation had ever offered.

However, that generosity came with the immense accidental risk givers often experience: being hated by the takers who see the givers as having too much control and power. When American troops entered Somalia to supervise food distribution to the local population and tried to pacify the country's internal civil war to provide relief and restore hope, two US helicopters were shot down. The dead crew members were dragged on the streets of Mogadishu. Months later, US troops pulled out of the chaotic Somalia conflict.

The fanatical Islamic terrorist group Al Qaeda reacted in a violent way, sending suicidal Jihad warriors to crash hijacked planes into the World Trade Center's Twin Towers in New York City and at the Pentagon in Arlington, VA, outside Washington, DC. Suddenly, the American superpower seemed not only vulnerable but defeatable. The incident appeared to confirm the ironic name Mao Zedong gave the USA: a paper tiger.

Angry American presidents decided to show the triumphant American flag to the world. They sent high-tech armadas to occupy Iraq in a manner reminiscent of the German blitzkrieg. The Muslim world perceived the preventive attacks as attacks on their religious establishment, and the rest of the world saw America flexing its military muscle to intimidate others.

The well-intended American concept of making the Earth a better place has created another problem: the near rejection of most other nations. In response to the United States' imperialism, its traditional Western allies (including reluctant Great Britain), which united under the Euro currency, have tacitly fought back against America's economy and the sacred dollar itself.

Once again, the superpower America did as it pleased, but a risk for doing so was imminent: the United Nations and NATO only minimally backed the US, and it received almost no support from the Euro nations in attacking Pakistan. France and Germany, with their large Muslim populations, refused to be direct allies in any new war. With too many serious problems of its own, Russia decided to wait and see to whom it might sell weapons. China, the next contender for the title of superpower, responded in a globally significant manner by manufacturing more and cheaper products to drive American companies out of business. China has developed a global market. Eventually, it will continue after 4000 years to have its own winning empire with the capacity to mobilize almost 200 million soldiers.

Geographic and military overextensions precipitate the decline of empires. The assertion is hard to refute as history bears it out. Nevertheless, the ultimate risk is right here at home, where the US public reacts negatively to the steady loss of its soldiers fighting abroad and where the cost of maintaining wars skyrockets the national debt. Historically speaking, a war brings plunder to the victorious nations. But, the United States' occupation of Iraq, with most of its wealth in oil, triggered an increase in the cost of gasoline for Americans. Additionally, the US is the only nation I know to help with the reconstruction of what their military destroyed during the war.

***

A recent unexpected invasion of millions of illegal immigrants is taking place in the US. They are consuming trillions of dollars of American taxpayers' money. The effect is that a prosperous civilization built by hard-working immigrants of the past is being taken down. By gradually losing control of its borders, the national culture, and even its traditional language, the country's sustaining institutions will become bankrupt, chaos will replace social law and order, and the government will become increasingly corrupt. These are some of the unmistakable signs of the decline of any empire.

The US represents only five percent of the global population, a number too small to generate sufficient military divisions and war equipment to keep international order on all continents and oceans. Coincidentally, the Roman Empire had the same proportional military resources for controlling the ancient world but failed in its mission after 400 years of bellicose imperial domination and fighting off devastating barbarian invasions.

Being a superpower has always come with risk. This risk is historically repetitive and easy to predict. Yet the title *superpower* itself is such a lure that we ignore history's lessons. Only a few modern empires experience global recognition and realize gains from their domination. Of the almost 8 billion people alive today, the majority live in poverty and need to be fed and taken care of. Such humane treatment is mainly achieved through American generosity. Local wars may cause financial ruin for existing empires. The result is increasing domestic protests and unrest, starting from the familial level and extending to the armed forces, partly due to increasing unemployment. Certain destructive social events cannot be predicted or controlled, and eventually, such accidents will collapse any empire.

For the time being, a significant number of the United States armed troops are deployed around the world in at least 170 countries to impose or maintain order in distant and rebellious lands. The entire situation is amazingly similar to that of the Roman Empire, which tried in vain to dominate three continents only to be crushed by barbarian invasions. Like a lion attacked by too many hyenas, any superpower finds itself in a vulnerable position when it tries to hold too many front lines. It will eventually collapse. The assertion that geographic and military overextensions precipitate the decline of any empire is a historical reality that is hard to deny. One may win the war but lose peace and the empire.

By historical analogy, the good news is that the US may have at least 100 years left of its superpower status before reaching what history indicates will be an inevitable decline. As Napoleon said, empires are built to be destroyed.

III. NOT PERFECT, BUT THE
BEST THERE IS

In 1973, I was 29 years old and came to the United States to partake in the dream of freedom and opportunity. Sofrone, my friend, brought me to New York City two months later, and I remember well the two weeks in February I spent alone in Manhattan. I had not pictured myself mingling with happy people. But, lost one day in the crowded streets, I sensed something emanating from the people walking in and out of the huge buildings: a determination to make it, an unbending will to beat the odds, a proud attitude and optimism. I noticed their genuine smiles and how they greeted strangers of all races and colors—and even me—with a polite, "How are you?" I felt like I belonged, and I was encouraged that a good future awaited me here. I had no doubt: the American character included true hospitality.

Their limitless devotion to their pets, considered part of the family, convinced me that no people treat animals better than Americans. The efforts many in Bridgeport, Connecticut, made to help me sealed my belief that compassion was another essential aspect of the American character. To me, Americans seemed to have a high tolerance for things that cause other people much concern. Americans patiently wait in still traffic, ignore the rain while walking calmly in it, and brave freezing temperatures with their coats wide open and their hair just washed. None seemed bothered by drafty open windows or squeaky doors, and they left electric lights on day and night. My broken English never made anyone nervous. However, they become aggressive over small nuisances, like another driver not signaling when they turn left or right. The wrong music in an elevator, a person trying to cut into a line, or a waiter forgetting to bring water with ice instantly infuriates many otherwise relaxed Americans.

I entered a young nation that had generated an adolescent society with people ready to act on an enthusiastic impulse—"I'll do it! Why not?"—and to take a risk and hope for the best while preparing for the worst. That kind of unrestrained optimism could be interpreted as naiveté, but that very level of sheer willpower has produced some outstanding technical marvels. On the other hand, it is no wonder that many have gone broke in the name of trying to achieve success. Yet, having learned a lesson and gained experience, many start all over again. To make it in this mercantile society, one must have a competitive nature. Here, heroes do not wear shiny medals; they wear power watches and expensive clothes. They do not march in formation to beating drums in order to intimidate the world but are driven in limousines to their offices inside skyscrapers, where they work to change the world.

Individuals are not judged by their culture, sophistication, manners, and elevated rhetorical skills but by their character and, ultimately, by their wealth. Heritage, which in the rest of the world is everything, matters very little in America if an individual is not rich. Money commands instant respect and power. The logic is simple and to the point: if you are bright, you will make money! Without money, nothing matters. In fact, the entire country would be better named the United States of the Dollar. The motto "In God We Trust" on dollar bills could be easily replaced with "In Money We Trust."

Hard work and the desire to make money can be perceived

as a need for instant gratification and even greed. Because money is made through sales, individuals are encouraged to buy more, buy better and buy cheaper. This national trend of thinking has created spoiled people who possess an "I want everything" attitude, regardless of whether or not they can afford the things they want. In no time, credit cards have created a plastic society with an "Enjoy now, pay tomorrow" logic.

The market reacts accordingly and will price a product to give the buyer the impression they can buy it cheaper. Thus, the dollar amount is printed in large numbers, to which 99 cents are added, printed in minuscule numbers. In this way, an item priced at $49.99 is perceived as not costing $50.00 (minus the one cent) but in the range of under $50.00, to which state tax is added later. Yet any "sale" or discount promotion, when examined, shows that a company still makes a profit, even if the price is cut in half.

By nature and education, Americans are trustworthy people, and the way they invest their money is a puzzle never to be solved. They are motivated to enrich themselves or by greed. Some will invest their hard-earned savings by trusting perfect strangers who print attractive business cards and prospectives or give financial seminars that convince investors they will earn an unrealistic ten or more percent. Most of those financial wizards build a Ponzi scheme, take investors' money for personal use and live in luxury until they can no longer send promised checks and declare bankruptcy. Too often, the charismatic providers of wealth who seem to offer successful business models and generous charitable giving, who come to be greatly admired and respected as pillars of society who offer hope for better living, turn out to be witty but ordinary squanderers. A prime example can be seen in the scandal of the Madoff case—he managed $60 billion and died poor in prison.

Everything in America sometimes seems to move quickly: fashion, jobs, residences, and even spouses are temporary. Yet, something magical holds this highly mobile society together. A Good Humor ice cream truck can sometimes bring children, families, and neighbors together more than schools or churches. Capitalistic practices keep the nation together as many fast food restaurants, hotel chains and other businesses are licensed or franchised and available in all 50 states, providing the same quality and similar price points no matter where one is. In this way, Americans are united in experience with minimal effort on their part. The practice contributes to relatively consistent cost expectations, as Americans can access services that no other country or nation could provide.

Yet, what keeps Americans united is that immigrants from all over the world are given the opportunity to integrate into our society and use their talents to work hard to prosper in business or politics in this vast country, which all can call home. Our society is diverse in color, nature and family values, but we share a collective American spirit of success to overcome hardships that make other nations collapse. In America, even among those who share differing political views, its citizens can make adaptations and create a compromise to solve a national crisis. Backed by an enormous industrial complex and the mighty dollar, which can adapt to any domestic or foreign demand, resilient Americans use their inventive spirit to overcome adversity and end as winners. Hopefully, they will continue to do the same for another 250 years.

***

After I became a US citizen, I rushed to travel abroad. I felt enormously proud of my American passport. It made me feel important, strong, and protected. I expected the entire world to admire me. However, how Americans perceive themselves is not always how the rest of the world perceives us. Abroad, American tourists often expect everyone to speak English, and they are considered arrogant, rude, and ignorant. "We know better" seems written on most Americans' faces as they rush to tourist sites and take hundreds of photos, as is their limited understanding of local traditions and self-focus.

Historically naïve and largely unaware of other cultures, Americans relate better to comic book heroes than to past civilizations' ancient heroes. As they talk loudly and dress casually, with clothes often looking like undergarments hanging down haphazardly, wearing baseball caps turned around, American tourists stand out in any crowd. Whether lounging on a cathedral's steps or sleeping in the corridor of a train station, their attitude translates as "I don't give a damn about what you think of me!" The world interprets such an attitude as a sign of faulty education or an inherent disrespect for others.

Yet, the "ugly Americans" who show a lack of manners by flashing their dollars and demanding instant service are the same ones who carefully toss their garbage into proper containers, patiently stand in line and say, "Excuse me" and "Thank you" in any circumstance. Their inviting smiles, fashionable clothing and approachable nature are irresistible to local youth who try to Americanize themselves by wearing blue jeans and t-shirts with numbers on the back, chewing gum, and saying "OK!"

It is an inherited international opinion to consider Americans for their lack of culture while they supply the entire world with the best of Hollywood movies, books, entertainment artists, and unique fashion industry. The US educational system may not rank in the top ten in the world, but the world sends millions of its best young minds to study in US schools.

Americans discovered everything from industrial electricity, the telegraph, telephone, radio and airplane, to the vacuum cleaner, refrigerator, air conditioner, frozen food, penicillin and the nuclear A-bomb. Americans continued to revolutionize the modern world with transistors, television, microwaves, industrial and personal computers, cellular phones and the global internet, complete with email. Today, Silicon Valley is the global center for technology in research, innovation and software manufacturing.

During the Trump administration in the pre-COVID-19 years, almost 62.8 million foreigners visited the US in 2023 (National Travel and Tourism). Over 140.6 million tourists, including 11.5 million international visitors, visited Florida's 1,300 miles of coastline, marveled at Disney World and Cape Canaveral, enjoyed Everglades National Park, the Miami area, and Key West.

Though much-criticized abroad, the American nation is the only one to have landed men on the moon and is the source feeding the world for free while it protects international laws and democracy. With 813 American billionaires owning $5.7 trillion, under the Trump administration, the country was the richest in the world. It had a GDP of $28.78 trillion and produced 23.93% of the total global economy (Investopedia Stock Stimulator). So, it is still possible to achieve the American dream, which would make half of the world want to live in the land of the free.

At home and abroad, America is well-known for its generosity. From the Marshall Plan that saved Europe after World War II to massive food and medical aid to undeveloped countries, its generosity has sustained life on Earth for countless numbers of people. Yet this aspect of the American human character is often perceived as a desire to control the world. When Americans are too eager to export freedom, democracy and prosperity, it often backfires against them. Their actions appear as the American New Order disguised as benevolence. Perhaps that is why America has won many wars but has lost much peace.

Former allies who could have perished without the help of the United States are now adversaries or reluctant partners. As always, givers are tarnished by takers, yet Americans hardly learn from the lessons of history. And that is another part of the American character: always looking forward and finding a way to do better. One does not need to be perfect to be good. For all there is, nothing matches "God Bless America!" and I always mention it in my prayers because it has been good to me for more than 50 years.

IV. VOX POPULI, VOX DEI

The phrase *Vox populi,* or "the voice of the people," implies that it represents the unified voice of everybody in a society. Yet, every society has many types of voices, each representing groups of people with varying levels of education, culture, income, business and political backgrounds, specific religions, ethnicities and genetic origins. But the common voice of the people was represented historically—and still is—through a collective vote that chooses a promising ruler, or rebels who want to replace a worthless ruler. However, there is a big difference between tribal, ancient Greek, Roman, and medieval times, as well as those of the post-industrial revolution. The modern *vox populi* was expressed by philosophers like Hegel, political reformers like Marx and revolutionary leaders like Lenin, Mussolini and Hitler, who expressed the nationalistic voice of their people for a New World Order.

Regardless of the specific leadership, the strongest voice for economic or political change does not come from an elite or privileged class but from the most numerous members of a society, who are generally poor but superior in number. Even if they do not vote, they can revolt and voice their demands. They may be defeated temporarily, but it is only a matter of time before the multitude wins their cause. As in any war, the side that is greatest in number and that achieves the most destruction wins.

The concept of *vox Dei,* the voice of God, which approves or disapproves of human decisions, originated in ancient times when God spoke to the people through prophets, orators, and other spiritually gifted humans who could connect with or hear what advice or decisions He made. Gradually, religious leaders, pharaohs, emperors, kings, and dictators impersonated the voice of God. Even today, to be a Catholic and not obey the voice of the pope, who is God's vicar on earth, is blasphemous. In the past, to be German and to doubt the words of Hitler, whom many saw as their messiah, was to deny what Providence bestowed on the future of the "chosen" Aryan race to rule the world.

***

When American politicians address an audience, especially before elections, they tend to target the middle class made up of small business owners and white or Latino citizens with average incomes, as that population represents the majority of voting taxpayers. These middle-class citizens want to identify with the future leader they will choose to represent them in the government to solve their problems and who will benefit their economic and political future. The system is possible only in truly democratic nations, where the citizens' vote is the ultimate final word, replacing the voice of God.

In the Communist bloc under tyrannical leaders, Marxist-Leninist slogans replaced the voice of Russians. Lenin and Stalin, the self-proclaimed man-gods, promised a future "golden age" of Communism for all proletarians who would unite under the Communist Party's red flag with its hammer and sickle insignia. After WWII, leaders in satellite Communist countries delivered cookie-cutter speeches originated from the Kremlin. Through these speeches, the Communist-controlled media glorified the Party's imaginary successes and denied the reality of the vital shortages of what was needed to sustain a normal life. When the people revolted, massive arrests and the execution of any suspected "enemy of the people" followed. Yet, in spite of the brainwashing Communist propaganda, the voice of people revolting caused the Communist Empire to collapse under its weight of lies, incompetence and corruption.

After WWII, the colonial-controlled system of Asian and African nations was abolished, and numerous new countries were supposed to have the voice of their own people. However, those voices were quickly kidnapped by Moscow and Washington, which competed to finance the leaders of the "freedom fighters" to become the new presidents and prime ministers of their own nations. The appointments, made by vote or revolution, proved not to be the voice of the people since, in no time, the new leaders became dictators and tyrants who stole the billions of dollars coming from abroad meant to help their poor nations. But those dollars came to be deposited in foreign financial sanctuaries. *Vox populi, vox dei* never took root in most liberated nations of the world.

***

The last bastion of *vox populi, vox Dei* is in the United States of America, the last true capitalistic country based on a free market, in which free enterprise allows people the chance to succeed and make money in any field they choose to live a better life. This opportunity is due to the Constitution of this land, which preceded the foundation of the country, which is now formed of 50 states, each with its own local government subordinate only to federal laws from the nation's capital in Washington, DC.

The First Amendment of the American Constitution protects the free expression of the voice of the American people. The rights it gives mean people's opinions can be made known through the country's mass media, including newspapers, radio, television, and other news venues. Ironically, the *vox populi* would come to be handled by intellectuals working for the media from their skyscraper offices—people without business experience, financial experience, or farming backgrounds, and those who never served in the US armed services. Rather, highly specialized experts, illustrious figures from the world of academia and leaders of respectable institutions, all with titles, merit awards and diplomas from the most prestigious universities, became the trusted commentators, editors, writers and reporters who explained to the public in convincing and detailed ways what they should think of what is going on in society and all other aspects of life. Thus, American mass media came to represent the *vox populi* (at least in its own mind).

At no time in history has any society been blind to its citizens' religious or racial status, and America is no exception, in spite of the "melting pot" trope drummed loudly by politicians claiming to be the *vox populi* for each segment of the population.

However, it took the voice of Dr. Martin Luther King, Jr. in the US and the voice of Nelson Mandela in South Africa to achieve economic, political and social progress for the Black population in their countries. Their movements achieved and guaranteed freedom for once second-class citizens to have a powerful voice in business as entrepreneurs and in elected political positions.

In the US, all who are elected to office have the mission to inform and influence the judgment and decisions of the general public about what is going on inside the federal government and various business, cultural, economic, political and scientific events, both domestically and in foreign affairs. However, almost all mass media serves two main political decision-makers: the conservative Republican and pro-socialist Democratic parties.

***

Proof that *vox populi* is alive and well for the American people can be seen in the re-election of California's governor in 2003. At that time, the state was experiencing an economic disaster. From 135 initial candidates came one winner, Arnold Schwarzenegger. The scenario seemed to come from a Hollywood script based on true stories. Schwarzenegger was a formidable bodybuilder and the winner of numerous Mr. Universe and Mr. Olympia contests. He showed amazing confidence and ambition and still remained a crowd-pleaser and an extremely popular hero.

Determined to win in any competition he entered, including in politics, the Austrian-born Schwarzenegger, with his thick German accent, decided to run for governor of California, though he could hardly pronounce the name of the state. With no political background, he compensated with qualities voters always want from a winning candidate: he was a leader with a good, credible record of achievements in business and other productive fields. He had the competence to handle important assignments—he came across as somebody who could solve problems, not become a problem, and as a leader who could inspire hope for a better life. Voters do not want empty suits spouting empty promises.

In Hollywood, by flexing his muscles in superhero roles, Schwarzenegger became the highest-paid actor of that time.

He was a Republican who married into the elite, Democratic Kennedy family. In addition to his other accomplishments, he won the position of governor in a recall election. The negative campaigning against him meant little to the voters who trusted a "real hero" to restore their confidence in the government and secure their jobs.

His undeniable charisma is rooted in qualities voters love to be a part of. Schwarzenegger was a powerful icon of a man with name recognition, destined for greatness. Ultimately, he became the Republican governor in the heavily Democratic state of California twice, which shows the power of the American electoral system to deliver what *vox populi* wants.

***

The credibility of the mass media is debatable when legions of brilliant analysts and wise advisers work for an owner of a newspaper, radio, TV network or any other news outlet, and that owner is who decides what is to be said, written or shown to the public. If he or she is a Democrat, the messaging can become a radical left socialist platform and even promote extreme communist ideas. Such outlets back up every decision of Democratic party politicians, regardless of how much they damage the taxpayers. Former Republican President Donald Trump, running for re-election in 2024, has called such outlets "fake media" since they always criticize him and promote the lies and mistakes of Democratic President Joe Biden and his administration as good for America.

An example can be found in the news coverage of the "peaceful" protests of the rioting in Minnesota in May 2020, in which looters and agitators were paid to riot as the voice of the poor.

Parts of the beautiful city were burned by rioters over four days, from May 27 to 30. The city police were not in a position to stop the vandalism and fires. Its mayor asked for the National Guard to quiet the violent demonstrators and protect private property and the city from the extensive acts of arson. But Governor Tim Walz vetoed the call so as not to infringe on the rights of what he considered a "necessary" demonstration. The mainstream media never condemned the rioters and arsonists, who were looters and agitators paid to show the voice of the people.

Once great American cities like New York, Los Angeles, Chicago, San Francisco and others are now sanctuary cities for millions of illegal immigrants crossing the open southern border. The taxpayers in the sanctuary cities suddenly became victims of Democratic party-led social and financial decisions. Democratic leaders have decided not to stop riots, arson and massive looting from stores because it would infringe on the First Amendment rights of the demonstrators against police brutality. Trillions of dollars were lost in revenue in "sanctuary cities" due to destructive riots, and countless thousands of businesses closed after being vandalized. Special but unaffordable budgets were created to provide for illegal immigrants even more than helping needy citizens. With no end in sight, the voice of the American taxpayer worries about "the vox dei," which would normalize their lives.

On the other end of the scale, the event on January 6, 2021, of Trump supporters and others entering the Capitol in Washington, DC, was judged by the Democratic Biden Administration and its biased media as an insurrection and a right-wing raid and former President Donald J. Trump was accused of being an instigator who needed to stand trial and be indicted and imprisoned over this incident. His Florida residence was raided and searched by armed secret agents in the night to collect proof that the former president stole important secret documents and was a traitor.

Eventually, former President Trump faced over 90 indictments to be judged in the courts. Those who brought the indictments hoped to find him guilty of anti-American conspiracies. Trump is accused of being a racist, a nationalist fascist, is often called Hitler, and is seen as a self-serving, rich, egotistical, and eccentric billionaire who wants to be a dictator. If convicted, he could not run for president in 2024. However, just weeks before the election, Trump was temporarily leading in most polls, which are supposed to represent the "vox populi," and some predicted he would be elected as the 47th president. Instead, he narrowly escaped two assassination attempts.

Trump accused Biden and his administration of being corrupt and crooked, recklessly spending trillions of taxpayer money and trying to destroy the middle class and the traditional, plentiful, and secure American way of life. By opening the borders to 10–13 million illegal immigrants who will step on America's culture and civilization and financially ruin American society, the general fear is that Biden's administration will change the once rich and powerful United States into a third-world country.

By granting citizenship to three million immigrants since he became president (Fox News, 8/14/2024), Biden shows he wanted more votes for his re-election. It turned out that his vice-president, Kamala Harris, became the presidential candidate who, in almost four years, did nothing to correct inflation or the illegal invasion of unwanted immigrants. Still, the "border czar" keeps the US border open for anyone to enter the country to steal, rape, murder, litter and rip off the benefits paid for by the American taxpayers. The worst of all is that they introduced new deadly "recreational" drugs, which have killed hundreds of thousands of American teenagers and adults. They illegally brought minor children, and some 300,000 vanished without a trace, most likely sold into the pedophile market.

***

The main problem with judging public speeches by politicians, the actions of agitators, and laws that maintain American freedoms and liberty is that the opinion of the vox populi on what is right is almost equally divided. The pros and cons of what is said into the microphone, as well as the actions taken by politicians and the government, are almost always debatable.

In brief, Democrats accuse Republicans of being xenophobic, racist, fascist, and individualists, who are only business-oriented, concerned about their own tax reductions and with competitive free markets. Democrats believe Republicans are in favor of individualism, nationalism, colonialism, and imperialism and that they do not support social progress for minorities, the poor, or people with special needs, including those who seek transgender medical treatments or have mental problems.

Republicans accuse Democrats of being left-wing extremists who support radical socialist thinking, which is only one step short of becoming communists. Democrats, Republicans believe, are more concerned with illegal immigrants' welfare than that of the country's own citizens and taxpayers.

The Democrats' open border policy brought some 13 million unwanted and not needed illegal immigrants. According to Fox

News (Laura Ingram show 8/21/2024), this policy will allow eight million illegal immigrants to invade the United States each year, which will change the existing culture and society and bankrupt the American way of life forever. Former President Trump, who built 570 miles of a border wall, wants to win the re-election to complete the wall and stop illegal immigrants from flooding into the United States. He is convinced he represents the *vox populi*.

Democrats tend to become socialists as they centralize the economy and create a one-state party in the style of communism, control the media and therefore eliminate the vox populi, leaving no opposition to criticize them. In an attempt to lower inflation by implementing price controls for food products, their model of government will destroy the capitalist system and its competitive marketplace. It will have an adverse effect by triggering severe food shortages, encouraging black markets, and increasing inflation while ruining the profits of businesses that will be doomed to close. Naturally, the vox populi will oppose anything that negatively affects their buying power.

In order for Democratic party leaders to establish "social equity," they will condemn all people to end up in the same place and situation—on the bottom. Corruption and bribery are rampant among Democrat politicians who seek to enrich themselves using their powerful political positions.

President Biden's son Hunter pleaded guilty to all nine charges of tax evasion of the $1.4 million in payments he allegedly received using his father's name during his past foreign business deals abroad. He was found guilty of three gun charges and falsifying a mandatory gun purchase form. Former President Trump built an election case on these undeniable illegal facts about the Biden family. On December 1st, 2024, President Biden unconditionally pardoned his son Hunter of all charges since 2014.

***

When it comes to choosing leaders, little has changed in voter mentality since tribal times, when the strongest, wisest, or richest person was entitled to lead the community. But in the modern American voting system, popularity contests have limits, as any candidate must confront the *vox populi,* who is entitled to ask questions about candidates' credentials, qualifications, future political and business intentions, integrity and character. They must earn their nomination. An exception to this well-established, democratic nomination system occurred when the Democratic Party granted Kamala Harris the party's nomination for the November 2024 presidential election. At the time, she was still Vice President for President Biden, who practically abdicated from political power as he was deemed unfit to continue his role as the party's nominee.

Harris, who was the first to drop out of the initial presidential candidate debates and was in charge of the border but did not close it, never achieved anything notable as vice president. Now running for president, Harris never passed electoral scrutiny, nor had a debate or even granted an interview before being nominated as the party's official presidential candidate. After a ruinous political career and almost four years as vice president without achieving anything good for the American people, Harris emerged overnight with a new, reinvented image as a competent, powerful, and efficient leader ready to "turn the page" forward and push American society into a socialist system.

In her new role, running to be the first female and non-white American president, she walked onto the stage at the Democratic National Convention in a fully undeserved light of glory, as if she were an acclaimed winning gladiator in the Coliseum. Along with her was her comical, Byzantine-acting vice president candidate, Tim Walz, who lied about his army rank and other personal achievements. Both accepted their nominations by the Democratic Party in the 2024 elections and shared the adulation of the costumed delegates and the vocally approving participants in the immensely expensive, glitzy, Hollywood-style decorated arena.

Harris, faithful to her scripted speech, barely mentioned the few political policies she would enact if elected president, and the circus-like audience went wild each time she denigrated Trump. Who needs policies when there is Trump to hate? For sure, the audience in the incredibly staged fairy-tale arena did not represent the *vox populi*, which in reality is not about liking or disliking a candidate or any made-up luxury to advance his or her image. What the majority of voters care about is whether the candidate is capable of serving their needs.

Yet, there are different voters whose power consists in their numbers who will vote for Harris because they do not like Trump as a person or they belong to ethnic, political or other groups that express their voices by traditionally voting for the Democratic ticket. If empowered to vote, millions of illegal immigrants that Vice President Harris allowed to invade America and take advantage of its reckless, expensive hospitality will certainly vote against Trump, who wants to deport them.

A divided vox populi leaves the vox Dei to decide right from wrong. Many citizens are looking for a safe and better life under a second Trump administration. In his previous term, there was low inflation, tax reductions, cheaper gasoline, a better quality of education, low mortgage rates, lower rental prices, and many of the government's unnecessary restrictions and spending were eliminated. Regardless of party affiliation, voters can ignore or overlook most things, but not financial safety, personal safety, and their own health. The result of the final vote counts as the vox Dei.

Until then, the *vox populi* cheered Trump with wild greetings and a chorus of "USA, USA" and "Four more years!" inside Bryant Stadium, where he watched the football game between Georgia and Alabama (Ryan Morik, Fox News, September 28, 2024). This was not the same welcome Tim Walz received, as the fans booed Kamala's vice-presidential candidate with "Get out of here!" as he left the Michigan-Minnesota game in Ann Arbor, MI, on the same Saturday (Bing.com/news).

Unfortunately, due to the numerous ways of voting and computerized vote-counting systems, millions of good votes can be erased at the touch of a button and replaced with votes to elect crooked liars and incompetent leaders. They will prove to act almost anti-American by undoing what was good and prosperous in the previous administration.

In this way, the 2020 elections produced laws that weakened the US economy with high inflation, increasing costs of food, gasoline and other vital necessities. Due to these increases, numerous small and large businesses became insolvent because of a lack of clientele or criminal activities. The US military power was eroded by the hasty and chaotic retreat of the defeated American troops in August 2021 from Kabul. They left behind war equipment valued at $7 billion, now in the hands of the former Taliban enemy during the 20-year war.

Yet, the most damaging decision of the Biden administration was to allow the American borders to be open to millions of illegal foreigners to invade and cross into the United States, jeopardizing the safety and prosperity of American citizens.

According to ICE (Immigration and Customs Enforcement) reports, thousands of illegal immigrants are criminals, sex offenders or convicted of assault. They are part of approximately 20 million illegal foreign immigrants by the end of September 2024. So far, they have cost the American taxpayers $60 billion to generously accommodate them (Fox News At Five, 10/14/2024). Maybe Biden liked to believe that the astronomical invasion would help him to be re-elected for a second term. However, he was pushed into retirement by his own Democratic Party, which nominated his vice president, Kamala Harris, to run in his place. To help her election, already in California, a major electoral state, it is illegal to ask for an ID to vote.

The voice of the majority of American people became angrier when, at the end of September 2024, two consecutive massive hurricanes, Helene and Milton, reached six southern states from Florida to Tennessee. On a destructive path of 600 miles, they left millions uprooted and homeless, with no electric or gas power, no shelters, internet, food or drinking water, surrounded by floods. All disasters were at a cataclysmic level never witnessed in America's recent memory. The total storm damage was estimated at $38.5 billion. To the victims, the Biden administration offered $750.00 in help for each person after an application is made.

With no internet, post office or even a mailbox around, millions learned that FEMA (Federal Emergency Management

Agency), in charge of the immediate response to any disaster to help victims, ran out of a one billion dollar budget which was supposedly redirected to help illegal immigrants (Fox News – The Big Weekend Show, 14 October 2024).

On October 3, former President Trump accused the Biden administration of spending FEMA funds for disaster relief "on illegal immigrants." Only $47 million was granted by FEMA for two catastrophic weeks of tornadoes, but it expects $20 billion to be approved by Congress.

Florida Governor DeSantis told Fox News that Kamala Harris had "no role" in the recovery effort, but she was "the first one… trying to politicize the storm" because of her presidential campaign. For that reason, he refused to take her telephone call on October 7.

To all these financial and political machinations, Americans expressed their revolt that the Biden administration would treat illegal immigrants to handouts better than the taxpayers badly in need of help, while the invasion of illegals proceeded in a full wave across the open borders or carried by commercial planes to American airports. It was the reason why 60,000 border agents endorsed former President Trump to stop illegal immigration, since he promised to begin the deportation of all illegal invaders on his first day as the new president.

The 2024 election will be remembered as the most pivotal event generated by the voice of the voting people. The result will provide to be the *vox Dei,* which will determine the future of the United States of America.

The voice of the American people was strongly felt in the US presidential election on 5 November 2024, as Trump made a historical 277-electoral vote comeback win. He became the second US president (after Grover Cleveland in 1892) elected to serve two non-consecutive terms. Trump's supporters rallied behind his first term record when they lived better and felt more secure than under the corrupt Biden-Harris administration.

Kamala Harris, the "joyful" far left-wing candidate, promised to "turn the page forward" and provide a new generation of leadership. Celebrities and rich Democratic politicians supported her, but she had no agenda. She had no answer as to why, in almost four years as vice president, she did not solve economic problems or stop illegal immigration. Perceived as a liberal socialist who wanted the highest title in the land without having cut inflation or stopped crime, she weaponized the judicial system and thus aimed for a communist society.

Trump campaigned on making America great again by promoting profitable business, cutting taxes and inflation, closing borders, deporting illegal immigrants and enforcing immigration laws. He will improve the educational system and regain energy independence, while re-establishing America's respect abroad. Trump already proved he was a reliable leader and is now providing hope for the American people. Giving citizens control of businesses and fighting crimes, his policies promote safety. He believes in a golden age. The political champion Donald J. Trump heard the voice of the American people, who entrusted him with a 312-vote Electoral College win and the biggest Republican popular vote. After being saved from assassination attempts, and after his crushing victory, Donald J. Trump seemed destined to implement *vox Dei*.

V. ON THE MATTERS OF LIBERTY
AND FREEDOM

Years ago, I lectured on "Life in Communism" in front of an audience of mostly retired, highly intellectual and well-educated professionals who had backgrounds of merit. Since I had lived for 29 years in Romania under the rule of the dictatorial Communist Party and was a published author, I had the proper credentials, and they trusted I would give a good lecture.

However, from the start, my lecture about Communism was not what they expected to hear, mainly because it was not a version of what they had learned in school, read in newspapers, or seen on television. I tried to clarify why Romania was an ally of Hitler in World War Two. No other major power wanted to fight against Stalin as he extended Communist domination in Europe. Four years later, because the Red Army already occupied Romania, it became the People's Republic of Romania, a satellite of the Soviet Union. Next, Russian troops, already stationed in the country, put the Romanian Communist Party in power, though it numbered only a few hundred misfits, including some who did not even speak Romanian.

Why, my audience wondered, after King Michael was forced into exile, would Romanians vote for members of the Communist Party? I mentioned Stalin's saying that while voters are important in any election, it's who counts the votes that is the most important. The most puzzling thing was that Romania was perhaps the only country that did not have food rations during the war, and the population never saw food coupons.

After the Communists took over, an epidemic famine killed untold numbers of Romanians. I explained how the Soviets looted the country's wealth. Romanian farmers, like the Ukrainians in the 1930s, did not have grain or seed potatoes and could not harvest crops. Since Stalin refused the Marshall Plan, the Communist leadership of Romania did the same, to deadly consequences. My audience listened in dismay, hardly blinking, following along as I pointed to a map of Eastern Europe.

I explained that Communist and Socialist ideas came from Marx and Engels, were implemented by Lenin, and enforced by Stalin, using the Greek word *democratia,* meaning "people's ruling power," to which Marx added that "democracy is the road to socialism." Preventable, the word "democracy" was never mentioned in the Declaration of Independence or in the U.S. Constitution.

The French introduced the revolutionary slogan, "Liberté, égalité, et fraternité," and Communists introduced the concept of "freedom" from exploitation. The term égalité is simple as it explains that to have a democratic lifestyle in any society, all people must have equal rights and obligations. Fraternité is self-understood: for all people of a nation to feel like brothers and sisters, they must belong to the same family.

Liberté implies a certain type of equality among members of a society. Politically, they are free to live and behave in the ways they want to pursue their own happiness, provided they stay within the limits allowed by law. *Liberty* implies one will not be politically harassed but has the right to be politically involved, to vote, to be free to do one's duty as a citizen, and to benefit from the rights a society allows to its rightful citizens. Regarding rights and responsibilities, liberty creates a balanced society. Even Lenin believed liberty to be so precious "…that [it] must be carefully rationed." Hitler stated, "if men were given complete liberty of action, they would immediately behave like apes." While the Statue of Liberty quote was offering hope to the "huddled masses yearning to breather free."

***

My difficulty began when the Communist ideologues introduced the sacred word *freedom*, which, in simple terms, implies one can make individual choices to act according to one's beliefs and change things without fear of arbitrary punishments. The fact is that once living in a society, one cannot live free from society's rules and obligations. Immediately, my audience asserted that freedom of assembly and the ability to speak freely without fearing persecution makes American society great. Indeed, I agreed: the guaranteed freedom of religion makes minorities and poor people feel they have the freedom to make choices. Everyone in the audience applauded my statement.

However, I argued, *freedom* is the most dangerous concept introduced in any society. I gave an example of Communist propaganda, which asserts that freedom is found in a classless society where all is shared in common (from which the term *communist* is derived). Communists believed that destroying private property freed the people from exploitation. Thus, by looting from and even killing formerly well-to-do and wealthy people, the Communists were able to take over. For believed humanity was to be free since all production, farming, and factory industries were to be owned by the Communist state.

My audience could now understand the joke that best summarizes the economics and politics of the competing systems: in the capitalist system, men exploit men, but in Communism, it is the reverse.

A communist dictatorship and its Red bourgeoisie took over, enslaving working people in the name of freedom. It affected not only working adults: from an early age, children in school are trained on what to think, not how to think, so their "freedom" came from obeying and carrying out Communist Party orders blindly. One was free to glorify the communist regime but not free to listen to the anti-communist radio broadcast of the Voice of America or Radio Free Europe. To do so was punishable by years in jail.

To provide an example more familiar to my listeners, I ventured to explain the danger of freedom in even the most capitalistic society, America. All in America can compete in the market, pursue artistic or creative endeavors, and join or begin any business. However, entrepreneurs are all subject to the law, rules, and regulations that cover everything from working conditions to paying taxes. My audience tacitly accepted this by nodding their heads.

But I, the defector from Communism, now lecturing those who made Capitalism great and who had accepted me, went further and I pushed the concept of freedom with a confusing, perhaps even murky logic for my increasingly nervous listeners. The point I wanted to make was that while freedom is great and people must be able to express themselves to be productive, one can practice freedom only within the limits of the laws of the land, and one must not infringe on the rights of the rest of society. Otherwise, one could ignore or even step on the freedom of others.

Under the definition of liberty, it is permissible to revolt politically and take down an unjust government. Still, an anarchist does not have the freedom to shoot and kill a crooked president or prime minister. When a local or federal government increases taxes on working people or allows inflation to rise, their ability to prosper and enjoy the fruits of their labor is minimized. The effects can reach dramatic levels, putting them out of business and condemning their families to poverty and unnecessary suffering. My audience casually accepted those reasons.

I criticized those who abuse freedom and thus harm society, especially in hooligan and criminal ways. They defy protective laws and instill fear and panic in innocent citizens. Those individuals who are born criminals or belong in insane asylums and prisons gain no true freedom as they set private properties, businesses and institutions afire or as they rob, loot, beat, and rape others.

A police officer who makes an unlawful arrest is equally as wrong as a person who attacks a police officer doing their duty. Agitators who set shops or streets on fire to protest police brutality claim to be victims only to cover their own crimes. They are not victims of society defending their "freedom." Instead, they are destroyers of law and order who often seek settlements of millions of dollars from taxpayers' money.

At this point, part of my audience protested that I was wrong. They claimed I misunderstood the meaning of freedom in America, which they did not want to see become a police state. Others applauded and smiled at me. Taking their encouragement, I went further. I warned about the dangers of total freedom when one does whatever one wishes. A person who believes in practicing total freedom is usually angry at the world because they likely find themselves at the bottom of society. They expect everything to be given to them but offer nothing in return. They may use illegal drugs in an attempt to find peace within. They may drop out of school and find themselves repeatedly fired from jobs. Thus, they become unemployable. What has happened is that they have become self-outcasts in society. They abuse their freedom to attack others. In the name of social equity, they destroy what they could never have built. Simply put, crime is the product of lax justice combined with an excess of wealth and freedom in any society.

Now, my liberal audience turned against me.

I blamed my poor English for any misunderstanding and immediately changed the subject from manmade freedom to freedom in nature, often symbolized as a wild horse running without restriction. Renowned aviator Charles Lindbergh once said, "Real freedom lies in wilderness, not civilization." I stressed that rivers run free to lakes or seas. But in response, my audience asserted that humans can build dams to stop their flow. I replied that the natural freedom of the river would ultimately break any dam, and I pointed out that humanity could never make raindrops fall upwards. Therefore, I asserted that changing the climate is impossible and that any other stance is only a political platform. Nothing can stop rain, wind, or love.

That statement redeemed my standing with them, and the audience applauded in unanimous acceptance.

I argued that so-called visionaries who are determined to try to control nature, who arm themselves with scientific data and examples of defiance of natural laws, will only get in trouble and discredit themselves. If one thinks that a mountain will come to him, that brilliant scientist better run: he is not Mahomet, and any movement he senses is actually an unstoppable mudslide, a rolling stone, or an avalanche.

To stop the resulting applause and laughter, I paraphrased Mike Tyson: while one may have glorious plans for the future, a punch in the face will instantly eliminate the freedom to implement them.

In conclusion, I advise all lecturers to start and finish with a good joke—not a politically accusatory or racist one—for their audience.

One should never argue the role of democracy or Newtonian laws!

VI. THE POWER OF ALCOHOL

Under the Communist regime, Romania suffered a food shortage, the likes of which it had never known before. It is enough to mention that during WWII, Romania was one of the few countries without food ration cards for its population because it was invaded by Stalin's Red Army, which plundered the Romanians' wealth and food supply. After the war, reparations for the destruction Romanian troops made in Russia included a huge delivery of food. Prior to the war, Romanians never died because of hunger until the years 1953–1954.

In the *epoca de aur* (golden era), Ceauşescu exported food, fuel, natural gas and electricity along with other vital goods to pay back billions of dollars he borrowed from the West to industrialize Romania. To his merit, he will be remembered in history not for his non-stop efforts to industrialize agrarian Romania, but for being the only leader to pay his country's external debts in full to foreign banks. In his case, it was 13 billion dollars.

For many years, food shortages nearly reached famine levels. In state grocery stores and supermarkets, shelves were empty most of the time. Foods were replaced with bottles of alcohol, which were displayed in abundance. Rampant alcohol consumption almost matched the levels in Soviet Russia. In Romania, domestic beer production was rushed to maturity to keep up with the population's demand, with laundry detergent mixed in to produce foam.

***

During human history, alcohol consumption has always been

part of life for common people, as well as for their leaders. It has been used to achieve various important purposes, many of which changed the world.

The former pagan Princess Olga brought Christianity to her Russian subjects after visiting Constantinople in the 950s. She was the Princess of Kiev, a stronghold which she burned down, and was still so revered that she was canonized as a saint. Her grandson, Prince Vladimir, was baptized, and he Christianized the barbarian Kiev people. It was not the New Testament which was translated into Russian and published 800 years later, but communion based on plenty of alcohol that attracted Russians to the Orthodox Church, and they later established its capital at Kiev.

Peter the Great, the tsar and emperor of Russia for 43 years until 1725, transformed his huge but backward homeland into an almost modern imperial power in Europe. He opened his country to the Baltic Sea and built the city of Petrograd to establish the Russian Navy, which he built after his apprenticeship in Holland. There, Peter was famous for his drinking orgies. His entourage destroyed furniture and invaded neighborhoods with loud screaming and litter. His drinking parties became legendary. A verse of the "Engineers' Drinking Song" was dedicated to Peter, the Great Drinker:

> *There was a man named Peter the Great who was a*
> *Russian Tzar;*
> *When remodeling his castle, he put the throne*
> *behind the bar;*
> *He lined the walls with vodka, rum, and 40 kinds of beers;*
> *And advanced Russian culture by 120 years!*

Regardless of the satire, Tzar Peter the Great indeed advanced the Russian culture, industry and society to keep up with the rest of Europe.

***

Another earth-shaking change took place in Russia in 1917, when the Great Bolshevik October Revolution (which happened in November) took place in Petrograd without Lenin, Stalin or Trotsky, who were abroad. At that time, Russian armies, fully armed, deserted the Western Front, and thousands of soldiers, aided by sailors, stormed to loot the Winter Palace. After they arrested the new provisional government, the armed mob discovered the palace wine cellars, the largest and best in the world. The wine was piped into the palace's drains, attracting additional thirsty mobs, and the entire night became dedicated to an alcoholic orgy which proved in the morning to cause the biggest hangover in history. It was the power of alcohol that changed the Imperial Russia of the Romanov dynasty into the Soviet Union under the late communist dictatorship of Lenin and Stalin.

***

The diplomatic banquets honoring Stalin and his foreign guests became world-famous. After the Molotov-Ribbentrop Pact (the Treaty of Non-Aggression between the Third Reich and the Soviet Union) was signed on August 23, 1939, at the Kremlin, Stalin offered Hitler's parliamentarians a lavish 24-course banquet. Before touching the food, Soviet Foreign Minister Vyacheslav Molotov dedicated a toast to all 22 participating members, and they drank a glass of champagne or vodka for each.

The Germans wanted to sit and eat, but Molotov continued. With a full glass in his hand, he declared: "Now we'll drink to the members of the delegations who could not attend this dinner." By now, everybody was drunk, except for Stalin, who only tasted a glass of wine with little alcohol content so that he'd be fully aware of what was going on. He listened to and flattered Ribbentrop, who could hardly express his admiration that the Russians' throats were better than those of the Germans.

A week later, the Germans invaded Poland. Sixteen days later, the Red armies did the same, resulting in Poland being divided between Hitler and Stalin.

Almost two years later, the Germans and their Axis allies invaded the 1,800-mile Russian border, believing that in a few weeks, Communist Russia would collapse.

If Hitler was smart, he would have given his soldiers not the handy MP1938 sub-machinegun, not the M42, the best machine-gun of the war, nor the unmatchable 88 mm cannon or the Tiger tank. If each one of the 3.5 million Soviet Union invaders had carried in 10 bottles of vodka to give to the Russians, they would have conquered Moscow, Leningrad and Stalingrad for Hitler. Actually, often before a deadly attack, Soviet soldiers imbibed alcoholic drinks, and they would charge forward singing communist songs and shouting Stalin's slogans, sometimes forgetting to bring their weapons. But, with their elbows locked together, they bravely advanced to the German positions, which machine-gunned them down until their barrels melted. Then, another group of drunken Russians would attack until the Germans ran out of ammunition.

It is true that Kamikaze pilots carried samurai swords but no parachutes in their planes. They were celebrated by a solemn ceremony with a cup of sake as a token of their one-way suicidal missions against American warships.

Alcohol intoxication and wristwatches were the main rewards for the Communist victors. It just so happened that in crossing into Germany, countless Russian soldiers died after being poisoned by drinking from abandoned German trains that were carrying fuel for V2 rockets. They wrongly believed they were drinking regular alcohol. Drunk or not, Stalin's armies occupied Berlin and won the war, extending the Communist Empire to the middle of Europe.

Stalin had good reasons to celebrate anything, and his drinking parties lasted all night at his *dacha* outside Moscow with his trusted chieftains. It included Marshal Semyon Budyonny, who used to make love with two women in a large barrel filled with wine, and Nikita Khrushchev, who was known as the drinking clown. "The Immortal Stalin," as he was glorified in communist propaganda, probably died from an alcoholic coma, drowned in his own vomit.

***

The next Soviet leader was Khrushchev, who denounced Stalin's crimes, and he was trusted to practice humane communism. Khrushchev, who only learned to read and write at the age of 22, could hardly sign his name. But he was the poster boy for success. After being born a poor shepherd and miner, by believing in the communist party, he reached the highest military, political and civil position in a communist society, mainly because he knew how to drink. He was an alcohol lover, especially on his hunting trips at home and abroad in Soviet satellite countries. Khrushchev enjoyed long drinking parties.

The Romanian leaders pleased him so much with their alcoholic hospitality that they convinced the Soviet Premier to move the Red divisions stationed in Romania since the end of WWII and return them to the Soviet Union.

In September 1959, Khrushchev and his family visited the United States for two weeks as guests of President Eisenhower. The two men looked strikingly alike. Khrushchev visited six states and caused a media circus with his ill-fitting suit, lack of manners, and angry tirades, which he highlighted by swinging his fists in the air. He was uncomfortable facing what was good in America, commenting that its farms' pigs were too fat and turkeys too small. He yelled back at hecklers. At the United Nations forum, he took his shoe off to bang the desk in protest and attract attention to his speech. The uneducated, poor, drunkard Russian peasant's characteristic temper tantrums never left his persona and brought about the downfall of this Communist leader.

When Khrushchev, now considered a *persona non grata*, died in disgrace, no state funeral was held, and not a single highly ranked Communist leader attended his burial since he was considered a communist buffoon with an inferior intellect who, once a devoted Stalinist, had turned into a bitter anti-Stalinist.

***

Khrushchev was toppled from power by the next in line, Leonid Brezhnev, who became the leader of the Communist Party and of the Soviet Union from 1964 to 1982. Along with Khrushchev, he was one of the chief political commissars during the Stalingrad battle. He was so drunk that he wanted to cross the Volga River at night on a wide wooden board. He fainted while trying and was saved from drowning by fishermen who pulled him into their rowboat.

Largely because of the rampaging epidemic of alcoholism in Soviet Russia, its economy was failing, social civility was declining, and there was massive corruption and theft of state property. The downfall was aggravated by the defeat of the Red Army, which itself had become tainted with opium and alcohol during its ten years in Afghanistan. Brezhnev declared war on alcoholism by raising taxes on alcohol, issuing limits on quantities available for purchase, and opening rehabilitation clinics. Yet, feel-good vodka toasts remained the key to settling issues and enjoying life in Brezhnev's golden era of communism.

The memorable 1973 diplomatic visit by Brezhnev to Richard Nixon's California compound revealed his love for alcohol, in spite of the fact that one year earlier, he had imposed an anti-alcohol campaign in the Soviet Union. Brezhnev drank whiskey before the puritanical American-style dinner and continued to drink afterward in the corridor, where Nixon bumped into the Soviet leader. The Soviet Ambassador to the U.S., Anatoly Dobrynin, served as translator between the two leaders when the drunken Brezhnev began to divulge Soviet Cold War secrets and details of the Kremlin's intrigues between members of the Soviet government. Fortunately, he could soon no longer speak or walk, so Dobrynin and Nixon carried the drunken leader of the Soviet Union and the enemy of the United States to his bed.

***

By the end of the 20th century, all leaders of the Soviet Union (except Lenin, Yeltsin and Gorbachev) were former high commanders in the Red Army, and their strict dogmatic rules kept Russians in line with the Communist dictatorship. In 1991, the dissolution of the Soviet Union took place, and eight years later, former KGB Lieutenant Colonel Vladimir Putin became the leader of Russia. In a militaristic manner, he restored order and law in the vast country, which extends over one-seventh of the dry land on Earth and has the world's biggest population of Caucasians. An ardent nationalist determined not to let anarchy and corruption rule the former Soviet Union, he restored it as a military superpower.

The sober Putin found a way to amass a fortune by creating *Rosspirtprom*, the Russian spirits industry, to control the vodka culture of the Russians, who were willing to pay any tax to keep their historic tradition. Before becoming president or prime minister of Russia, Putin used to joke: "There are three ways to influence people: blackmail, vodka, and threatening to kill." Certainly, he knew what part of the joke was the most efficient. The power of alcohol also proved to be useful when during economic crises, many Russian state employees, including teachers, were paid not in rubles but in bottles of vodka.

After the fall of Communism in Russia, Russians celebrated their freedom by drinking heavily. They labeled a new brand of vodka *Kalashnikov*, named after a military mechanic who copied the German automatic assault rifle STG 44, which is now the most-produced weapon in the world.

***

Russian capitalists wanted to include a weaker drink, like beer, as part of its alcohol industry. To compete with Western Europe, a food scientist was sent to Munich to study the secrets of the famous *Hofbräuhaus,* which boasted over 400 years of beer brewing tradition. The venerable scientist Ivan Ivanovich was trusted to spy on its practices to see how the Russians could copy the original Bavarian beer makers. The Russian expert was given ten days to steal the secrets of the historic beer hall, where the ascetic Hitler had begun his Nazi Party and where he came once a year with his old comrades to celebrate his first political speech.

The studious scientist was immensely impressed by the beer hall's vibrant atmosphere, with its live Bavarian tuba and accordion music, the female servers who carried eight huge steins of beer at a time between countless tables, and the friendly nature the locals showed to the tourists, who busily took pictures of the iconic drinking establishment.

Ivan Ivanovich ordered a beer, which was served immediately. The beautiful blonde waitress placed a round, thick coaster on the table before putting the heavy stein on top of it. Ivanovich slowly sipped the beer and wrote in his secret notebook about the white foam, its taste, and how long it took to evaporate. He measured the quantity of alcohol, its color and temperature, and swished the beer in his mouth like it was wine, noting the smell, bitterness, and feel of it. He drank in small gulps and larger ones to feel the impact going down his throat. He noted many other details.

Ivanovich was so pleased with the taste of the Hofbräuhaus beer and the elegant serving method with the absorbent cork coaster that he decided to have as many steins as he could in one day to study the effect of having multiple drinks instead of drinking only one beer a day.

Noticing that the coasters had disappeared, the waitress suspected that the Russian stole them, and after serving his sixth beer, she placed the next full stein directly on the table.

The drunk scientist secretly secured a sample of the beer and of Bavarian water to analyze back in the Moscow laboratory. For the rest of his nine days in Munich, he visited a few Russian immigrants he knew of the 10,000 that had migrated there. They celebrated their reunions with shots of imported Russian vodka. With a painful hangover, Ivanovich returned to Moscow with his secret beer notes intact.

***

Back at his important academic job, Ivanovich was invited to speak about his Bavarian beer experience and his secret findings. His lecture was inspiring and well-applauded. One participant asked if Bavarian beer and its worldwide success could be duplicated in Russia. The scientist scratched his head, put his glasses on his forehead, and answered: "The secrets of the beer can be duplicated by our advanced science, which the entire world recognizes. But I forgot to save any samples of the delicious Bavarian round cookies I ate. They call them *coasters*. Without them, the beer does not taste as good."

VII. THE FISHPOND

Day One

Without a competitive spirit, one can accomplish nothing. I was feeling ambitious the morning I decided to start digging a fishpond. Of course, I could have hired the excavator working across the street where a new house was being built, but I'd wanted to build a pond by myself all my life.

The urge coincided with a time I was alone for a few days— long enough, I thought, to take on and complete my project. A second motivating stimulus was that no rain was predicted for the rest of the week. With confidence and determination, I dressed like I would be playing basketball. I put a shovel and ax in a wheelbarrow along with a pair of thick new work gloves. An old Chinese saying states that a journey around the world starts with a first step. With this Confucian concept in mind, I happily stepped out of the garage and pushed the wheelbarrow down to the tiny stream in my backyard.

Within moments, I encountered a problem that would plague my project: the temperature was 95 degrees and climbing with high humidity. The conditions were a far cry from the comfort of the 73 degrees inside my air-conditioned house, where my working spirit was at its highest motivation. The stream was hidden among a green jungle. I began pulling apart and chopping up rotten trunks and fallen branches, moving them farther into the forest as I tried to locate the stream's elbow, which had vanished under the wood's debris. The more I moved piles of wood, the more the mess seemed to multiply. No matter which way I turned, I tangled with wild roses, poison oak, and vines hanging from the trees.

An hour later, dripping with perspiration and covered by yellow dust, suffering from swollen bruises and bleeding cuts, I realized I was fighting an uphill battle. It was time to take a break and regroup. I needed better tactics to clear the area for my fishpond. If I had listened to my instincts, I would have quit right then and lived happily after. However, my pride pushed me to continue.

So, I washed myself off with the hose to get rid of a few layers of dirt and sweat, and though the temperature was above 100 degrees Fahrenheit, I continued to work. After a few more hours of digging, I'd finally dug a straight line to outlet the pond. Dripping perspiration, with mud all over me, I reached for the hose again.

I looked at the manicured part of my yard and saw my beautiful flowers and bushes drooping from the heat. I sprayed them and was rewarded minutes later with their perfume. *Water nourishes life*, I philosophically reminded myself.

I went to the garage, where I pulled off my wet tank top and replaced my sneakers with a pair of green Crocs. I grabbed a handsaw and headed back to continue my deforestation project. Itchy from the poison oak I had uprooted, I remembered Kentucky forests are infamous for that irritating plant. Since I was allergic to it, my project should have ended right then, but the mud on my skin had a soothing effect, so I continued working.

I smiled to myself, thinking that a few years from now, young people would probably not even know what Crocs were—just as today's students do not know what a typewriter is, and young mechanics have never worked on carburetors. I recalled a time when I went to buy a cassette tape with tango music, and none of the young employees at the Sam Goody store knew what a tango was. When I explained it was a dance, one of them asked if it was an Irish dance and suggested I might be able to find it in the Irish music section.

As I dug in the mud, my mind kept itself busy with all kinds of oddities. *Today,* I thought, *a new employee might not even know what a cassette tape is because they've only known compact discs.* Once, I was looking for a "gentleman's valet," and no employee from any clothing or furniture department store I visited knew what one was. One told me that they did not carry books, another asked if it was perfume, and another if it was a drink. What I wanted to buy was a free-standing wooden coat rack, the kind with a little shelf on top where I could put my wallet and change. How ephemeral everything is! Perhaps hieroglyphs might eventually reveal now-vanished tools or descriptions of long-lost rituals if we can ever decipher them. *One thing that never becomes obsolete is military uniforms,* I mused, *though their details change over time.*

After another hour of fighting branches and stubborn roots, I went under my cool deck, where I could be shaded by grapevines. I drenched myself with cool water. Refreshed, I went to the garage to get my pickaxe. The menacing look and weight of the pickaxe made me feel more confident about my efforts to liberate the stream elbow from the jungle. Indeed, armed with the pickaxe, I demolished almost everything I did not like. But the feeling of empowerment the pickaxe provided came at an alarming cost—my energy plunged with every swing of the heavy tool.

I straightened my aching back and surveyed my work. I was

disappointed to see I had made little progress, and each muscle in my body seemed to have its own distinctive pain.

By now, the temperature was well over 100 degrees. The sun was high and its rays began piercing the thick layers of tree leaves. The green vines looked like twisted ropes encircling and creeping up each tree trunk. They made deep dents in the bark, ensuring a firm grip. The strong, living ropes were, in fact, strangling the trees that supported them, all while birthing countless new young vines that climbed with the same suffocating mission. As I looked closely, I noticed many of the trees were dead. They had appeared healthy and alive to me because they were ornamented with nets of vigorous creepers covering their lifeless trunks and branches. It occurred to me that the countless vines were my most stubborn enemy by far.

Itchiness, sweat, and fatigue forced me to take a break. I analyzed the parasitical system of useless vines killing robust trees. I noted a striking similarity between healthy and productive humans who are invaded and taken over by opportunists and swindlers. Little by little, posing as a help to productivity, they attach themselves to thriving groups. Soon, the intruders inch their way to the top of the business canopy and take over their generous, reliable host. In the case of the invasive vines, the host is a thriving tree. The at-first timid, hanging visitors become permanent settlers. The climbing vines, like a certain category of people, are takers, sucking the life out of their hosts and shading young trees, stopping them from growing. Then, having totally drained the tree, which eventually gives up and falls, the vines immediately climb onto the next tree, and the damaging cycle repeats.

Determined to stop that cycle within my small corner of the woods, I headed to the garage for a strong pair of clippers. The urge to render punishment was never stronger.

Blaming all the broken and fallen trees on the worthless vines, I furiously cut them at ground level and got a big kick out of seeing their upper parts hang and swing lifelessly in the air. I wondered how long their green color would last without a ground root. Suddenly, I understood that building a fishpond was not only about digging the pond itself but also about preparing all the things around the pond. As with everything in life, there is an intricate interconnection between elements. On a modest level, I felt I was avenging an injustice for the beautiful trees. For decades, they could not get rid of their sneakily parasitic side-stabbers.

However, my proud victory lasted only until the moment I discovered that the vines' roots, crawling under the bed of dead leaves, were all interconnected! Cutting one did not do much harm to the rest. In fact, previously cut vines had already connected themselves to younger ones, and new vines with what looked like grape leaves grew quickly from other trees, choking those trees out. Infuriated, I sat down, forgetting about the poison oak and mosquitoes. I saw how the young vines had tucked their tendrils into each crevice of bark so they would be undetected by someone like me, their true enemy.

I noticed, too, that weeds grow faster and more vigorously than flowers and useful plants. No drought or storm seemed to damage the weeds. *Evidence,* I told myself, *that evil is sometimes more powerful than good—the bad crop is taking over the fruitful one.* Nevertheless, I was determined to be in charge of my little piece of turf. So, I continued to cut the vines and their roots. I would replace them with a fishpond. What a great feeling to be able to do the right thing!

Under the merciless hot sun, which I'd begun to judge for its destructive power, I quit for the day. I cleaned my tools as my father had once taught me. He believed a worker could be judged by how he kept his tools. If they were clean and packed in an orderly way, their owner was reliable and able. I took one more look at my worksite—actually, at my newly created mess—and shook my head in disapproval: the job looked barely begun; there was little sign of progress. I'd even made the stream's bottom disappear.

Discouraged but not defeated, I went inside. Contrary to what one might expect, I was not hungry or thirsty. But I took a well-deserved hot shower to eradicate any contamination with poison oak. Despite my fatigue and many small injuries, I still felt great overall about my project, like anyone on a mission. I could not stop thinking about the clever, mimetic, devious tactics the vines used to kill the trees. Watching a business news segment on TV that evening, I immediately spotted various "vines" and "trees," represented by crooked money moguls and the fact that none of the ruined investors killed the swindlers.

It is amazing that a thug can kill someone in cold blood for a few dollars, but none of those who lost millions of dollars would shoot the one responsible for so many ruined lives. Instead of acting like righteous cowboys once did when they hanged criminals, today's victims wait and hope for justice to put crooks in minimum security prisons with tennis courts and swimming pools, from which they will be released for health reasons a few years later, ready to start their schemes all over again—not that

I advocate vigilantism!

Well, over the course of a few hours that day, I had done my cowboy duty. No vines were left hanging around my future fishpond. I'd cut them all. I ate a good soup I'd made and went to sleep that night feeling great about my hard but noble work. As I drifted toward sleep, I could not help thinking about those who laid down the railroads all over America and those who had built skyscrapers. But itching and covered with blisters and bruises, I could not sleep much more than an hour at a time. Finally, I collapsed and woke a few hours later, unable to move because of muscle aches and pain in my joints. No wonder no one wants to dig ponds by hand!

Day Two

Nothing is like the first day of doing something destined to bring happiness. The next morning, despite my aches and pains, I encouraged myself to continue since there was no one else to do it. Wearing only boxers and Crocs, I went down to my worksite with unbroken confidence and determination to make more good progress. It was already 90 degrees. As two brown bunnies hopped away from a bush next to me, I wondered how many other creatures were watching me work—that is, besides the ever-present, attacking mosquitoes. Before grabbing the shovel, I carefully looked for snakes since they strike only if you step on them. To my relief, the area looked safe. I saw there still was not a drop of water in the streambed near where I intended to have my pond, even though there was plenty of water further up.

My work gloves were still wet and dirty, and they scratched

my hands as I put them on. Once I grabbed the shovel, the gloves quickly molded to my hands. So, I began to work eagerly along the elbow of the stream, digging and unloading one full shovel after another as I looked for water. An hour later, dripping with perspiration and unable to straighten my back, I stopped. Breathing hard, I looked around. To my left and right were chunks of dirt that I would have to remove again sooner or later to make room for the pond. Obviously, my main concern was finding water. I decided to dig a furrow straight across the bend to find the water, which somehow disappeared right before it reached my worksite. In the meantime, the mosquitoes realized I was an easy target and mercilessly sucked my blood. But I was unabated from my mission.

The temperature rose to 100 degrees. I used the garden hose to douse my head and took a few gulps before returning to digging. Little by little, the dirt I removed became moist, and soon, at the depth of one shovel, I struck water! It was a "Eureka!" moment as if I had discovered a gold nugget. No wonder the gold rush of California and Alaska attracted so many miners: they'd felt as I did, but in a more profitable way (and maybe without so many mosquitoes). I kept digging and rationalizing that what was good about water, like gold, was that it always runs to the lowest point, and nothing can stop it from doing so.

I kept digging and soon, happily, I was standing in mud that seeped into my Crocs. It gave me great pleasure that soon changed into continuous suffering. I took a break and another look at my messy work. I needed a better plan. I determined I needed to trace the stream's long main line and dig around it. The line included the elbow since it contained water. I felt very good about making such a decision that would materialize in my useful and economical work. I wondered how many men at that moment were spending their free time working in garages and basements or digging in their yards while others went to air-conditioned gyms to work out and sweat?

I did not eat breakfast or lunch. I kept on going. In many places, I could not push the shovel into the ground. Too many thick roots and large stones were at the surface, which required heavy effort to remove. The shovel proved not to be the right tool, so I seized the pickax and swung it with all my strength.

When my attempts to remove stones and roots proved impossible, I decided to go around them and change the design of the pond. But I realized I was out of energy. Sweat dripping in my eyes, I took a break. Countless mosquito bites had become itchy blisters. The water hose never looked more inviting, and the water from it never felt more relieving. That relief, combined with sitting in the shade under the deck, refreshed me a bit. Scratching all over, I surveyed my work. Inspired, I went inside the house to get my camera and document it.

I know how to take a picture that can tell a story. Years ago, I studied to be a movie director. I learned the meaning and value of composition: a photo should show the viewer what is happening. In my case, each picture was to document the progress of clearing the forest, starting with the first shovel as I looked for water and how I hopefully succeeded in turning a muddy mess into a fishpond and fulfilled a dream of mine.

I have a thing about people taking photos without thinking about the setting. On many of my trips, whether in the Rocky Mountains or on the beaches of Florida, in Yellowstone, or in

Paris and Monte Carlo, I have noticed tourists taking pictures of each other with a wall behind them, ignoring the incredible scenery around them. Tourists in Manhattan do not direct the camera toward the Empire State Building as a background, but without thinking, have the traffic in the background. In front of the Metropolitan Museum, they sit for a picture on the steps, which could be any steps in the world, and miss the glorious entrance and the writing above it. Standing up above their small children, parents take pictures of them, practically focusing on the pavement instead of kneeling in front of the kids so the photo can show the surroundings. In brief, each photo should tell a story. In my case, each of my photos would show the creation of the fishpond as an accomplishment of my stubbornness to do the hard work. Thus, I began my photo documentary, which I would continue for the duration of my endeavor.

I went back to work, trying to cut the thick roots and break up the large stones in the stream bed. My itching was coming not so much from poison oak as from mosquitoes who found an ideal food source in my half-naked, sweating body. I suddenly envied cows, horses, and other large animals with long tails and their ability to shake each section of their skin to stave off the shameless bloodsuckers. Since I had none of those natural defensive weapons, blisters covered my body. I dug faster since sudden movements seemed to keep the annoying buzzers away.

Once in a while, I stopped to use the end of the shovel or pickaxe to scratch my back as hordes of mosquitoes attacked the rest of my body. The only way to evade these mini vampires was to use my reliable water hose and blow them away with a powerful jet of water. The itching persisted, though, and got worse each time I scratched. I went inside the house and doctored myself with various ointments, all proving ineffective. I realized I was no Robinson Crusoe or frontier man. Sadly, I returned to my gruesome work.

As I dealt with the stubborn ground and horrible insects, I remembered an entire French army of 22,000 workers died of malaria and yellow fever while digging the Panama Canal. By 1889, the entire nation of France was in bankruptcy because of the minuscule buggers—the insects of Panama. Fifteen years later, the U.S. Army Corps of Engineers took over the near-im-possible task of building the canal, and their first task was to eliminate the region's mosquito infestation. By 1913, when the canal was finished, another 5,600 workers had died of disease and work-related accidents out of an army of 75,000. My point is that it was not a huge elephant, blood-thirsty lion, savage tiger, predatory alligator or crocodile that causes the most danger, but minuscule, whizzing mosquitoes that kill nearly one million people yearly.

During WWII, the GIs in the Pacific Islands carried out a similarly successful war against mosquitoes, using some 50 million cans of repellent (at a cost of a few cents each). This turned out to be a decisive factor in their ability to defeat the Japanese armed forces. I wondered, *How many other frail and hard-to-see insects are out there able to decimate populations of giant humans?* The thought was so depressing that I quit working for the day.

After cleaning my tools, I took a hot shower, hoping to wash away all the infestations I had accumulated during my frustrating work, which so far had resulted in little visible progress. I remem-bered my father digging post holes with a long, heavy crowbar.

I jumped in the car and drove to several hardware stores until I found exactly what I needed. Back home, I could not resist going to the pond site to try my new heavy tool at once. One end was shaped like a narrow blade; it smashed anything in its way in pieces. It was also a great lever; I suddenly envisioned how the Egyptians may have built their pyramids five thousand years ago.

I have seen many documentaries and have listened to experts about how those huge pyramids were built. Some architects even re-enacted how the stone blocks were cut and dragged to the top of pyramids using rolling logs, and so on. None of those theories satisfied me. However, I always suspected that extra-terrestrial giants with advanced tools, immense powers, and sophistication were able to build those incredible prisms. Thousands of years later, the Egyptian pharaohs took credit for building the mono-lithic pyramids and temples, adding their hieroglyphs to describe their achievements, which have lasted to our days, leaving us to wonder about the truth.

Regardless of who built the giant monuments and temples during the flowering of the Egyptian civilization, they lasted till now because around them was a sea of sand, not a jungle which swallowed other great past civilizations, proving that Mother Nature always wins against mankind.

It amazes me how my mind worked and what kind of ideas I had when struggling, sweating and enduring insect bites, trying to convince myself that countless people before me did much more while experiencing much worse. Probably, this is the final wisdom of the Bible: to instill humility in every rebellious human who tries to adapt to the hardships of life. Indeed, just about every other verse of the Holy Book underlines someone's previous experience that went from bad to worse, just to teach the reader patience and faith in God. *No argument there,* I reflected that night, also thinking that besides God's fingerprints, in addition, others' fingerprints have lasted in the many changes from the original.

I called a few friends, complaining about the incurable mosquito bites. From one, I learned what the Bible didn't point out, like rubbing apple cider vinegar on the bites calms the itching and cures the irritation in minutes. Nevertheless, I was not going to ignore the teachings of the Bible, and I said to myself: If God made the entire Earth and everything on it in six days, how long can it take me to finish a fishpond?

Encouraged, I ate my home-cooked soup and thought about the invention of canned food for the Napoleonic armies and the can opener that came 50 years later. I recalled reading a piece of trivia about a big reason the Union soldiers won the Civil War: they were provided with canned food. While the Confederate troops had to canvas the land to obtain food instead of resting or battling, the Union soldiers were ready to fight at any time— without being hungry and weak. Indeed, as Napoleon pointed out, an army marches on its stomach. Canned food has since become an important "ingredient" of any war, and every soldier develops a lifelong affection for his most versatile gadget, the can opener and a versatile Swiss pocket knife with all its eating gadgets.

I also wondered why obesity tended to be rampant in the poorer populations. It was because most donated food for the poor consisted of canned items with much salt and sugar. Is canned food responsible for the fact that today, there are more people alive than all humans buried since the beginning of recorded history? During Roman times, the known world population was a little more than 200 million people. During Napoleon's time, the world population reached almost one billion. Famine, wars and sicknesses kept the population in check at 2.5 billion until 1950. Today, more than seven billion people are in the world, and that number is rising. Probably because of reincarnation, billions of newborns are added, and the ready availability of food in cans feeds them. Obviously, mosquitoes may reincarnate as well!

Day Three

I woke up unable to move any part of my body, but thanks to the vinegar, the itching was gone. To outwit the little bloodsuckers, I worked much earlier in the morning, before sunrise, when the temperature would be the lowest. Dressed only in trunks and Crocs, I had a terrible time fitting the stiff, dirty, still-wet working gloves over my aching hands. When I grabbed the crowbar, I felt an instant repulsion toward all I saw around me—I'd created an awful mess that still lacked shape, and I was losing hope. My feet were already wet, and they sunk into the mud. My first (and probably healthiest) thought was to turn around and leave that spot that was already responsible for so much pain and anguish. I wanted a pond, but not at the price of so much discomfort and pain.

It is incredible how a little detail can go wrong and compromise an entire activity. In the summer of 1941, when German tanks invaded Soviet Russia and almost reached Moscow, they had to stop for nearly two months to overhaul their engines. The reason? No one in Berlin had thought to provide the mighty Panzers with dust filters, which cost just a few cents each. Because of the long delay, the Siberian winter caught these Germans in trenches covered with snow drifts, as once again, no one in Berlin had thought to provide the soldiers with winter uniforms. General Winter of Russia won the war against the Germans and saved Moscow! In my case, because I did not buy a pair of work gloves, I could hardly dig my pond, and I kept suffering, and I kept digging.

I reminded myself that probably billions of workers faced similar painful tasks that I was doing of hard labor each morning for the duration of their lives, and they were happy to have their jobs. I grew up in a remote village in Romania, where life had not changed in the last 500 years, where I walked barefoot from April to November. Life was hard in the mountains, even for a child. I carried piles of dry wood on my back, which I had collected in the forest, so we could burn them in the medieval-style stove used for cooking and heating the room. I plowed the garden with a shovel, but because I was too light to stick it very deep into the earth, I needed to jump on top of it a few times.

Look at me now, I thought. *Life in America since I came 38 years ago—my hands have become delicate and my muscles soft.* Even though my Carpathian character had changed little, here I was, a shadow of my younger, hardened self who never used to know the meaning of quitting. To my credit, I would not allow myself to be defeated by gloves or mud.

So, I went back to digging my fishpond, working non-stop in 100-degree-plus temperatures. I had never been sick in my life, but already past middle age and depleted of potassium and electrolytes, I felt dizzy. I collapsed and passed out. Luckily, I was in the shade. When I woke up, I was in a hospital bed with a diagnosis of A-fib or atrial fibrillation.

All this because I avoided giving 20 dollars to the excavator operator across the street to dig my fishpond in 20 minutes.

Most of all, I learned from my own self-destruction experience of challenging Mother Nature on my miniscule scale, and I failed to clean a few square feet of dense vegetation. Actually, I was in the good company of many glorious past civilizations whose megalithic structures vanished under the vast green canopies of triumphant jungles. Again, somehow, after so many ignored warnings, humans refuse to recognize that Mother Nature always wins.

VIII. A BRIEF HISTORY OF
THE ROMANIAN CHURCH
UNDER COMMUNISM

Since the dawn of creation, humans have feared and believed in something more powerful than themselves and worshipped miracles. They have considered shamans, prophets, mighty kings and pharaohs to be demi-gods of divine origin. Humans are born with a God gene, which animals do not have. That is why *Homo sapiens* is the smartest and most versatile creature in the world. They are born with the intellect to speak, develop skills of many kinds, and are spiritually inclined towards philosophical investigations about the meaning of life and belief in God. Animals have strong instincts to kill for survival, fear being unsafe, and desire to dominate and multiply. They have no spirituality or consciousness, no mercy, compassion or regrets, and have no remorse to stir them on to repent or try to correct mistakes.

When Marx, Engels, Lenin, and Stalin proclaimed that God did not create humans but that humans created god, they replaced divinity with slogans to promote brotherhood among a godless and revengeful poor people. Religion was declared an illness of superstition or hallucination. Belief in miracles was considered an inherited, abnormal behavior that must be eliminated from any Communist society. Marx denied the role of God in human life, Lenin decreed that religion was the opiate of the people, and Stalin, a former seminary student, declared himself an immortal man-god.

Ironically, Stalin, frightened by German invaders at the

Moscow gates, had the clergy bless the Red troops going to save "Mother Russia." His name was mentioned in their prayers. When the "immortal" died in March 1953, church bells announced his death throughout the Communist Empire, perhaps as a sort of eulogy (or was it to celebrate the happy event?). By the 1980s, only approximately 7,000 churches were left in the Soviet Union, with a population of 293 million.

***

In ancient times, Romania was called *Dacia*. Christianity was introduced to the region by the anti-Christian Emperor Trajan when he occupied Transylvania, a Dacian province rich in gold, silver and salt. He stationed the Legion V Macedonnica and Legion XIII Gemina there, renamed Dacia Felix. Both were heavily Christianized. When those legionaries retired, they married local Dacian women, baptized their children, and thus introduced belief in Jesus and the Holy Trinity.

Christianity spread all over Dacia, and for the rest of history, the Romanian Orthodox Church faithfully served the country's princes and kings, preaching blind obedience to their divinely inspired rulers who held indisputable rights. None of the barbarian invaders, even the Ottomans, could make the Romanians change their devotion to Christianity.

When Soviet troops occupied Romania in 1944, and puppet Communist leaders took over the country, they tried hard to please Stalin by arresting openly anti-communist priests and spreading terror among the Christian population. Members of the Romanian Communist Party and their families, all state employees, and students were forbidden from going to church.

Otherwise, they would be punished with dismissal from their institutions.

***

The ambitious Romanian Communist dictator Nicolae Ceaușescu was born to strict Christian parents and baptized in the church of the village Scornicesti. At age 11, he went to Bucharest to become a shoemaker's apprentice. His limited time in school later helped him to enroll in the illegal Romanian Communist Party. He needed to find a place where he felt he belonged. His meteoric ascent through party ranks happened after Soviet troops occupied Romania because he only involved himself in political matters; the least of his concerns regarding socialist Romania was Christianity's role. Most of the old priests (former fascists) were arrested, and many were murdered. The current seminaries for the new priests' generation followed the party's educational goals, which nearly took on the priority of the doctrine of the New Testament.

With the exception of a few priests, the young, freshly ordained priesthood turned into informants who used confessionals to spy on anti-Communist parishioners. They were arrested and, under torture, further "confessions" were extracted from them and used in the Stalinist kangaroo trials.

The young priests tried to gain the respect and wealth of the old priests. However, they were more interested in living the good life that socialist society offered them. Many were sent to the West to penetrate the anti-communist activity of the independent Romanian Orthodox parishes of the old timers and of the new generations of immigrants who escaped from Stalinist Romania.

***

In Bucharest, just a short walk from the impressive building of the Central Committee of the Communist Party, there is an old brick church always open to visitors. It's astounding that the Communist leaders looking out their windows at this religious symbol did not demolish it. It still stands as a triumphant miracle of Christianity over Marxist-Leninist doctrine, which denies the existence of God.

On a bright summer day in 1971, the church's front door was open to all, but the only person inside was a volunteer there to clean the church and replace the burned-out candles. She was an old woman with a bent back, dressed in black. She moved slowly but maintained the church beautifully so that it was always ready for the next service.

She worked without stopping until the afternoon when a familiar car claxon made her walk outside. A red sports car was parked outside the church. At the wheel, a young man with a red baseball cap (nobody plays baseball in Romania), a goatee, and large sunglasses signaled her to come closer. Walking carefully and wiping her hands on her black apron, she approached the car, which was still running.

"Good afternoon, Father!" she said and kissed the driver's hand.

In a hurry, he said: "Hello, Maria. Is there anything new with the church?"

Maria shook her head from side to side.

He continued: "Did the man whose baby I baptized come with the money?"

Maria shook her head again.

"Did the fireman inspector come?"

Maria again shook her head *no.*

The priest remembered, "Did the man deliver the candles I ordered?"

This time, old Maria opened her arms and shrugged her shoulders, answering, "No, but I went to his shop to pick up the candles, but he wants to be paid first..."

This time, the priest shook his head and sobbed. "Ah Maria, yet another one who could not donate anything to our sacred church..." He wiped his sunglasses with a special silk cloth taken from a custom-made case. Suddenly invigorated, he exclaimed, "Ach! I almost forgot why I stopped by the church," and he handed a piece of paper to the old woman. "Remember that big-shot communist's secret wedding when I married his son in his house a year ago?"

Maria nodded her head.

The priest continued, "Come to this address tonight at eight o'clock because I have to baptize his newborn grandson. Bring all that is needed for the baptism, and do not forget the prayer book. Maybe this time, he will arrange for me to move into a real house, and I will give you my apartment. So do not forget!"

Maria crossed her heart. "Have I forgotten any of the other secret church services we've done for those atheist top-dog Communists?"

"Okay, okay. Do not be late. Bring that beautiful tablecloth with the big cross in the middle of it."

Glad to comply, the old woman bowed a few times, saying, "I will, I will!" as the priest quickly accelerated away, driving his flashy convertible down the empty main street of central Bucharest.

***

Romanian Communist dictator Nicolae Ceaușescu destroyed 22 churches in Bucharest to make room for his megalithic "House of the People," the second largest building in the world after the Pentagon. To make room for his vision of a modern capital and vast port for the Danube River (some 400 kilometers in the distance), valuable, artistic, cultural establishments and countless historical buildings were destroyed. Entire districts were demolished. Unfortunately, Ceaușescu's era was riddled with compromises that leaders of the Romanian Orthodox Church made in collaboration with the regime's secret service. Despite being a genuine Romanian nationalist, Ceaușescu was sentenced by the people he had trusted and promoted. He and his wife Elena were executed on Christmas Day, 1989, inside an Army garrison where he believed they were safe from revolting Romanians. No priest was present at their execution or for their burial.

IX. THE LOST SHOULDER BAG

I was staying in a boutique hotel located on the central water canal in Copenhagen, one of my favorite cities in Europe. The canal was lined on both sides with vintage boats and sailing ships. Between the boats were large platforms for parking bicycles, which were one of the most useful means of transportation in the city. The platforms accommodated thousands of bikes, neatly stacked one above the other, and all very easily accessible.

One day, I noticed a restaurant a few doors down from my hotel that specialized in serving herring, a slim fish found in Nordic waters. I sat at a table and told the waiter I had never been there before, and I didn't know what to order. The young man spoke English better than I did (as I found was the case all over the Baltic nations). He said he wanted to surprise me. Soon enough, he placed a round platter in front of me with eight herring cooked in various ways and attractively arranged like the spokes of a wheel. The first few bites from each were delicious, but I realized herring was an acquired taste that I simply did not have. Thank God for the Danish beer with its high alcohol content. It helped me wash the taste from my mouth after I tried each one. I could not finish the platter, but I would give a solid 8 out of 10 to the cooked herring.

Finally, I asked for the check. The meal was surprisingly cheap, but I could not pay. My wallet was missing! In fact, my small shoulder bag that contained my wallet, almost $3,000.00 in cash, my passport, plane tickets, notebook, camera, and 50 postcards with stamps I bought at the train station that morning was nowhere to be found. The waiter smiled and asked me to pay the next time I came to the restaurant, and he said he would be glad to help me find my shoulder bag. He returned 10 minutes later and advised me to take the same bus I took to and from the train station and to tell the driver about my lost bag. Twenty minutes later, an elegant double-decker bus with velvet-covered seats and the pleasant smell of air conditioning stopped not far from the train station. The driver from another similar bus coming in the opposite direction stopped and came running, carrying my shoulder bag, which he gave to me. Before I could say thank you, he had already run back to his bus and was driving away while waving to me.

To my surprise, even though the bag's zipper was open and the $3,000.00 in cash was visible, nothing was missing from the bag I'd left behind on the bus that morning. I experienced a revelation about how God made people good and honest. I crossed my heart a few times, and I swore I'd be good for the rest of my life.

X. REFLECTING ON VENICE

I traveled using a European train pass, valid from Madrid to Helsinki and from Athens to London. I was in Venice at 6:00 in the morning. Guided by the Dodge Palace Towers, I walked into San Marco Plaza, where hungry pigeons dove towards my feet, asking for food. As there was almost nobody around, I took my time to admire the ancient bronze statue of the four horses placed on the terrace above the entrance of St. Mark's Basilica. They were taken from Constantinople (also known as Nova Roma) when, in 1204, the Crusaders captured and plundered it instead of liberating Jerusalem from Ottoman occupation.

Cleaning crews used large, slow machines to shampoo and rinse the most photographed plaza in the world. I noticed an imposing restaurant with many tables outside that would open at 11:00 AM. With this precise schedule in mind and having only a shoulder bag as luggage, I began to explore the unique vintage city built on some one hundred small islands united by water canals filled with gondolas and connected by bridges. The gondolas supplied the aquatic metropolis with food and other necessities, as well as collected garbage from the properties, a task completed routinely each morning. Once in a while, a speedy motorized police boat, a medical emergency boat, and others used for postal delivery, as well as other daily services, went by.

They left v-shaped wakes, the waves of which broke against the ancient walls of the decorated marble buildings with their large entrance steps leading to the waters.

To my knowledge, during the battle of Lechfeld in the year

955, the German knights of Emperor Otto I destroyed the invading Magyar hordes who had pillaged Europe up to France and the Danish Peninsula of Jutland. Thus, the Germans saved the civilized continent from further destruction by the Asiatic barbarians. Those left from the Magyars and their allied warriors found refuge in the marshes of Venice, as the heavily armored Germans and their horses were unable to follow them.

In time, many Venetian islands were settled by the fugitives of Europe. Many were rich, and they were protected by the surrounding marshes. Due to its easy access from the Adriatic Sea, Venice proved to be an ideal location for the merchants and pirates of the early Middle Ages. Prosperity gave birth to the powerful city-state, which had no competition except from Dubrovnik, which was too far away to pose any real threat to the newly rich republic.

Using enslaved labor, the industrious settlers began to compete. They built monumental mansions and mini palaces with foundations in the mud of Venice, which was endangered by flooding from the Adriatic Sea. In time, the rather safely located Venice became a major commercial and military power due to its armada of sailing ships, which crisscrossed the waters of the Mediterranean and Black Seas.

There I was, leisurely walking over bridges, observing as a tourist the way Venetian citizens lived above the watery environment in houses with small gondolas parked in front of them. Almost every dwelling had a small, fenced garden on the side of the building. In a few square meters, they grew vegetables and flowers and had tree-shaded barbecue decks protected by a barking dog.

I kept walking within a visible distance of the tall buildings of the Great Canal and was surprised I was not arrested for trespassing on private property as the owners slept.

Led by the well-known fact that getting lost in a strange place is the best way to discover it, I continued walking while taking pictures. I wondered how the sewer system worked since any connecting pipes had to be submerged in the canal waters, and there seemed to be no good explanation of how to get rid of the waste. Indeed, the waters were yellow and murky and emanated a strange odor. Maybe that gave Venice another mysterious charm about what its waters were hiding.

***

As I continued my stroll, I became hungrier and was glad to find my way back to San Marco Plaza. At this point, thousands of tourists had flooded the area. At 10:00, I was crossing the famous Rialto Bridge and entering a large shop specializing in the best of Italian leather products. I bought an expensive leather belt that others always admired when I wore it. I was attracted by the irresistible smell of cooking coming from the open windows of a restaurant. I later discovered it was the best eatery for the famous Rialto liver fried with onions in butter. It was one of the main reasons I later returned to Venice three times, just to once again taste and treasure the flavor of that cooked liver. It was enough to make one forget any hardship.

The sound of beautiful music coming from San Marco Plaza drew me there in time to arrive for the 11:00 opening of the plaza restaurant, where uniformed waiters arranged chairs and metallic tables covered with red and white tablecloths as they awaited their customers. At that time, I was the only one watching the musicians dressed in 1920s-era costumes. Violins and other instruments warmed up, including a magnificent large accordion playing "O Solo Mio/My Sunshine." They played mainly tangos, waltzes, and tarantellas.

An athletic-looking waiter politely invited me to sit next to the orchestra, which was beginning to attract attention from the large groups of tourists there feeding the pigeons. I was fascinated by the accordion player, who played chords and embellishments in perfect synchrony with the drummer's beats.

The waiter came to ask me in his melodious English if I had looked at the menu and decided what to order. I responded, feeling a little intimidated, that I would like their best Italian pizza. He smiled and informed me that they make 42 different kinds of pizza, but the best one is pricey. I showed him my large roll of liras and stated I would pay whatever it cost. He placed a green bottle of "gas water," which was seltzer water, on my table. I continued to enjoy the repertoire of beautiful music from the band, led by the accomplished accordion player.

The sun was out, and it was getting hotter, so it was time for the waiters to open the umbrellas above the tables. The musicians were shaded by a large awning resembling the Italian flag. Soon, all the tables around me were filled with tourists loudly speaking strange languages, the sounds of which interfered with the sweet music I was enjoying.

Finally, my waiter came with a sizzling hot plate, which he skillfully placed on a round metallic grill in front of me. To my surprise, instead of my familiar-looking pizza, I saw on the crust two sunny-side-up eggs with two bacon strips placed crosswise on top of the eggs, all topped with a large strawberry and basil leaves arranged around the plate. Judging by the black lines on it, the pizza dough had been grilled over a fire.

I felt nearly revolted. I asked the waiter, "Where is the red tomato sauce, the stringy melted cheese, and the pepperoni?"

The waiter rearranged his immaculate white towel on his bent arm. Smiling, he said in his melodious English with Italian intonations: "You, sir, must be coming from New York City!" And he moved on to the next table.

XI. THE TRAJAN COLUMN

My Italian experience in Rome was quite different. It was raining. From the airport, I took a taxi, a small red car with small funny wheels and almost no room under its hood for an engine. The traffic was hectic, aggravated by the presence of what seemed like thousands of Vespa scooters driven mainly by beautiful women. My hotel was built on the side of Emperor Trajan's Forum at the bottom of the former Quirinal Hill, excavated 20 centuries ago by thousands of Dacian prisoners after Roman legions occupied part of the immensely rich Transylvania. Their excavation of the hill stopped when they reached 130 feet, which matched the height of Trajan's marble columns with 155 sculpted friezes depicting the two wars against the Dacians (101–106 AD), the ancestors of the Romanians.

The famous column still stands, but the 300 meter/984 foot long, 185 meter/607 foot wide Trajan forum lies in ruins. It was the reason I stayed in the Forum Hotel—to research and write my book *Dacia: Land of Transylvania, Cornerstone of Ancient Eastern Europe*, which I later published.

To get to my special hotel, the petite taxi had to drive down the street the Dacians originally built. It had since been paved over with cubic stones. They were wet from the rain. As the driver increased speed, the car slid as it competed with the many other cars on the road. I asked the driver, who was dripping with perspiration, to slow down. He said he could not, or he would cause an accident by not keeping up with the other larger cars. I had never seen such a reckless driver except in Istanbul, where my taxi driver backed his car up against the oncoming cars on a one-way street.

I spent the next few days around Trajan's Forum studying the immense column with its elliptical marble frescoes, which went upwards to show the Romans' final victory. Unfortunately, the column was under restoration, but I was able to take excellent pictures. Amazingly enough, one after another, tourist groups with their guides came to visit the column, but never once did the guides mention that the Romans fought the Dacians. A guide with an Israeli group described the scenes as the Jews fighting the Roman invaders. Later, I saw a small white plaque on the retaining wall of the shopping mall built by Trajan, the first of its kind in history. Indeed, the writing indicated that Emperor Trajan built and erected the column to immortalize his victory against the Dacians. It made me happy and even more determined to write my book about the history of Dacia.

XII. ITALIAN TOURIST EXPERIENCE

If there is a happy place to visit in the world, it is Italy's Adriatic shore, especially the Amalfi Coast. When I left the airport, I saw many private drivers holding large signs with names from all over the world calligraphically written in fancy, italic-style letters. My name was on one of them, and I signaled to the middle-aged gentleman holding it. He was impeccably dressed in a black suit. He wore shiny high boots and a black chauffeur's hat, and he had a large, gentle smile under his large black mustache. He came to me and carried my wheeled carry-on luggage to the car. I noticed he wore a thick gold chain with a large gold cross resting on his chest and many bulky gold rings on the fingers of his left hand. His name was Giannini. He looked to me like an actor from a high-budget movie about a mafia boss.

He made precise, elegant movements as he opened the limousine door and invited me inside. The other drivers who walked past saluted him. I was greatly impressed and felt a bit uncomfortable since I was only a poor tourist from America. That feeling increased when Giannini slowly drove towards the airport exit, as many limousine drivers approached the car to kiss the rings on his left hand, which he hung outside of the driver's window. In very good and charming English, he told me he'd lived in Queens of New York City for six years, where he made enough money to buy a house, marry, and start his tourist business. "It's too bad," he explained, "my only son, age 20, instead of picking you up at the airport, is probably still sleeping after partying all night. I spoiled him because I love him too much." But now, he explained, he was trying to motivate his son.

We drove up into the mountains. My chauffeur stopped to show me where Nuriev, the Russian ballet dancer who defected to the free world, had bought an island. I could see below to where he built a castle, where he eventually died of AIDS. For the next two hours, my driver continued driving me up the many hills, stopping here and there in small village plazas to let me browse the flea market tables. He took pictures of me and asked if I was hungry because it was noon time. We drove a few more miles and stopped at a sharp turn on the steep roads, where there was a parking space in front of a closed restaurant. He beeped his horn. The owner appeared. He looked almost identical to Giannini—perhaps they were brothers? He kissed Giannini's hand and invited us for a private lunch of spaghetti and meatballs and grappa, a high-alcohol liquor made of grapes.

Giannini snapped his fingers, and the owner presented me with a bottle of grappa shaped exactly like the high boot of the Italian peninsula. I wanted to pay for the meal and the grappa, but Giannini protested, saying it was on the house. I still have the empty bottle to remind me of the pleasant time Giannini showed me during the trip.

We drove further through the picturesque small mountain villages while my chauffeur shared Italian history. The most interesting story was about Mussolini. Giannini said he was very good for the Italians, but his disastrous alliance with Hitler and being afraid he would miss the German victory parade in Moscow, Mussolini volunteered to send the Eighth Italian Army of 235,000 men to fight along with the Germans. The near-annihilation at Stalingrad was his undoing. Laughing, he told me Mussolini got rid of the Sicilian mafia, but then Americans liberated them from the prisons because the gangsters declared they were anti-fascist victims persecuted by El Duce. Eventually, most ended up in America to work in the casino industry and take over unions.

He believed it was not the Italian patriots who executed and hung Mussolini half-naked upside down, but British secret agents sent by Churchill to confiscate the briefcase El Duce always carried with him. Inside it were letters of thanks and admiration that Churchill had written to Mussolini before the war. But after his execution, they became accusatory proof against the British Prime Minister.

Giannini was not a fascist nor a communist. He knew a different history of Italy, and he wanted to share it. Indeed, when I was with him, Italy was shaken by electoral fighting between its left and right parties. In one town, Giannini stopped in the plaza where thousands of spectators had watched the Communists with red bandanas and red armbands club the Fascists, who were dressed in black and used small chains to whip their adversaries. Suddenly, the fighting stopped, and the previously belligerent parties shook hands and entered a pub to have lunch together as good neighbors do. One hour later, the enemies went home, each satisfied their fight had taught the other side a lesson in respect.

Sometimes, Giannini would stop to show me a certain monument, cross, or plaque that commemorated heroes and their heroic deeds. I felt exactly like the Americans felt when I tried to tell them about what happened in rundown Communist

Romania—I *tried* to look interested. Giannini gave me a memorable tour of the Amalfi Coast and then drove me back to my airport hotel. And he was very appreciative of the $300.00 tip I left him.

XIII. THE HEALER

What happened to my friend is so powerful and unusual it deserves to be known by all. It proves how little we know about ourselves, our profession, and what is around us.

A few years ago, right before Christmas, my friend, a strong and still agile 70-year-old, decided to cut off the top of a pine tree that was pushing against his house. Two practical reasons motivated him: the tree was bending the gutter, and the portion he planned to cut would make a handsome Christmas tree for his grandchildren. Armed with a chainsaw, he climbed the aluminum ladder and began to cut the lush evergreen treetop two feet below the gutter. The more he cut, the harder he pressed against the tree and the faster the ladder began to slide away from the house. Realizing the danger he faced, he stopped cutting and wrestled the chain blade out of the cut. Suddenly, the ladder collapsed, and my friend fell some twelve feet onto the icy ground.

A former pole vaulter, he managed to land on his feet with his knees bent, and he instinctively rolled on his side to break his fall. But the ladder fell, its entire weight landing on him, breaking all the bones in his right ankle. Shoving the ladder off, he tried to get on his feet, only to experience an explosion of pain. He collapsed, roaring with cries and moans. His foot was twisted in an unnatural direction and was completely, lifelessly limp—he had no control of it.

Alarmed by the noise, his wife rushed outside the house and quickly evaluated the severity of the injury. Her husband's foot was rapidly swelling and looked like it was held in its awkward place only by the skin.

"Help me get in the car and drive me to the emergency room!" cried my friend.

But his wife, a registered nurse, knew better. Running inside the house, she called 911 and briefly explained what had happened. She then ran back outside with a thick blanket, a bunch of towels and a rope. First, she made a tourniquet below the knee to stop the bleeding and wrapped the towels around the ankle that was now so swollen it overflowed the sneaker. Next, she pulled her husband onto half of the blanket and covered him with the other half. The pain was so excruciating that he could hardly breathe and had already run out of strength to cry aloud. Wanting to keep him as calm as possible, she spoke soothingly and brought him a glass of strong brandy.

Within minutes, they heard the ambulance siren, and shortly thereafter, colorful flashlights announced its entrance in the driveway, and the white van pulled up near the fainting man.

After a brief look, the paramedics lifted my friend using the blanket and placed him on a flat metallic bed inside the van. A painkiller was injected, and an IV quickly connected to one arm. Then, with my friend's wife aboard, sirens screaming and lights flashing, the ambulance headed straight to the hospital. The ambulance floor was covered in blood, and the tranquilized man was silent and half asleep.

By the time he was wheeled into the operating room, he was unconscious. A 50-year-old surgeon left my friend's sneakers on as he cut into his training pants, which were soaked in blood. He called a few strong male nurses to hold my friend tight on the operation table. The surgeon pulled with all his strength, putting the hanging foot back in its correct position. The sleeping man jolted as if hit by a thunderbolt, letting out a wild scream and many curses. Then, he began to fight with the nurses who held him down tighter. Another strong injection calmed him down while the doctor examined his ankle, now larger than the knee. It was still bleeding, and bone marrow dripped from the wound. A mask was placed over my friend's face, and he inhaled strong anesthetics, quieting his moans and sobs as his crying wife waited for news from the surgeon.

Four hours later, eleven wires, screws, pins, and other titanium enforcements had been installed in the ankle to rebuild the joint. Finally, my friend was rolled into the recovery room where his wife was waiting. The doctor explained to her that some half inch of the bones directly above the ankle bone were so smashed by the sharp edge of the ladder that the tiny pieces had to be cleaned out, which left a gap between his foot and the rest of his leg. Steel gadgets now connected the separated bones to keep them steady so the marrow wouldn't leak into the flesh, but, the surgeon explained, her husband would never walk again by himself.

Within the span of a few hours, her healthy husband had become a crippled man.

***

For the next few days, a team of doctors and medical students stopped by my friend's bed several times daily, shaking their heads as they looked at the X-rays. Heavily sedated, my friend believed that despite his injury, he would be dancing by Christmas. Indeed, he was dismissed from the hospital before the holiday. He was confined to a wheelchair, and his damaged leg was bound in a plaster cast, held straight and parallel to the floor. Dancing was out of the question, and sleeping was possible only with the help of many pills.

At Christmas, the grandchildren received their presents and played around their armchair-bound grandfather, who tried to smile while tears leaked from his eyes. Relentless throbbing and sharp pains inside his ankle indicated his flesh was fighting to acclimate to the invasive metal gadgets as his loose nerves tried to reposition themselves.

At the next visit to his surgeon, my friend and his wife heard nothing but bad news. It was the same during the second and third visits when they were told that the surgery was a success, but missing parts of human bones do not regenerate, and the ankle joint was held together only by wires, screws, pins, and metallic plates. The reality was that my friend would need a wheelchair for the rest of his life.

***

Back home, he sat in front of the fireplace reading or watching holiday specials on the television as he sipped tea laced with rum and munched on a few sweet cookies. Felix, a big reddish male cat, hopped up on my friend's lap so he could quickly snap up the crumbs from the cookies. Then, the cat walked on the leg that was held straight forward, resting on a small chair and lay down on the white cast with all four paws hugging it. Happy with the cookie crumbs, the heat from the fire and the comfort provided by the round cast, Felix would begin to purr louder and louder as he fell deeply asleep.

The cast became Felix's favorite place to sleep. He spent hours each day lying on the cast, hugging it with his paws and loudly purring. He even jumped on the bed when my friend went to sleep to resume his place on the cast, purring contentedly through the night. The weight of the big cat and his loud purrs comforted my friend. Bit by bit, his pain lessened, and the swelling receded.

At the next appointment with the surgeon, new X-rays were taken. It looked like there had been considerable improvement, surprising the doctor, who had no explanation of why for the medical students, who also examined the X-rays. A calcification process had begun, enclosing the smashed ankle. The doctor said he had never experienced such a case in his entire career and could only credit my friend's exceptional genes.

My friend, however, believed Felix deserved the credit for what was happening. When he returned home, he greeted Felix warmly and smiled as the big cat wrapped his paws around the cast, closed his eyes, and purred.

***

By May, my friend began to put his damaged foot down more. Soon, he could stand and walk slowly while pushing the wheelchair, using it as support. Each time he sat down or lay down, Felix joined him, laying his heavy little body on the leg and purring loudly.

At his next scheduled visit with the surgeon, my friend walked into the office—slowly but upright and by himself. The surgeon and his office staff were stunned. My friend credited the healing to Felix, an absurdity that the doctor immediately dismissed. But, indeed, X-rays showed that the missing portion of the ankle bone was totally rebuilt!

To everyone, this was a miracle recovery, and the surgeon received high praise for his outstanding surgical work. He began to write a paper about the surgical procedure. During one of the follow-up visits, the surgeon laughed hard when my friend declared he had healed because of his furry feline, who continued to purr while lying on the ankle, now freed of its uncomfortable cast.

A few weeks later, the surgeon phoned my friend and invited him to the office for some important news. My friend arrived with his wife. The surgeon opened with a surprising statement: "I have never done this in my life, but I must offer you and Felix my professional apologies!" Arranging and rearranging his thick glasses and ignoring incoming phone calls, the middle-aged doctor, who was going bald and growing a round belly, explained that he had watched a medical report on TV about mother cats purring between 25–50 Hz while nursing their kittens. The purrs, the report stated, acted as special therapeutic waves that fed the kittens' bones and made them stronger and more elastic. This, in fact, is the main reason that felines can fall from high places and land on their feet without breaking them. The surgeon realized that it was the same bioenergetics process that Felix had applied to his master.

A few days later, the doctor removed all the wires and metal pieces from my friend's ankle that he had thought would be there permanently. The ankle was a little crooked but very functional, with no pain. Without a doubt, my friend would dance the next Christmas!

As for Felix-the-healer, he passed away at the respectable age of 20, as if he had waited first to heal his master, who provided him with a good home and a good life. He was never credited for "felinotherapy," nor mentioned by name in any medical papers. He was buried right on the spot where his master broke his ankle. My friend's eyes get moist each time he sees the little mound covered with colorful flowers, marking the eternal resting spot of the best healer he ever knew.

PART III

FROM THE WEST...
CAPITALISM

$

1. IN A REFUGEE CAMP

International immigration laws are clear: any refugee, including illegal immigrants, from any nation must stay in the first country they enter until they are officially approved by a consulate to immigrate to another country. I was in Austria in the refugee camp in Traiskirchen, a small city 20 kilometers south of Vienna. I spent my first eight days of freedom in quarantine, locked up on the top floor of the main building. It's likely that Austrian authorities asked the Romanian government if I was a member of the Communist Party, an anarchist, a polygamist, a homosexual (or sexually deviant in any way), a prostitute, a drug user or dealer, a disabled person or beggar. They needed to know if I had a criminal past or was involved in any illegal activities. All were reasons to deny an immigrant a visa to the United States of America, where I wanted to live. While I was in quarantine, a doctor gave me a general check-up and took my blood for testing. After I passed, I was released into the camp community.

A refugee employee who spoke little Romanian showed me various offices, the mess hall, the main gate where mail was delivered, and finally, my dormitory, which had 74 bunk beds for refugees like me. I noticed nobody had made their bed and that a few fully dressed men were snoring in their beds. A few, speaking in low voices, curiously followed my movements with their eyes. I waved to them but received no response.

No sun rays could penetrate the dirty windows in the dormitory. The slippery floor was covered in spit, phlegm, vomit, blood, and garbage, including cigarette butts and empty alcohol bottles.

I was told to choose any empty bed with a rolled mattress and to later go to the supply office to sign for a pillow and blanket.

My tour continued along a littered, cement-floored corridor that led to the bathroom facilities. The smell coming from the military-style washroom with its long, dirty metallic sinks made my eyes burn and my nose drip. The odor of urine permeated the room. A urinary trench lined one wall. A violent stench came from the Turkish-style toilet holes in the cement floor. There were dried stools all over, even plastered on the walls, which were inscribed with notes in many different languages. There was no toilet paper. It was apparent nobody from the camp administration ever entered this area.

Later, I was told as a joke that ever since 1955, when 2,000 Russian soldiers were garrisoned in the same buildings, no one had cleaned the place. A year after Soviet tanks put down the anti-communist Hungarian Revolution, some 6,000 freedom fighters who escaped annihilation were interned in these same facilities, initially built in 1900 to house 500 Austrian cadets and officers. When I entered the camp in September 1972, it was said that more than 3,000 refugees populated it. There were separate wooden barracks for women and families.

Most of the refugees were from Eastern Communist countries, but there were also Semites, Orientals and black Africans. A few political refugees from the Soviet Union were housed in a long, clean room with only eight beds. It had a large, sparkling clean window facing the camp's fence. However, the feature proved to be deadly when a sniper killed a prominent Soviet scientist housed there. As the camp was located near the train station, the killer easily escaped by hopping onto the next train.

He was never caught.

***

For the rest of the day, I took my time inspecting the camp. There were big grey buildings with red tile roofs. Many people went in and out. They walked in ethnic groupings, each dressed the same and speaking the same language. All seemed to be rushing somewhere. I saw a neglected volleyball court with a long, single wire for a net and a soccer field with goals marked by large stones. Men of various nationalities tried to prove their athletic abilities and patriotism in their matches, occasionally refereed by Herr Frank, who had to explain in many languages why he used his whistle to stop the play.

Herr Frank was a small middle-aged man who looked like a pleasant Italian barber or an accordion player, down to his middle-parted black hair and pencil-thin mustache. Born in the former Austro-Hungary, he'd lived in many countries. He was an accomplished polyglot who spoke at least ten languages, including Romanian and English. As a valuable camp employee, he had his own office, and he was in charge of many functions that required translators, including the supply room and police investigations. Often, foreign consulates called on him to assist with immigration interviews.

I went to the supply building to get my pillow and blanket for my bed from no one other than Herr Frank. He learned that I was a teacher and a coach in Romania. Seeing my city outfit, he called me "Professor," and I was known by that name from then on in the camp. He was unhappy to hear which dormitory I was assigned to and said, "Let me know if you have any problem there, and I will find you a better room." He smiled and handed me a small package. It had a few words written on it in English: "A gift from the people of the United States." In it was a "Welcome to freedom" letter inside a plastic maroon wallet stamped with a golden international refugee seal.

I returned to my dormitory with a personal emergency kit, which contained an oval bar of soap, toothpaste and a toothbrush, a towel, a pen and paper, a nail clipper, white and black thread with a few sewing needles, and a few wrapped mint candies. I was very moved, for I knew of no other nation that would give such a gift to a perfect stranger without a country. Except for my pillow and blanket, I put everything inside my blue shoulder bag, which I placed under my bed. In the bag, I had my own towel, a pair of underwear and socks, soap, toothpaste and toothbrush, my son's small teddy bear, and a harmonica, which I could play really well. I sat on my bed and looked around at my roommates, who were of an obviously low intellectual level. They argued amongst themselves and their manners were not civilized. Tears came to my eyes as I felt pity for myself and my situation. I remembered what my father once said to me: "Pity anyone who leaves his country to look for a better one."

***

It was supper time, so I walked outside. Following the smell of cooked food, I entered the noisy dining hall, which looked like an oversized hunting lodge. There were parallel rows of long wooden tables with long benches on each side. In the middle of the rows of tables, an ample open space led to the kitchen counter. Refugees waited in a long line, and each was served a meal in an aluminum bowl placed on a large tray with a big, triangular piece of dark bread and a plastic cup of milk.

I noticed a few groups of people whom I'd seen rushing ahead of me to the mess hall. They talked among themselves while eating. Holding my tray carefully not to spill the precious milk, I sat alone at the end of a table and concentrated on my food. In the bowl was a thick bean soup with chopped vegetables and pieces of the Austrian version of hot dogs. The dessert, a thick round cookie, went well with the milk. The entire meal tasted delicious to me.

I walked around after I finished and overheard some Romanian being spoken, but I learned later that less than 20 Romanians were in the camp, including an intellectual couple who occupied a private wood cabin with their own Romanian-made Dacian car parked in front. Popular opinion was that most of the civilized refugees were Czechs and Poles who stayed away from the rest of the ethnic Slavic immigrants and from everybody else.

The biggest community was made up of loud-talking Hungarians who seemed to cross the border into Austria by foot anytime they pleased. One night, a Hungarian family pushing a baby carriage also brought a 92-year-old man along with them into Austria. The most disliked were two young Albanian students with goatees and mustaches. They slept with their black ties still on and acted superior because nobody understood their ancient language. Moreover, they talked to each other in butchered English with horrible diction.

Soon, I realized most Eastern European refugees did not want to work, especially the young ones who, to gain their freedom, had braved the bullets of border guards or swam through the freezing currents of the Danube. They expected to be treated as heroes and be paid accordingly for the spectacular, dangerous risks they took. Later, I learned many were thieves, drug dealers, sex offenders and other criminals who had escaped to avoid their countries' justice systems. (Perhaps governments should pay such people to *leave* their countries because it costs too much to keep them in jail.) Some stayed in international refugee camps for years because no country wants savage troublemakers immigrating to and hurting their societies.

I went to the clean bathroom in the mess hall to avoid the one in my corridor, where I anticipated that bad things might happen.

I walked out into a darkness broken only by a few lit lampposts and some pale lights shining through the windows of the building. So far, I had not spoken to any of my thousands of co-refugees. I was amazed that I saw no police officers or camp security guards patrolling the grounds. Maybe there were more than I knew. Perhaps they were dressed in civilian clothes. Regardless, their presence was badly needed. I saw them only once when a bunch of newly arrived refugees brought a heavy ATM full of cash into camp, which they'd stolen from the Vienna train station.

On the way to my dorm, I heard screams and cursing in many languages. Men were running around fighting. There was loud laughter from the drunkards, and ethnic music blared from portable radios turned to maximum volume. In the dorm, lights from a few electric bulbs, covered by flies' yellowish excrement, hung from the ceiling by black twisted wires. Everything was enveloped by clouds of cigarette smoke, combined with other strong smells. Under each bulb, agitated, noisy men played poker and backgammon on the top bunks. Not too far from my bunk, near a wall with an electric outlet, a loud group speaking a language I had never heard before was frying sizzling, garlicky sausages on a hot plate. As if they were celebrating something or somebody, they sang a march-like song punctuated by the sounds of beer cans being opened.

Finally, I reached my bottom bunk. I identified it because of my clean pillow and neatly folded blanket. Nobody was around it so far. Getting undressed or taking off my suede shoes was not necessary and could even be dangerous—I didn't want them to be stolen. I laid down on my back and wrapped my head and ears with the clean towel to buffer the Tower of Babel-like tumult.

Thankful to be free at last, I crossed my heart. Exhausted, I fell asleep immediately.

***

I do not know how long I slept without moving, but when I awoke, I jumped up and hit my head on the metal lattice of the top bunk above me. A wild shout of foreign words, no doubt a long string of curses, shook the previously silent room. Someone jumped from their bed and helped roll a massive man not far from me onto his bed. He had missed it because he was drunk. Thankfully, the drunk man did not wake. He was deeply feared by everybody, for he was the strongest and most unpredictable refugee in the camp, known to carry a long dagger and pistol.

Days later, I learned the mysterious man who blurted out the curse words was a former sergeant in the French Legion who had fought warlords in Africa. With only weeks left before he was set to retire and receive a large pension and benefits, he and two other legionaries were sent to search out enemy lines in the jungle at night. After a while, they became disoriented and decided to return to their military camp when they were taken prisoner by an enemy squad of black guerillas who disarmed them and tied them up. Hours later, on the edge of a river, two of the captured legionaries were stripped and executed, their bodies butchered into pieces, grilled on a large fire and eaten. The massive man was spared that fate because he was a sergeant. They planned to torture and extract information from him.

The strong sergeant loosened the ropes tied around his feet and ran for his life, deserting the French Legion. He returned by plane to Europe and landed at the Vienna airport, where he asked for political asylum. That was why he was in the refugee dorm, drunk and still haunted by the vision of cannibals eating his comrades. His drinking, fighting, and nearly killing innocent black refugees caused him to become the oldest camp veteran for the longest time. All his requests for immigration visas were denied.

I was unable to sleep the rest of the night. I noticed a few early risers leaving the dorm, dressed in work clothes and wearing heavy yellow boots with tool belts around their waists. I got up and followed them to the mess hall, where they met up with others. Herr Frank translated for them: they had secured a deal to work for a road building company, which paid very well. They ate their breakfasts—scrambled eggs with sausages, a large slice of dark bread with margarine and real marmalade, all washed down by diluted hot coffee from an aluminum canteen.

I told Herr Frank I wanted to work as well. I explained that I had left behind a wife and a small son, as well as my poor parents, who needed financial help.

Herr Frank looked critically at my city clothes and my gold Tellus watch, which was gifted to me by my mother after I graduated from the Sports Institute of the University of Bucharest.

"Nobody will hire you dressed like that," he warned me.

I told him I worked in construction every summer, but he shook his hand to deter me, saying, "You are not dressed in a way that says, 'Ich gut Arbeiter.'" (The phrase means "I am a good worker" in German.)

But I insisted I was ready, so Herr Frank advised me to go to the front of the church, where locals hired handymen from the camp daily. "Perhaps you'll get lucky and be hired."

I quickly ate breakfast, and then I ran outside, asking directions all along the way till I found the church where a hundred other refugees, none of them Romanian, were looking for work. Many ran after every car that slowed down, hoping to be hired.

I tried to remember the three German words from Herr Frank.

$$\blacksquare \, \$ \, \blacksquare$$

2. ICH GUT ARBEITER

At seven o'clock in the morning, I was on the church steps with many other refugees waiting to be hired by local Austrians as daily laborers. Even though I was young, strong, and had more knowledge of construction than most, I didn't look the part. I was dressed like a sissy city boy compared to the rest, who were dressed in well-worn work clothes marked by large spots of paint, dirt, and even holes and rips, as if in testament to their past labor. They deeply inhaled cigarettes. Their work hats, muddy sneakers, boots, and tool belts gave them the visual credentials they needed to be hired ahead of me. Indeed, many had already been hired and were waiting for Austrians to pick them up in their cars and drive them to their worksites. As for me, I did not dare to move from my spot; if nothing else, I would observe what to do in the future to be hired. By eight o'clock, my co-refugee job hunters were gone, regardless of whether they'd been hired or not.

Alone and feeling humiliated, I sat down on the church steps. I looked across the street. There, in a schoolyard, a fifth-grade gym class marched together in lockstep, learning how to stop on command. They did calisthenics in various formations. Some worked on how to start a race, practiced long jumps that filled their athletic shoes with sand or threw shot put. I could not help but reflect that in Romania, I'd taught high school students and trained competitive athletes at the sports club. I was so successful that I was in line to be promoted as a national coach, a position that came with a good salary and an apartment. However, I could have that position only if I first became a member of the

Romanian Communist Party.

However, I could not become a member because my father was in a Communist jail and sentenced to 20 years of hard labor. He was believed to be an enemy of the people. After ten years, he was released and deported for four more years to prove he was rehabilitated. My mother was forced to divorce him so I could continue my studies.

I was only four years old when my father was arrested. After, my mother was fired from many jobs, and I was expelled from school. For me, being an anti-communist was almost an inborn instinct. I never believed in Marxism-Leninism, never supported Stalin's dictatorship, nor could I accept the rampant corruption and nepotism under Ceausescu's oppressive regime and personality cult. I never wanted to be around communists.

I refused to sign the application to join the Communist Party because I knew the United States of America did not allow members of the Communist Party to immigrate.

I continued to enjoy watching the school activities until ten o'clock when I returned to the refugee camp to look for any fellow Romanian citizens. As I was alone among 3,000 people at the refugee camp, I realized I had the same feeling about the Romanian Communist Party: I did not belong in either.

***

Soon, I found a Romanian refugee. His name was Dudescu. To defect, he bought a green jersey with ROMANIA written on the tricolor red, yellow, and blue flag on the front and the back. To aid his travels, he planned to ride a racing bicycle he bought along with four extra inflated tire tubes, which he carried over his shoulders, two on each side. In May, he traveled by train to the closest train station to the Danube River border, which was secured by Romanian border troops with dogs and hidden flares, explosives and traps to stop any defector from crossing into Yugoslavia. With a sports bag on his back and the extra tire tubes around his shoulders, he had begun to bicycle towards the well-guarded border when he was stopped by a patrol to check his ID.

Dudescu pulled his legal documents out of the sports bag, including an official letter stating he was in long-distance training around Romania for July's international Tour de France. It was stamped and signed by the Sports Federation of Romania on the proper stationery—a perfectly fake letter done by Dudescu. The patrol asked why he was riding on the military patrols' frontier path. Dudescu innocently replied, "Indeed, it is the best path to ride a bicycle since the rest is only stones and thorns." The sergeant saluted and let him ride away.

Dudescu kept riding until he saw a large cluster of bushes leading straight into the Danube River. He stopped, pulled off a branch from a leafy bush and planted it between his bag and jersey to cover his upper body. Then, he drove his bike straight into the water of the second-largest river in Europe. The four inflated tubes over his shoulders kept him afloat, swimming on top of the bike, showing his head only enough to breathe, and he was otherwise well-masked by the bush. He'd worn waterproof long johns, so the cold May water was bearable. He hit a current that brought him to the Serbian shore, and soon enough, he was riding his bike into Yugoslavia and heading to Austria.

But not as fast as he thought he would get there.

Riding on a paved road that paralleled the Danube River,

Dudescu believed he would reach Vienna as the final leg of his escape. A highway police car signaled him to stop. Fortunately, without knowing it, Dudescu was riding in the former Dacian land now named the Serbian Banat, which had a large Romanian-speaking population, including the police officer. He'd seen many Romanian defectors aiming for Austria. Dudescu took the risk of admitting his trick of claiming to be in training for the Tour de France. The policeman was amused, admitted no one had used that stunt before, and he offered to help Dudescu. He took the fugitive home, fed him, let him take a shower and sleep.

One may wonder if Nicola Tesla's family was not from this kind of older Romanian, living in Serbia for centuries. His father's family name was Draghici, a pure Romanian name, but nicknamed Tesla, after the tool that looks like an ax with a blade across the top, used in their carpentry business. It is common in Romania to have families named after the tools they use to make a living. The name *Topor*, for example, is the word for broad ax or lumberjacks, and *Ciocan* means hammer, referring to a black-smith's hammering.

His father, Milutin, who was an Orthodox priest born in Raduc, married and moved to the Croatian village of Similijan, where Nicola Tesla was born. Obviously, he was baptized in his father's church, which may have Romanian parishioners, considering that in the same region 100 years before, there were more than 1,500 families of Vlachs (also a name for Romanians) in the churches of the Serbian Orthodox Vlachs and Roman Catholic Vlachs. Also, Similijan village was not too far from the many thousands of Romanians living on the Istria peninsula since Dacian times.

Did Tesla, who spoke eight languages, including Latin and Italian, also speak Romanian romance, which was one of his father's languages? For sure, Tesla abbreviated his name *Nicolae* to *Nicola* to simplify the pronunciation in English. This is just some food for thought. Now, back to Dudescu's story.

The next day, the police officer, who happened to be the same size as Dudescu, dressed him to look Serbian and gave him a note to show to a priest who spoke Romanian and served in a Belgrade church. Dudescu reciprocated the favor by gifting the officer his racing bike. The officer's note asked the priest to help the fugitive reach Vienna. Dudescu arrived in the capital of Yugoslavia by train, and the merciful priest paid for his fare to ride a bus with some 40 Serbian workers hired by an Austrian contractor. At that time, at least one million Yugoslavians commuted daily by train to work in Vienna, making Tito's regime look good as he enriched his people. Thus, Dudescu asked for political asylum at one police station, and he ended up in the Traiskirchen refugee camp.

A little over the age of 30, small in stature but very energetic, Dudescu was a good soccer player. He became famous for having a large pressure cooker, its cover locked with a key, that filled the dormitory with delicious smells while stews and soups cooked as he showed off his soccer skills outside. Born to be an entrepreneur, he soon established himself as a trusted dealer of conveniences. He provided various services, from exchanging foreign currencies for Austrian shillings, buying goods from Vienna and selling them for a profit in the camp, and being the barber because he had an electric clipper and an old-fashioned razor.

At his advice to look more like a "gut arbeiter," he clipped all my hair to the skin. Now I looked more like a convict who had escaped from prison, which was much worse than looking like a city sissy boy. But encouraged by my new look, I decided to go back and wait on the church steps to challenge my record of not being hired. When Herr Frank called after me to take my picture for the camp photo ID, he scratched his head and said, "I do not know, Professor. You could have waited another day to cut your hair. A copy of your picture goes to the American consulate, where you will be interviewed for visa approval. The American government has not sponsored any immigrants since 1924, and I have to look for someone to sponsor you... with this haircut?!" He took my picture anyhow.

***

Since it was impossible to sleep the entire night in my filthy, noisy dormitory, I began to make a habit to be at the church at seven o'clock each morning. But I always ended up being alone there after everyone else was hired, watching the physical education class until ten o'clock. Returning to camp one day, I received advice from Dudescu: "Stop washing your face and hands each day to look tougher."

In the meantime, Herr Frank asked me to come to his office, fill out the immigration forms for America, and write my biography, which he would attach to my forms. In half an hour, I wrote everything I knew about myself and my parents, for I had nothing to hide. He looked over my CV, approved it, stapled my picture to it and promised to register my dossier in Vienna with the American Consulate in charge of immigration visas. Then he handed me my camp ID, and I saw his valid concern that I looked too headstrong and not appealing enough, which did not help my case too much. He gave me two copies of my picture in a small envelope, just in case I needed them.

On Monday, a camp minivan took eight of us to a Vienna medical clinic, where a few doctors consulted me, taking blood samples and x-rays of my lungs. The American Embassy wanted to make sure I had good sight and hearing, did not have epilepsy, tuberculosis, syphilis, other venereal diseases, or cholera, and to ensure I was not demented. I passed the exam with flying colors, and I received a clean bill of health.

For an entire week, including on Sunday before church services, I found myself alone on the same steps. Back at camp, I avoided Dudescu and Herr Frank because I was humiliated and did not want to report daily on my rejection as a hired laborer.

I got to meet the Romanian intellectual couple at the camp. She was a dentist, and he was an accountant. Both were indeed different from the rest. We related to each other because they had two children they left in Romania. That was the reason they received passports and approval to take their Romanian-made Dacia car on their trip to Western Europe.

We discussed many topics, including books, movies, history, and politics. Once in a while, they invited me to have dinner with them since they had access to a small kitchen next to their bedroom. We would review and learn English expressions from my tourist dictionary together, and they took me to a weekly free English class offered by the camp. I learned very little since the young Austrian, himself a student in an English college, translated everything into German. The couple made me feel better about myself even as I hopelessly continued to wait each morning in front of the church.

***

On one Thursday morning, as usual, I lingered on the stone steps of the church before returning to the camp when a long green station wagon slowly approached. The window rolled down, and the largest head with reddish hair and penetrating blue eyes looked at me and said something in German. I clearly understood the word "Arbeiter."

I shouted back, "Ich gut arbeiter!"

The huge man smiled and signaled for me to get in the car by opening the passenger door. He kept explaining something in German, to which I repeated my standard "Ya-ya-ya," without understanding anything as he drove outside the city on a country road.

After some twenty minutes, he drove the car through a gate of barbed wire into a muddy space with a very large house just being built. A large hole was in the ground in the back of it. A wood shack nearby was filled with digging tools. The six foot, six inch and maybe at least 300-pound Austrian took me to that tool house and pulled out a wheelbarrow, a pickaxe and a shovel, all covered with dry clay. From the edge of the hole, he pointed at lines that had been dug that ended at the side of the house. Then he gestured a digging motion with the pickaxe and shovel, showing me a large, long uphill path of wide, strong boards that went from outside the hole in the ground to where to unload the diggings. All this time, I approved everything he said by repeating my same "Ya-ya-ya."

His explanation was over. I put the two tools in the wheelbarrow, and I pushed it back next to the tool shack, where there was a hose attached to the water pipe. Under the amazed eyes of the owner, I took my shoes, socks and all my clothes off, except my boxers, and I hung them on the barbed wire fence. Then, I turned the nozzle onto a strong jet of water and remembered my father's advice to work with clean tools; otherwise, I would have spent twice as much energy on achieving half of the work I was doing. I removed all the dried clay from the three tools. Then, ignoring the mud, I walked barefoot inside the hole, which was to become a swimming pool.

Determined to show my skills, I began to crush the dirt with the pickaxe, shovel it into the wheelbarrow and run uphill on the boards to empty it. On the way back, I noticed the green station wagon driving away back toward the city. I ran my way back down the boards. I dug, shoveled and rushed up the board path to unload the dirt, over and over, sweating heavily under a scorching sun. After a few hours, the sun began to set. I washed myself off with the hose a few times to refresh myself, regained working momentum and continued digging and running up and down the boards to load and unload the dirt I was excavating, now up along the lines which marked the square border of the hole. I moved then to begin digging to the side of the house.

After hours of digging with the pickaxe and transporting and unloading the dirt, I felt a pat on my shoulder. I turned around and saw the big owner signaling me to stop digging because I almost went under the house. He signaled it was time to go back, and he went to his car. I cleaned the tools off and put them away. I took my boxers off, washed them, and hung them to dry on the barbed wire fence to wear the next day. Then I washed myself. At this point, I was happy I'd had my hair cut so short. I brushed the water off my skin as best I could and put on my clothes, still warm from the sun.

The Austrian drove me back to my camp. On the way, he held up all his fingers and pointed to the church. I understood he wanted to pick me up at ten o'clock the next day. I showed him seven of my fingers, and happily, he approved with a "Ya-ya-ya." He put a roll of money in my shirt pocket and took off. It was 200 shillings—my entire salary in Romania for one week's work.

***

I walked inside the mess hall feeling like a different man, down to the new calluses on my palms, with the roll of money in my pocket, and knowing I had work the next day. Dudescu had been worried by my absence. He almost jumped on me while I ate my meal of potatoes with cubes of ham. He rushed out and came back with Herr Frank, and they both listened to my employment story. When I finished, Herr Frank said that I was working for a rich veterinarian doctor who bought land in the countryside where he was building a mansion with a swimming pool. The doctor came to him to ask for workers, but he fired all of them, sometimes on the same day. I worked two more days for 400 shillings, and on Sunday, I was off because it was church day.

My two intellectual Romanian friends drove me to a shopping mall. I bought a pair of blue jeans and a jacket, overalls of the same material with straps, high rubber boots, two work shirts, t-shirts of different colors, underwear and tank tops. I kept what I did not wear daily in my shoulder bag in their cabin. I felt great when, a week later, I sent money home to my wife and son for the first time.

To make a long story short, in a few days, the owner trusted me to be partly in charge of the project. He gave me the gate keys to the property and asked me to hire masons to build the walls of the swimming pool with cement blocks. I knew a Romanian refugee who used to work in construction, and he chose two others who knew heavy carpentry and scaffolding to be his helpers. Because I worked to help them, they respected me, calling me "Professor." They recognized my ability to organize the project and have their materials delivered on time. Also, they knew I could fire them if they stole tools or materials like those who had been fired before had done.

The owner was so happy that he picked us up from the camp to do our jobs and had us in his home for lunch. In the evenings, though, he was too busy with his many small children, and we had to walk for more than an hour back to camp. I do not know how much he paid my workers, but he now paid me 350 shillings a day. I was probably paid more than anyone in the entire camp.

With the weather getting colder, the owner hired one more mason to handle the cement blocks. He was a huge, strong Austrian dressed in white coveralls. He slid the blocks on long vertical iron rods through each of the blocks' three large holes. Finally, all were sealed with poured cement. The owner wanted the swimming pool walls in place before the freezing weather came. One late afternoon, we ran out of concrete blocks. Everybody left early except for me. I always cleaned everything for everyone after a workday. I arranged the tools in the shack and locked the premises.

***

All was going well when a five-ton truck and a small car stopped in front of the barbed wire gate. The driver realized I did not speak German. Pointing to his wristwatch, indicating six o'clock the next morning, he made clear with gestures that whatever concrete blocks were left in the truck at that time, he would drive away with. As usual, I nodded, saying, "Ya-ya-ya." After the driver lowered all sides of the truck, he jumped in the little car with his friend, and they drove away together.

Left alone, I began unloading and carrying the concrete blocks, each weighing more than 50 pounds, to the swimming pool. One by one, I lined them up around the unfinished walls so the masons could properly slide them onto the rods and cement them to finish the walls. I was tired and hungry, but I was determined to empty the truck. After a few hours, it began to rain. Wet to the bone, the cold rain combined with my hot perspiration made me cough, and the weight of the large blocks made my hands numb and slippery. I began to drop blocks in the mud. Many times, I fell into the mud, rolling after the dropped blocks, but when the night was over, I had all the concrete blocks neatly arranged in two rows around the unfinished swimming pool walls.

I tried to wash my face, but my swollen, muddy hands were so dirty and full of open blisters that I just dirtied my face more. I decided to rush to the camp and take a hot shower before returning to work at the swimming pool. Now, I had to negotiate walking on the slippery country roads. I was exhausted, so I slipped and fell again and again as the rain intensified. Seeing the city lights and then the monolithic buildings of the refugee camp made me almost run to my smelly and mildewed dormitory.

Hardly able to walk up the steps, I entered my room as if it were a palace, and I rolled onto my bed, dirty as I was. I fell asleep immediately. Dudescu started to shake me, trying to wake me up.

"Professor, professor, professor, did you see the note I left for you?" he whispered in my ear.

"What note?" I mumbled, trying to open my eyes.

"Herr Frank left a note for you to be at the American consulate at 9:30 this morning for your visa interview. Move over to find it."

He pushed at me, and I moved enough for him to snatch the note from under me. I jumped up, hitting my head on the metal lattice above my bed. The pain and panic woke me up well enough for me to run to the train station.

$

3. THE INTERVIEW

Without time to wash or change, I got on the seven o'clock train to Vienna. I stood on the platform so I wouldn't soil the seats. Once on the Vienna streets, I wanted to jump in the back of the first available taxi. The driver, though, asked me to sit next to him. He put the floor mat on the seat for me to sit on. I pulled out the note, which had the address of the American Consulate written on it, and the driver looked at me as if I were coming from Mars.

He stopped directly in front of the main gate, where a Marine stood sentry. I gave the driver a good tip, and looking at his dashboard clock, I realized that in 19 minutes, my destiny would be decided for the rest of my life. Tears came to my eyes.

The Marine, with a Colt 45 in a half holster on his white belt, looked at me, at the note signed by Herr Frank, again at me, and he snapped a sharp salute. He pointed me to the door on the right. In just a few seconds, I was standing in front of a secretary's desk with many telephones on it. She read the note. Trying to smile, she said something in English and gestured for me to take a seat. I moved near the wall and remained standing. She seemed to appreciate my concern and returned to her typewriter, rapidly firing away at its keys. A telephone rang. She answered, then after a pause, said, "Yes," which I understood.

I assume she then told me that the consul was waiting for me. She showed me to a massive, tall door. According to the wall clock behind the desk, it was exactly 9:28 AM. Underneath the clock was a portrait of President Nixon. He seemed to be smiling at me. Without hesitation, I knocked on the door so hard I felt a sharp pain in my knuckles. I heard "Intra" ("Come in" in Romanian). I entered and closed the door behind me. To my surprise, I saw Herr Frank. He was there as the translator for my interview.

The American Consul was a young gentleman dressed in a blue suit with a blue and white tie and a matching pocket handkerchief. I could easily study him because he stood frozen in position, looking at me. His eyes were blue, his brown hair was perfectly parted to the left, and he had a chiseled face. Behind him, President Nixon kept smiling at me. On the right side of the consul's desk was a standing American flag, half folded. Neatly lined up across the desk were even more telephones than on his secretary's desk. Herr Frank sat to the left of the desk.

The silence was interrupted by the consul, who asked Herr Frank something as he lifted a document from my dossier with my "tough" picture attached to it.

"Is that you?" asked Herr Frank.

I answered in English, "Yes!"

The consul asked something else, and Herr Frank answered, "No!" (I figured the consul asked whether I spoke English.)

Again the consul asked Herr Frank something, who then asked me, in Romanian, to explain what had happened to me.

The consul sat down and invited me to take a seat in the leather armchair in front of his desk. Herr Frank jumped up and placed a large newspaper on the seat. The consul smiled, which encouraged me to tell the entire saga from the previous night. I set the scene by describing the cold rain. I explained about the cement blocks that had to be removed from the truck, how I'd dropped the blocks because my hands were numb and slippery, and how I fell in the mud. I paused after each description to allow for a good translation.

Suddenly, the consul stopped Herr Frank's translating. Looking at my hands resting at the end of the armchair, he asked me to make a fist. Herr Frank demonstrated to me to make fists with both my swollen, muddy, blistered hands. Immediately, I did it, and my overstretched skin broke—blood sprang forth from my knuckles. The consul was perplexed for a moment, after which he took a large stamp and noisily placed it on the document with my picture.

My interview to immigrate to the United States of America was over. Later, Herr Frank told me in secret that I was approved.

My life would never be the same.

$$\text{———} \$ \text{———}$$

4. A GOOD MISTAKE

My immigration visa was approved by the American consul, but to fly across the ocean, I needed to book a cheap flight, which could take months. With the first frost coming, my swimming pool job was soon to end. Herr Frank told me that a refugee who worked in a mustard factory in Vienna was flying to his new country, and I might have a chance to replace him. He gave me a letter of reference and the address of the small factory. Early the next morning, dressed in work clothes, I took the train to Vienna. There was a stop on the street where the mustard factory was located.

Looking for the address, I found myself in front of the heavy gates of a medieval mini fortress. High walls surrounded a massive, low building. There was nobody inside. I was too early. I paced back and forth until a middle-aged, well-dressed woman came to unlock the gates with the largest key I had ever seen. I showed her the recommendation letter, and she shook her head and arms in a negative way, slamming the gate in my face. Curious, I waited to see how many people worked there. One by one, four women and three men rushed to be inside before eight o'clock.

I was dressed in overalls and an old coat, which the veterinarian's dog once slept on (I rescued it from being thrown away when the German shepherd received a large round pillow). As a bonus, the good doctor also gave me an old conical hat the dog used to play with. As I sent most of my earnings to my poor family and my parents in Romania, I appreciated the two gifts, which I thoroughly washed. Now, they kept me warm. (I still have a picture of myself standing in the middle of the swimming pool construction project, dressed in the two warm garments.)

Early the next morning, I traveled on the same train and arrived at the same historic gate, and again, the secretary gave me the same negative news. I came back to the factory so many times that in order to save money, I paid for a train pass with my "tough" picture ID. Fifty years later, I still have it. By now, all the factory employees knew me and saluted me with kind but helpless smiles.

My persistence paid off. One sleety morning, the secretary ran out and led me inside the inner court of the old building, which smelled like a sandwich shop.

Right there, like in the worst déjà-vu, was a five-ton truck packed with sacks, each weighing 150 pounds. My job was to unload the truck and deposit the sacks in a large supply room inside the factory. I was glad to do it. By 1:00 PM, the truck was empty. I was totally soaked from the freezing rain and my perspiration.

I sat in the corner restaurant across the street. It was a treat offered by the factory office. I ate a schnitzel larger than my plate, drank boiled red wine and got warm again. Plus, I had 200 shillings in my pocket.

For the next three mornings, I was in front of the same heavy gate, waiting for the sleet to stop. The secretary ran out and gave me a big hug, speaking fast in German, and she pushed me inside to the office. Led by hand as if I were blind, I was taken to four mixing machines in a long workroom and presented to an older man with the bluest eyes I had ever seen. He held an electric mixer handle, which shook his body like a jackhammer in the

most comical way. The secretary told him something while pointing to me. The machinist shook his head, "Yes," though maybe
more so than normally would because of the powerful machine's
vibrating effect.

Later, I understood what had happened: the regular machinist was carrying a heavy sack with the ingredients for the grinding
machines when he fell and broke an arm in a few places. He was
rushed to the hospital, and I was called on to take his place, as I
had proved that even in heavy sleet conditions, I did not fall while
carrying a heavy load on my back. (Somehow, previously carrying
those cement blocks proved to be good training.)

The owner of the factory was a half-bald young man with
a blonde mustache and blue eyes. He came to shake my hand.
Next, he brought a large 4x4 foot piece of plywood. He wrote out
the names of twelve ingredients I would feed into the tower-like
mixer. He showed me how to let the mustard flow into a barrel on
wheels almost as high as I am and then how to stop the grinding
machine when it was full. Next, I learned to wheel the oak barrel
into the fermenting room and return with an empty barrel to be
filled by the mixer. Most importantly, I had to have a full sack to
feed the mixer. He went on and on with other instructions I did
not understand. I figured out why the Germans lost many wars: it
was due to their rough language with its unpronounceable, long,
barking words. No other nationality wanted to learn or could
even tolerate listening to the German language.

The owner left the plywood instructions in my full view to
ensure I added all the measured seeds, water, sugar, salt, powders
and the right quantity of acid into the mixer. I knew from the New
Testament that yellowish mustard seeds were very small, but I saw

with my eyes for the first time how they really were only one or two millimeters each. As for the acid, if I dropped some, it would make a hole in the cement floor. The vapors from the mixing machine made my eyes water, my nose drip, and I sneezed and coughed. In a week, I learned everything about making industrial amounts of mustard using the powerful machines, while the old expert used the electric hand mixer for smaller, specialty orders.

I was paid well (with a check the office cashed for me), and the owner offered me a free lunch each day: one bowl of soup, one entree, a salad, bread, a large, creamy éclair and one glass of red wine or beer at the restaurant across from the factory. I became its most known client, among a few older Austrians who all wore the iconic green hat with a feather sticking out. They all talked at the same time. I believe it was about the war. None had any idea that I did not speak German or understand them. They kept asking for my approval, especially when I was taking a mouth full of food. I nodded my head along, saying "Ya-ya-ya." They had twinkling blue eyes and red noses. They laughed, agreeing with my opinion, and patted me approvingly on the back.

The restaurant owner was Viennese and married to a Hungarian woman who was the best cook when it came to goulash, potato casserole with sausages, bacon and boiled eggs, and my favorite, the oversized and unmatchable schnitzel. In the beginning, I asked for *wasser* (water) with my lunch, and they all laughed, mimicking my request and telling me to go wash my hands in the bathroom since, in a German restaurant, everybody drinks beer—not water. Each week, I tipped the owner with a plastic bucket filled with the specialty mustard he wanted.

As I was a graduate of the Sport Institute of the University of Bucharest, when I went back to work, energized by the red Tokai Hungarian wine I'd had at lunch, if I passed through the washing room, I would stop to do press up handstands, walk upside down around the barrels' edges, and do cartwheels and forward flips (handsprings) one after another on the cement floor. This amused the older women, who applauded when they saw me entering their hot, steamy atelier. However, the biggest hit among my coworkers was when I played Viennese waltzes with my mouth harmonica. They sang along as they washed the containers returned from restaurants. Everything was reused, from the largest containers to the smallest shot glasses.

I was strong and willing to do the job of three workers. I manned the three big mixers, pushed barrels back and forth, carried heavy sacks to feed the three machines, cleaned the work area around them, washed the shop at the end of each shift, and helped the washing ladies move heavy boxes to and from the delivery vans. I learned to sleep on the commuter train to make up for my lack of sleep. The conductor used to wake me before my stop.

All in all, with my steady, well-paying job, my life was good compared to the thousands in the refugee camp doing nothing except eating, sleeping, gossiping, and lying about what rich big shots they were back in their countries. Most wanted to go to Germany, Canada, and the US, where they thought they would receive money without working.

***

Herr Frank moved me from the crowded, filthy dormitory into a room with just eight beds, occupied at the time by three Russians and one Romanian from the Soviet-occupied area of the

Bessarabian land taken from Romania by Stalin after the war.

His name was Alexandru. He spoke Romanian as well as I did. He was previously a student at a chemical college when he decided to defect to Romania, believing it was a free nation since no Soviet troops occupied it. Braving the presence of Russian border guards, he swam across the Pruth River into Romania one night. When he arrived in Bucharest, he went to the American embassy to ask for political asylum. In front of the iron gates, a few Romanian militiamen formed a cordon to keep the hundreds of Romanians with passports safe, all of whom wanted to ask for tourist visas valid for the United States.

Alexandru was happy to hear about a visa and approached a uniformed Romanian man, telling him about how he had defected from the Soviet Union to immigrate to America. The blue-uniformed law enforcer asked Alexandru to wait, and he ran to find his superior officer. Seeing both look alarmed, the Bessarbaian ran for his life. Arriving at the Danube River, he illegally boarded an anchored Austrian coal barge and buried himself in a coal pile. After three days of hunger and thirst, he jumped back into the Danube River in Vienna and finally ended up in the refugee camp.

The Russian Sergey was in the same room. An old art critic from Moscow, he'd been sent to Vienna for an international art symposium, only to end up in the "luxury" room in the Traiskirchen refugee camp. He read all the time. One day, he came into the room after a day visit to Vienna, and he said he was in love with a young, beautiful Muscovite artist whom he had met at an art show. In spite of all official and friendly warnings, Sergey kept going to meet the adorable Russian, who proposed that they live together in Vienna.

That was the last time he was seen. Weeks later, Radio Moscow announced that the well-known art critic was disgusted with the decadent, capitalistic way of life in Vienna and that he had returned to the motherland. In reality, Sergey was drugged by his lover, kidnapped by Soviet agents, and put in a Soviet embassy container. Even if they'd known, Austrian authorities had no right to take control of a diplomatic parcel. Sergey was flown on Aeroflot Airlines straight to Moscow and imprisoned in the KGB's Lubyanka prison. The art critic disappeared from friends, the art world and public life.

In the same room, another important defector from communist Russia was killed by a sniper, but the fact was that I could sleep a straight seven–eight hours each night there, so nothing else mattered to me. After all, I was a nobody in Romania, easily replaced and totally forgotten. I bought a winter coat with a black fur collar and a pair of warm shoes lined with felt, and I could still send money to my needy family and to my empty-nester parents. I was free, still young, healthy, strong, working in a warm factory, and eating daily in a very good restaurant. I could not thank God enough for watching over me.

***

The first snow covered Vienna in white. The colorful, angular mosaic roof of Saint Stephen's Cathedral looked more majestic than ever. Its Romanesque tower, 450 feet/136 meters high, conducted the prayers of its visitors to heaven. When I walked inside and looked around, especially up into the vast ceilings, I became dizzy from the enormity of the arches and their columns. In later years, I felt a similarly overwhelming feeling inside the cathedrals of Köln, Notre Dame in Paris, and the Episcopalian Saint John the Divine in Manhattan.

As the great city of Mozart, Beethoven, Schubert, and Johann Strauss began to get ready to celebrate Christmas, each Sunday, I would go on Mariahilfer Strasse Street to see which shop window had set up its spectacular pre-Christmas display. The scenes made my heart beat a bit faster as hidden emotions were stirred from my Romanian childhood in the mountain Muscel region. I realized how poor but happy I was then, as I observed the wealth and abundance of German life as it represented Christmastime in imaginative, breath-taking winter scenes. The non-stop choo-choo toy trains filled with presents whistled as they entered and emerged from tunnels between miniature white mountains and villages. Santa surveyed all from his sleigh pulled by flying reindeer, while forest animals danced below.

Visitors could not get enough of the displays of sweet candies in all shapes and colors, gingerbread in all conceivable shapes, colorful homemade cakes, pies, tarts, and baked pastries. The extravagant treats were also on display in the outdoor markets, along with many kinds of grilled sausages and spiced, boiled wine sold in collectible mugs. Millions of dazzling colors of Christmas lights shone, and chandeliers were suspended above the streets and open markets, which were flanked by charming Christmas trees.

Prosperity extended to the sidewalks where well-dressed, red-cheeked people strolled, many carrying presents wrapped in colorful paper and striking bows. Everyone exchanged merry greetings. Old men lifted their hats to salute if a pregnant woman walked by, a respectful gesture I never saw anywhere in the rest of the world.

Historically, the beautiful imperial Vienna was often attacked by Eastern barbarians and Ottomans, and it was partially destroyed by the Allies' 50 bombing raids before the Soviet's unstoppable assault in the spring of 1945. Some of the most beautiful historical buildings were leveled. The Russian occupation of Vienna and invasion of Austria came with massive looting, rape and the unnecessary killing of innocent civilian Austrians simply because it was Hitler's birthplace.

After the war, Austria gained independence in 1955 as a republic, but its geographical position in the middle of Europe as a buffer between the East and West made the country into an international center invaded by refugees from the Iron Curtain, as well as from India, Pakistan, African countries and much of the world. These political and other asylum seekers were facilitated by refugee camps, which hosted millions of people looking to migrate to better parts of the world. They greatly impacted the 7.5 million Austrians, their national budget, as well as their traditional culture and civilization, as no other small country in the world suffered more abuse at the hands of aimless and ungrateful foreigners.

***

As for me, the master of mustard making, I kept doing the same thing until one day, after entertaining the ladies with my gymnastics, I saw something new on the slippery corridor in the middle of the washing room. The ladies were washing thousands of small glasses, not larger than a cup, that had mini paintings of Scottish bagpipers in traditional tartan kilts, high-collared shirts with black ties, woolen knee socks and solid soldierly boots. The figures sported traditional oversized bearskin hats, leather belts with big buckles, sporran pouches of fur or leather with long fringes, and large mantles draped over their shoulders. The small, painted glasses were truly objects of art. I took a few different colored glasses for their uniquely dignified Scottish looks. Even the Romans were historically afraid of the Scottish, and Emperor Hadrian built the famous Antonine Wall to stop their invasion.

Days later, the factory owner came with another 4x4 foot piece of plywood with some 12 bullet points written with the names of the ingredients I had to use to make eight barrels of mustard for a large Scottish corporation. This time, he described the list in English, noticing that I was studying my tourist guide with the English translations. Ever repeating "Ya, ya, ya," I understood one thing: it was a special order that would be used to fill the painted glasses as Christmas presents. After consuming the mustard, people would keep the glasses for drinking their whiskey.

A few times, I took the plywood with me to the big storage room to ensure I picked up the right ingredient sacks, which were labeled with Gothic letters. Soon I memorized the labels on each sack, and I rushed to deliver the first barrel. I had only two weeks to make this special mustard. I finished the order, and the ladies filled the glasses a week later. Dozens of boxes marked FRAGILE and THIS SIDE UP were sent by plane to Scotland. I must say I was mighty proud to be trusted to make such a great quantity of special mustard for export.

Christmas came for me in a most festive way: across the street, near my restaurant, there was a somber-looking medieval convent for nuns, from which came the sounds of what I believed to be the Vienna Boys' Choir rehearsals. The small windows of the convent were open, and I opened the windows on my side of the mixers' zone. I could hear the most angelic voices singing beautiful carols. Ignoring the grinding noise of the machines, I felt transported to another world.

For the Christmas day off, I wanted to dress up. I went to a few thrift stores and bought myself a pair of greenish slacks, a white shirt, a red tie, a blue jacket, old-fashioned, elegant shoes and a long cashmere coat. The first three items still had their original price tags, telling me they were once rejected gifts, but they were good for me. The last three were slightly worn, which reminded me that in England, rich lords often let their valets break in their new shoes and clothes to make them comfortable.

Freshly shaved with my hair long enough to be parted on the right and dressed as a successful young man, I showed up for the factory family party. It was held in the paneled conference room with an ornately decorated Christmas tree. Nobody recognized me until I opened my mouth to greet them in English, "Have a holly jolly Christmas!" I'd learned the phrase from my tourist dictionary. I accepted their applause, shook the hands of the men and kissed the hands of the ladies, making an excellent impression. I was kissed in return a few times by half-drunk ladies.

The food from the open buffet and the many types of wine were very tasty. I received a gift from the owner—a box with 12 different bottles of alcohol, including champagne. I believe I was asked in German if I wanted to stay and live in Austria. I automatically responded with my usual "Ya-ya-ya," collecting another round of applause. For the first time since I left Romania, I felt like a man who counted for something and that I was important.

For the New Year, I went to a restaurant and ended up sitting at the table with a happy group of Viennese, apparently well-known socialites. After midnight, I visited a very large house decorated in a heavy Baroque style. Again, I shook hands and kissed gloved hands, ate, and had a good time responding with "Ya-ya-ya" to all questions. I was not a drinker, but I knew how to dance. I was invited by a few ladies whose husbands were drunk to sit at their table and talk with their friends.

The dance floor was in a large entrance hallway with heavily ornate high columns. Waltzing with large pirouettes, I was afraid they would rotate as well and fall on me. I had no idea what my dance partners and other people told me, but I nonchalantly responded, "Ya-ya-ya." I must admit that for the first time in my life, I realized what a luxury it was to be rich, and I liked it a lot. It was too bad that instead of learning the English or German languages of prosperity in my school, I had eight years of learning the Russian language of poverty without the letter "H." That East Slavic language sounds like it should either put one to sleep or scare one to death with its thunderous sounds. I'd also had four years of Latin, a dead language. Both had an impossible grammar to learn. Communist schools teach students what to think, not how to think.

As for the party, I developed a new philosophy: regardless of how many ugly things happen in one year, if one has a few days of joy and happiness, that is enough to give one hope to go forward.

***

On January the third, my birthday, I was back to work in the mustard factory. I expected to have a wonderful day celebrating because before I would turn 30, I wanted to start my life over again in the United States of America, where half of the world's achievers and losers want to live. However, before lunch, the young owner, holding a piece of 4x4 plywood with its list of ingredients written in gothic letters, briskly entered the grinding machine room shouting a long accusation in German. In broken English, he repeated the entire recipe in an angry tone. I understood only the keywords from his entire rage: *mistake* and *money*.

He asked me to turn off my machines and follow him to the supply room, where earlier he'd noticed a full lineup of untouched sacks of important ingredients, which were to have been used in the mustard sent to Scotland. He pointed out the name written on the 4x4. Instead, I had used another line of sacks filled with seeds *not* to be ground for Scotland. I had mistakenly put them in the Christmas mustard that had already been sent off, packed in the beautifully painted glasses. The mistake was all because I was unable to properly read the embellished, calligraphic Gothic letters. The two names were easy to switch. The owner was afraid he'd have to pay thousands of dollars back to the Scottish corporation. He angrily said he would be lucky if no one died eating the faulty mustard I had made. I explained the huge mistake with one word: *confuzia*. The owner was ready to fire me.

I went to my locker to pack up my fancy clothes and leave when the jubilant secretary ran to hug me. She showed me a telegram from the Scottish corporation addressed to the owner, who almost fainted reading it. It was brief, written in English, and confirmed that the Christmas mustard was the best ever tasted and requested eight more barrels without any change to the recipe. She took me to the office, where the young man was still confused between the bad and good news. He promised to ask for social security for me and my permanent residence in Austria. I thanked him without telling him I had already been approved to immigrate to the United States officially.

***

When my flight confirmation came, I decided to send all the money I had saved to my family and my parents, unsure when there would be a next time I could show my generous compassion. Left without any money, Dudescu, recognized as the "camp dealer," bought all my fancy clothes and work wear to pay for my room and board at the camp. I was told by Herr Frank that out of tens of thousands of refugees, I was among the few who paid those dues in full. Still, I was left with $42.00 to take with me to America, where I would find money on the streets, as Dudescu informed me. He gave me a bunch of postcards with pictures of Manhattan he'd written notes on, addressed to the suckers from Romania who were after him. He wanted to show them that he'd made it. He added, "You mail them for me from Manhattan and make sure you use airmail stamps."

What I kept to take with me were my winter clothes and the blue shoulder bag in which I kept my most precious possessions—my towel, underwear, and socks, the emergency kit from camp, the little toy teddy bear, my harmonica, tourist dictionary, and the folder with my immigration papers and the letter of recommendation attesting that I was a good worker for the mustard factory.

Three weeks later, I was flying on TWA. I landed at Kennedy International Airport in New York City. It was the day in Romania when the union of Wallachia with Moldova was celebrated. They were two sister principalities of the same people with a common language, and they'd become one independent country above the lower end of the Danube River. With $42.00 and a shoulder bag weighing six pounds, I wished to unite myself as an immigrant with the American people, a nation of immigrants, especially after I learned to speak English and could be useful in any capacity in my new country.

One day, I would call myself an American.

■ $ ■

5. FINALLY IN AMERICA

I left Kennedy Airport in the evening on a bus filled with other new immigrants. Some 20 different languages could be heard, every speaker exclaiming amazement at each new view. The biggest expressions of excitement came at the top of the Triborough Bridge, which looks down onto many highways ending in overlapping circles that head off from many suspended levels into a straight line to cross into Manhattan. When the vast panorama of Manhattan suddenly appeared across the East River in an explosion of colorful lights that reached toward the snowy sky as if belonging to an extra-terrestrial colony from outer space, the decibels of screams doubled, and most of the newcomers, including me, had tears of happiness in our eyes. It was a moment never to be forgotten—what America first was for us.

Driving in the night through the colorful streets of Manhattan, I twisted my neck once in a while, pushing my head against the bus window to look up. I never could see the tops of the many skyscrapers. Rivers of cars, most notably yellow taxicabs and long, shiny limousines, honked their horns as they drove alongside our bus. At short intervals, the bus stopped, and our guide would read the names of those who should get off the bus, take their luggage from the compartments underneath, and then follow another guide into a hotel.

At one stop, one name was called in the wrong way. Of course, it was my name. The guide wanted to open the luggage door under the bus, but I showed the driver my six-pound shoulder bag. I stepped off the bus into the snow outside and followed my guide into the main hallway of the hotel, where she went to the desk, pointed to me, left a paper and, waving to me, returned to the bus.

The black hotel clerk handed me a key attached to a small, soiled wooden ball with the number 211 barely visible on it. Showing two fingers, he told me something and pointed to the squeaky elevator which was coming down. The first Americans I saw were two young white men wearing leather jackets and three black girls with leather miniskirts and furry jackets. All five were smoking and laughing, and they almost ran into me.

***

I pushed the second button and walked into noisy shouting and loud music on the second floor. I found room 211 and unlocked the door. I entered the room. It smelled of cigarette smoke and mildew. After turning the light on, I saw the black walls change into white, and bed bugs and other insects ran onto the dirty floors. The bed had not been changed recently, but it was a bed, and I was happy to have a sink with hot and cold water in my room. I pulled the curtain open to see the immaculate snow, and I saw something I'd always wanted to see: next to my run-down hotel was the Empire State Building. I could check that site off my bucket list.

Too bad I did not have a camera and only 42 dollars, but nothing could make me more curious than the incredible building into which an American B-25 air fortress plunged into the 79th floor in 1945 and was stuck in the hole that opened to the floor above it. The huge building did not even move, a testimony to its fine construction and the daily efforts of 3,500 construction workers, mostly immigrants, including many mighty and fearless Mohawk Indians who did the ironwork assembly. Fourteen died accidentally.

I discovered how good Manhattan tap water was for drinking, and I washed my hands and face. After that, I ate a bread roll I'd saved from the airplane, and after drinking a lot of water, I had a full stomach. I took the hotel stationery and the pen and put them in my coat pocket. Because there was so much noise and so many people running through the corridor, I waited a while to go to the bathroom and then quickly returned to my room. I slept fully dressed with the lights on until screams and the noise of firecrackers woke me. Totally disoriented, I locked the door and put the chain in the hook above the door handle.

***

In the morning, the snow had stopped before I walked out of the hotel, and I quickly found out that it was very cold. The weather did not affect the bumper-to-bumper traffic on the famous Broadway or on the expensive Fifth Avenue. I was overwhelmed seeing so many people looking so different from one another, walking in all directions without touching or looking at each other. I stopped in front of the Empire State Building's entrance, which was flanked by street cart vendors with smoked chestnuts, hot pretzels, and the best-smelling boiled hot dogs served on long buns with mustard and boiled sauerkraut for only 50 cents. It reminded me of the Vienna street vendors' grilled sausages, and I wondered, "Why are they called hot dogs?" It obviously was not an animal, hot or not. However, it made a most delicious breakfast, though it lowered my budget to $41.50.

I entered the immense building and joined a group of French tourists going down the escalator. Before I knew it, I was flying upwards in the Art Deco elevator to some floor, from which we took another elevator up to the observation deck on the 86th floor, where the doors opened into a large, well-heated gift shop. Outside on the circular observation deck, guarded by a tall iron fence and a strong net, I felt the winter wind would whisk me up and parachute me down to the minuscule streets below, where people and cars looked like they'd been reduced to the size of ants. Very quickly, I realized two things I did not have to protect me from freezing: warm gloves and a fur hut.

From that height of almost a quarter mile up, I spent a lot of time looking in the distance in all directions at the highways coming to and from Manhattan, the enormous bridges, the large rivers, and the countless skyscrapers competing with each other in height and shape. A few Gothic churches and other megalithic buildings stood out to me as well. It was too bad I had no idea what their names were. They were all lined up on straight avenues and streets, except Broadway, which followed the same cows' path from one end to the other of the 13.4 miles/21.6km long and a few miles wider island. In the middle of everything, a rectangular park served as a reminder of how beautiful and necessary it is to have a patch of nature among manmade canyons of steel, cement and glass.

In 1626, a Dutch merchant bought the entire island from a native tribe for 60 guilders (then worth $24.00 and today $1,150.00). He wanted his own land to build a trading post, where one could exchange fur pelts for trinkets, beaded necklaces, small mirrors, knives, axes, blankets and the most desired of items:

bottles of whiskey. Gradually, more and more Dutch immigrants settled in the area and engaged in the profitable fur trade, but they also became farmers, hunters, and fishermen. They formed their own colony named New Amsterdam. Fifty years later, the mercantile British bought part of the island and named it New York, after the Duke of York, the future King James II. The name stuck for the entire island and its surroundings as New York City, and it became the main port for millions of American immigrants who built what is there today.

Energized at learning so much history, I forgot about the freezing wind and that I was the poorest person on this magnificent island. But because I was privileged to be standing above its more than one million inhabitants, plus at least another million working commuters, I felt good about myself. I did not speak English, I had no employment, and I did not know anybody, but I felt immensely proud and happy to be accepted in and belong to a society that built such incredible monuments to prosperity and had become a global superpower. I looked around at the foreign tourists who were realizing what the United States is really made of. At that moment, I felt pride, and I felt privileged that one day, I would be named an American.

***

I was filled with dreams of making it in my new country, as millions of others who came before me had succeeded in building a civilization like none other on Earth in just 200 years.

When I later exited the Art Deco interior of the once tallest structure in the world, I stopped after taking a few steps on Broadway to look through the large windows of a luxury restaurant. Right there, I recognized one of my sports heroes. He was gazing outside, maybe at me. It was Jack Dempsey. I once had his picture as a bookmark, and now, it was hard to believe, I was unmistakably looking right at him, the famous world boxing champion who earned the first one million dollar gate after beating French champion Georges Carpentier in 1921 in Jersey City.

Now, more than 50 years later, he looked older and heavier. He had distinguished salt and pepper hair, neatly combed back and was dressed in a blue suit with a blue tie and breast pocket handkerchief to match. He was greeting an important customer who was flattered by such an honor. I felt like I was shaking his hand. Again, I felt so important just to be in America.

I stepped back and looked up at the five-foot high oversized red neon sign: JACK DEMPSEY'S, and underneath, in smaller letters, BROADWAY BAR. I regretted having so little money and not being able to afford a meal in Dempsey's restaurant, and I thought, "One day, I will eat here."

I turned around to find a grocery shop to buy myself something to eat for dinner. I returned to my dingy but warm room with a pack of sugar and two loaves of bread, having spent another two dollars. In two weeks, I would have no money left to eat. Finding work was my priority. I never thought about paying for the hotel since Herr Frank told me that the hotel would be paid for by an international refugee organization. I could not sleep all night because youngsters fought and screamed, men and women chased each other in the hallways, and my door was constantly hit by passers-by, yet the two days' past events kept my hope and euphoria going.

***

The next day was even colder, but after eating my bread with sugar and water, I felt confident enough to go look for a job. I noticed posters in shop windows with the words HELP WANTED. I especially noted those in food stores that would feed me. But, due to the language barrier and the way I was dressed, never mind that I did not know how to fill out job applications, some of which asked for my measurements in *inches* and *pounds*, words I had never heard, I was unsuccessful. With my hands and head freezing, I congratulated myself on my sturdy working shoes and two pairs of socks. They allowed me to walk through the cold to knock on doors for half a day. I tried restaurants and fast-food places, but again, my lack of even a minimum of English vocabulary was against my luck.

I quickly learned that I could get into any big museum for free if I joined a group of visitors with a guide, just like I had in the Empire State Building. The advantage was that in the museum, there was always wrapped, untouched food in the wastebaskets. I could eat very well there. If there was a cafeteria, I could sit down at any table where people left food behind, and sometimes my lunch was very good. The busboys did not mind me, because I always cleaned the table I'd sat at afterward.

I made the best of my poverty, and I spent many memorable days in the Metropolitan Museum of Art and the American Museum of Natural History. Besides eating there and staying warm, I acquired an irrepressible knowledge I could not find in any other way. I took a lot of notes on hotel stationery, and I think many visitors believed I was doing research, just as many artists sketched or painted some of the objects on exhibit.

***

Everything seemed to be going well, but after a week, I could not unlock my hotel room door. I went to the desk to complain, but the clerk put my blue shoulder bag on the table and asked me to pay $100.00 in advance for another week because the refugee organization paid only for the first eight days. The clerk said only Romanian refugees came to his hotel. That night, I tried to sleep on a bench in the back of the reception room. In the morning, I was kicked out. With my bag filled with bread and sugar, I went about the same daily routine I had established. What else could I do?

One night, I slept in Grand Central Station's large waiting room until a police officer forced me and others like me to leave the building. Other nights, I walked on the freezing streets and warmed myself above the subway grills, where warm air rose like steam. The problem was that as I walked on the freezing streets, my wet clothes became coated with ice. It was so cold I felt my brain might freeze, and my hands were numb even in my pockets. Only my work shoes kept my feet warm. I did what other homeless people did, padding my coat with newspapers from the streets' garbage cans. The newspapers proved to be very good insulation. Because I was unshaven, unwashed, and dirty, going to the museum was out of the question. So I'd go inside the underground mini city of Rockefeller Center or across the street to Saint Patrick's Cathedral, the safest places I could find. A young priest there looked at my papers and wrote down the address of the Romanian Church in upper Manhattan.

In one hour, I was at the church, which was inside a brick apartment building. It had been remodeled to look like the inside of a church. I waited on the second floor with a few other Romanians who knew each other. The priest there had one day per week to receive visitors, and when my turn came, he exclaimed, "Why doesn't a Romanian carpenter or bricklayer come to America?!" He gave me a check for $25.00 and wished me good luck. Happy, I went from bank to bank to cash it, but I did not have an account or a driver's license to show my identity. After a few days, I returned the check to the old priest, who tore it apart.

***

I bought more bread and sugar, and I went back to my hotel to get warm. The old clerk was busy, and his replacement let me sit on an armchair in the hallway, where I immediately fell asleep. I felt someone shaking my shoulder. Opening my eyes, I saw a young man, well-built with a long face, large black eyes, and long hair. He was looking at me and asking in Romanian, "You are a Romanian, aren't you?" I answered, "Yes." He nodded his head a few times and said, "If you do not come with me, you are going to die on the streets of Manhattan." I answered, "I will go any place with you because I cannot take it any longer…"

He understood, nodded his head again and helped me get up from the armchair. Pointing outside, he said, "I have a car. Where is your luggage?" I showed him my shoulder bag, and he tried to swallow a lump in his throat. He walked ahead of me. I noticed he was dressed in tight black velvet pants, an open red jacket and fancy but sturdy European shoes. With a short but skillful wheel maneuver, he moved the car out of the tight parking space and headed to Uptown, driving at a speed to catch all the green lights in a row. Indeed, he had a beautiful blue 1963 Buick Riviera with aerodynamic windows and, on the hood, a large gold American eagle with its wings spread.

He drove onto a marginal avenue without tall buildings, but the buildings it did have had fire escape stairs on the outside, which I had never seen before. The stores, tightly pushed against each other, looked modest. The customers were poorly dressed and the children were bundled up. Some pulled dogs on leashes along. Narrow doors led to stairs, which went up to the residential second and third floors. The rooms had small windows, some of which were frozen shut, with peeling paint and curtains that had faded from their original color. Christmas trees were thrown all over on piles of black garbage bags. Dirty, tall snow drifts were pushed up by snowplows at street corners every three to four streets.

"Are we still in Manhattan?" I dared to ask.

"Soon, we will leave it behind. We are headed towards Highway 95, which goes to the state of Connecticut, where I live. I bet you are hungry now, but we'll eat at my house in Bridgeport if that is OK with you. Do you like steak?" he joked. Seeing my sad smile, he pointed to the left toward the George Washington Bridge, with its two levels built at an incredible height above the Hudson River. I had never seen anything like it before. "It connects Manhattan with the State of New Jersey, but there is another one much bigger than this: the Verrazzano-Narrows Bridge, the longest in the world, which goes to Staten Island. My friend, you happen to be in the richest and most powerful country in the world!"

After we drove under crisscrossing highways, all dripping from above, my driver stopped talking so he could carefully concentrate on driving the frozen, slippery roads. He exited off the narrow road, leaving its high walls behind. Suddenly, the highway entered open land, going into what looked to me like the countryside. My driver looked relieved and hollered, "Let's go!" and pushed the peddle to the metal to 90 miles per hour. I had never experienced such speed, and the sensation somehow made me feel like a winner. I trusted my future with this new friend, who looked like a man's man. Now, I truly was in America, and I was going to make something of myself.

— $ —

6. IN THE BEGINNING

The young man, who looked very muscular and sure of himself, had a history that would amaze anyone familiar with it. In Romania, he was a stuntman in the movie industry. He was popular for his humor, easygoing nature, being a good person, and because of his distinct origin, coming from an Aromanian-Macedonian family. His first name was Sofrone, evidently from the ancient Greek name *Sophronios*, meaning "a sober man to be trusted as a savior." His friends called him Greco, but his family called him Hronciu, a baby name. Sofrone should have been in the *Guinness Book of World Records* for illegally crossing five borders until he ended his journey in Paris, where he was hired as a stuntman by a popular cowboy-themed attraction park, but he wanted to go to America and do stunt work in Hollywood.

When I heard that Sofrone was a Macedonian, I remembered that my father, who was in a Communist prison, often mentioned that the most admired and trusted cellmates were the unbreakable anti-communist group of Macedonian captives. Their integrity and bravery in any dangerous or humiliating provocation, and the fact that none of them ever was a turncoat, was respected even by the brutal guards. I could look at Sofrone and see the good genes he inherited from the forgotten ethnic people persecuted in all the Balkan countries.

They were the descendants of the Dacian shepherds, who were stranded south of the Danube River when the Romans withdrew from the occupied Dacia in the year 275 under Emperor Aurelian. He granted those Dacian Rhomanoi (Romans), mostly of the Moesia, land renamed Dacia Aureliana with its capital at Serdinca (Sofia), today's Bulgaria and extended into the southeast of today's Serbia. They were mostly shepherds who spoke Dacian mixed with a strong Latin dialect, later including Greek and Slavic vocabulary. From 1185, they were called *Vlachs*, and just like the Wallachias of Romania, they had their own Valachian kingdom for 200 years that included Bulgarian migrants. Being strongly related to the Romanian people and their language and culture, they were also called the Aromanians and Macedo-Romanians.

After the Ottomans took over, the Aromanian shepherds retreated into the mountains as a distinctive ethnic group, but wars that shifted borders sent many of them to diasporas in Albania, Greece, and nations along the Danube River. After WWI and the Greek-Turkish War, most were living in Bulgaria and Greece as victims of the partition of the defunct Ottoman Empire. The Aromanians lost the vast pastures for their numerous herds of sheep, goats and cows. Their crisis was solved in 1925 by the Romanian government, which needed settlers for the newly regained Danube province of Quadrilateral. Considering the Aromanians were part of Romanian heritage, it gave each family ten hectares (almost 25 acres) to settle on. Many with buying power settled in Bucharest as they were prosperous traders and had other money-making businesses. Their children went to good schools and graduated from universities, and many became important personalities in the culture and politics of interbellum Romania.

As loyal Romanians, they joined the Fascist Iron Guard, an anti-communist and anti-Semitic party. After the Romanian

Army crushed this ultra-nationalist movement in January 1941, many members filled the royal prisons. Then, after the Communists took over Romania in 1948, more of them were arrested. Renamed *Macedonians* but still Romanian patriots, they resisted the Communist regime and the Soviet divisions occupying Romania. They formed groups of partisans who were freedom fighters and pro-Americans. Once again, the captured partisans filled the Communist jails, where my father met them.

***

However, many Aromanians-Macedonians migrated to the US, and one of their more significant communities settled in Bridgeport, Connecticut, where Sofrone brought me to his rented house on Howard Avenue. It was a big house with many bedrooms, a large kitchen and a wraparound covered deck. It was next to the Armenian church, which local Black residents soon purchased. He and I were the only White persons from State Street to the railroad tracks. To me, it was heaven, especially after the first meal Sofrone served me: a cowboy steak with mashed potatoes and a Greek salad with colorful vegetables and feta cheese. After starving for so many days in Manhattan, I ate with tears streaming down my face while my friend, who always proved an excellent cook, looked at me to see if I was alright.

The house had central heating, and after so many months of collapsing from exhaustion on smelly beds and dirty pillows, I slept in my own bedroom. I do not know how many hours I slept, but afterward, Sofrone asked me to shave, shower, and change into some new clothes he lent to me (we were the same size). We had been invited for lunch by a friendly family.

Thus, I entered the Macedonian community, where I learned that my father spent eight years of hard labor in Communist prisons and did hard labor one mile deep in a lead mine where the toxicity and lack of oxygen extinguished the carbide lamps. Sofrone's many friends made it in America because they worked hard and knew how to invest their money. They owned homes and many cars and knew how to party.

I met former politicians and intellectuals, including Aurel Ciufecu, Professor Emeritus of Romance languages, who spoke eleven languages. His brother was arrested by the communists, and he worked in the Baia Sprie mine with my father, which made him cordial with me. The much-respected professor was an ardent champion of the international campaign to have the Aromanian communities recognized as an official ethnic group by the Balkan countries.

He initiated the uniting of intellectuals and patriots from the Macedonian diasporas, inviting them to participate in the Macedo-Romanian Cultural Congresses he arranged to be held at the Sacred Heart University of Fairfield, Connecticut, where he taught. I was the only Romanian present to honor these true cultural international meetings at all three congresses. There, I read my thesis, which was connected to the Aromanians' history, and I participated in discussions from the Romanian point of view during the congresses. Unfortunately, Professor Ciufecu died in 1996 at age 88, and that was the end of the important effort to unify the Aromanian-Macedonians who spoke a Romanian dialect strongly mixed with words from each country they resided in.

$

7. A NEW LIFE

As I correctly judged, Sofrone was a young man with good character and rare determination. After only one year in America, he succeeded in settling down in Bridgeport and gained respect from his Aromanian community. At the time he found me, Sofrone was in a vocational school. The school was financed by the Bullard Machine Tool Company, perhaps the largest employer in Connecticut with a great industrial tradition and thousands of employees. He took me to the school where 60 students, men and women, mostly young and illiterate immigrants, learned English and the skills to work in mechanical shops or as office clerks. Sofrone chose to be an auto mechanic and was already working in the school's repair shop. He took me to the administration office to enroll me in the same school, but I ended up on a waiting list. When one student graduates, one on the waiting list enters the school. I met a few of the teachers who praised Sofrone as one of the best students since he spoke Romanian, Aromanian, French, and Greek, and he had recently learned to speak Spanish fluently.

One thing was remarkable about my friend who kept working out with heavy weights to keep his chiseled body and perfect six-pack abs in shape so he could become a Hollywood stuntman, his ultimate dream. It was his cooking talents to produce the most aromatic and tasteful meals with a minimum kitchen inventory and basic ingredients. Besides his best cowboy steak and Greek salad, which is a multitude of colorful vegetables enhanced by feta cheese, one dish that has never left my memory and whose taste has lingered in my mouth is his elaborate omelet. His recipe is still fresh in my mind.

With a folded red bandana tied around his head, Sofrone perfected the kitchen sink omelet by adding a few tablespoons of oil and small pieces of bacon to a large frying pan heated on medium. He chopped Polish kielbasa, onions, mushrooms, added slices of colorful bell peppers, sautéed all together until tender, and sprinkled with salt and pepper.

While these simmered, Sofrone whipped four eggs in a bowl with a dash of milk, salt, pepper, and finely chopped dill. He poured the egg mixture over the sautéed ingredients and let it set. He carefully lifted the edges of the omelet all around to let the watery mixed egg cook to the bottom and skillfully turned the omelet over with one flipping move of the heavy pan. When the omelet was fully cooked, he sprinkled the top with cheese or used sliced cheese and then folded the omelet over the cheese.

At the same time, he was finishing French fries covered in hot oil in another frying pan, and he'd bring out from the refrigerator a bowl with Greek salad, which he placed in the middle of the table. It was a complete meal, including his cowboy steaks for any time of the day and for the rest of life, there was no reason to eat anything else.

***

It was already the end of winter, and I was busy learning to read and write English words to prepare myself for school. Occasionally, we drove to Manhattan, where Sofrone had a friend, and we would go for a drink at the restaurant on the corner of 57th Street and the Avenue of the Americas. Because I had never driven a car in Romania, both insisted I should learn how to drive.

Days later, Sofrone took me to deserted parking lots by the Bridgeport seashore where I could make mistakes without hurting anyone. His big Buick Riviera was perfect for me to learn the maneuvers for the driving test. I also prepared for the written test for my driving license.

When I thought I was ready, Sofrone took me to the Department of Motor Vehicles. I passed the written test, and soon, an officer sat in the passenger seat next to me in the driver's seat in Sofrone's car. He spoke something very fast while I rearranged the rear-view mirror, the seat, and the two side mirrors of the Riviera.

He asked me to drive. I correctly exited the parking space, but misunderstanding his directions, I made a right turn instead of a left turn, causing the instructor to shout. Scared, I made a U-turn in the middle of the very narrow, one-way, busy street. My instructor kept shouting something while covering his eyes. Cars zoomed by us, beeping their horns, and I sped between two oncoming cars. The officer yelled at me and ducked under the dash. His hat flew off into the back seat. He kept yelling at me to stop the car, which I did in the middle of a two-way street. He jumped out of the Riviera right there and ran back to the motor vehicle building.

Sofrone ran out to take over driving his car and returned us to the parking lot. He began naming the many mistakes I had made while waiting for his car's registration form to be returned from the office. A different officer came out on the building steps and began calling out the names of those who had passed their driving tests. Neither Sofrone nor I had any hope that my name would be called. The officer tried hard to pronounce a complicated name. It sounded like *Ein Gurr Metze*. Sofrone ran out to get my new little green driver's license. My name was spelled correctly, and the license was valid for the next five years.

We looked at each other in dismay, without understanding the mistake someone in the office must have made in giving me the driver's license. My driving instructor came out to claim his hat from the back seat. Smiling, he gave me a thumbs up—probably because I didn't cause an accident.

I could not believe what had just happened, especially not that Sofrone let me drive for the first time on the highway back home. He instructed me to stay only in the right lane and follow the car ahead of me, which took the first exit. I dutifully followed it. Sofrone hit himself in the head with the palm of his hand, rolled his eyes, had me pull over, and took over the driving.

Sofrone drove to a friendly family's home, where we celebrated my success with shots of tzuica and hot stuffed cabbages along with *mamaliga* (polenta). I felt so good about myself.

The next day, I felt even better when I received my notice to start at the vocational school in the mail. I would be paid $75.00 weekly for attending. I really didn't expect so many good things to happen to me for doing nothing to deserve it. I said, from the bottom of my heart, "Thank you Sofrone," and "God Bless America!"

***

Yet, more changes took place in the few coming months. I began the school where I was the only student to never be late or miss a day. The teacher was surprised at how smart I was, and she enrolled me in a typing class instead of the auto shop classes that Sofrone had done. However, being dyslexic, I failed to learn how to type. I did so badly that I ended up in the auto shop, where I was the only Romanian student. Somehow, I was the first to learn how to diagnose a defective car using a large, red computerized machine with many dials and cables connected to the car's various parts. My paycheck increased to $90.00 per week, and the Bullard Company recruited me to work there after I finished the training program.

Fate changed all my plans when Sofrone decided to move to Hollywood to be a stuntman in the movie industry. I was left alone in a large house in the middle of the black community. His departure was made less painful because he first helped me buy a 1966 Chrysler New Yorker. It did not run, but I overhauled it in the school's repair shop as part of my training. I put $300.00 of new parts into it. I did such an excellent job that my car could go from 0 to 100 mph in only eight seconds. I continued to learn English and used the dumbbells Sofrone left behind to get into good shape. The days passed very quickly. One Saturday, I decided to drive to Manhattan.

$

8. STILL LUCKY

I arrived in Manhattan around noon and parked my car on a side street near a bar I used to go to with Sofrone and his friend. When I entered, the bartender remembered me and offered me a drink on the house, which I politely refused. I asked instead for a hamburger and French fries and sat next to an older man dressed in a training suit. In a heavy Russian accent, he asked me where I was from. I explained I was an athlete and had graduated from the Sports Institute in Bucharest. After I finished my meal, he paid for it, then asked me to go upstairs with him to see his gym.

We took the elevator to the 21st floor, which was a duplex with three exercise rooms downstairs and two other smaller rooms upstairs, plus a sauna, dressing rooms, showers, a reception and waiting area and other accommodations. He talked about business being good there. I noticed large wall mirrors with ballet bars in front of them in all of the rooms, blue mats, rings, a trapeze, and parallel bars, which were all very familiar to me as I had trained on them for four years.

Alex, the owner, asked if I knew anything about the equipment I saw in his gym. Gladly, I took my shoes off, placed three mats in a row, and began to demonstrate the gymnastics floor routine that I used to do. I began with diving somersaults and press up handstands. Then I rolled forward into a half-split, laid on my back into a backbend, flipped one leg over into a standing balance on one leg and arms apart, rolled forward and turned around into two cartwheels. I did a back spring, jumped into a straddle, and…

Alex stopped me. He pointed to the rings. They were my favorite. I began with a pull-push into an "L" position, rolled forward into another "L" position and into an upside-down shoulder stand. I arched my legs into a handstand, followed by a large forward swing and a back flip to plant a firm dismount with my arms apart.

Alex was impressed. He asked me to follow him into the dressing room, where he had me wait. He returned with a sports bag, said something, and left. I sat on the bench, waiting for him. He came back after a few minutes and pulled out from the bag a blue training suit in my size and a pair of white gymnastics slippers for me to put on. Pointing to his watch, Alex said my class would begin in five minutes and I would be paid $6.00 per hour, more than double my factory wage.

He put his arm around my shoulder. Smiling, he walked me to the gym class, where six young women in leotards sat on a mat waiting for me. Alex introduced me. He told the class that my name was Ion, and I was a former Romanian champion.

After he left me alone in front of the class, I asked for anyone to show me the routine they had learned so far. Since I was a professional coach, I demonstrated a few elements that needed to be done correctly. My small audience applauded.

From then on, I worked for Alex. He allowed me to sleep at night in the small gym. In return, I had to clean the entire studio, including the bathrooms, showers, and sauna, until I could find a place to rent.

I agreed. I took my Chrysler to Queens to a friend of Sofrone who owned a house with a large yard. I started the next day, working 10 hours in the gym, teaching gymnastics, weightlifting, and calisthenics with a one-hour lunch break.

Soon, I found a small room, 10 by 10 feet, to rent. It was on the upper floor of a building. It had a skylight, a sink, and a refrigerator for $70.00 per month. I paid for three months in advance. I happily slept on the floor until I found a single-sized metal rollaway bed on 73rd Street between Broadway and West End. With two large blankets from Alex, I now had a good place of my own. I shared the bathroom with two other tenants, both very old.

Soon, I found a perfectly good television and a folding table left out on my street. I bought a new mattress, a pillow, a large two-gallon blue pot, and a hotplate with two burners. I purchased utensils and began to cook once a week, usually soup, which I refrigerated in my International unit, which had not been man-ufactured for 20 years. If it was too hot, I opened the refrigerator door and sometimes opened the skylight for cross ventilation.

I was probably good-looking because, at the gym, the students kept asking me what vitamins and supplements I took and what my diet was. In reality, my cooking menu was very limited, basically meat boiled in a colorful mix of vegetables: more colors, better taste. Here were my six "secret" recipes: veg-etable soup with marrow bones (free of charge from the butcher) and a lot of French green beans and parsley; chicken soup with egg noodles with dill and parsley; bean soup with smoked ham or hooves, colored with tomato paste, added bay leaves, a little sugar and dill.

I cooked the potato soup the same way. Oxtail soup with egg noodles, soured in the dish with lemon juice and sprinkled with lovage, a favorite of Romanian cuisine; meatball soup with diced tomatoes and sauerkraut. All soups contained chopped onions, celery, and carrots; some needed parsnip. Other vegetables I added according to the soup being made once a week in a heavy blue enameled steel two-gallon pot with a lid, which I used for the next 50 years.

It was my daily main meal of eight servings, which did not cost me more than ten dollars a week. Others spent that much for one meal, and they never had any money left from one paycheck to the next. For dessert, I had a slice of Sarah Lee coconut cake and a glass of sour milk.

In the span of two weeks, my life could not have been better. I had an address in America. I ordered address labels with an American flag on them to send my letters to Romania. Once again, I declared, "God bless America, the land of opportunities."

$

9. AT THE GYM

Three full-time and three part-time instructors staffed the gym, including me, plus Alex. Each one taught a permanent class or private lessons at varying levels based on students' age, skill, physical qualities, and frequency of participation. As a new instructor, I was a floater. I'd help in a class with more than six people, replace an absent instructor, and test new students.

Even though I was capable of demonstrating any exercise or executing any element on rings, trapeze, or parallel bars, I soon realized how little English I knew, especially concerning gymnastics terminology. To avoid embarrassing moments, I began secretly taking notes on how American instructors spoke to their classes and what they called each move or exercise.

I was good at observing why most students turned blue, their faces and eyes bursting with perspiration, as they tired very quickly: instead of breathing out, they held their breath during heavy exertion. Also, I noticed that the instructors only counted from one to eight during any movement and encouraged the students to merely expend extra effort in order to improve their routines.

Therefore, being too focused on using their muscles, speed, coordination, flexibility or endurance in an attempt to gain power and stability, they held their breath to the point they were ready to faint. As I had competed in track and field, I knew how to breathe to coordinate lung activity with the movements of the arms, legs, and full body. The trick is to exhale carbon dioxide through the mouth before inhaling freshly oxygenated air through the nose in a rhythmic, timely, reflexive way. Moreover, before any event begins, one must exhale and inhale deeply a few times in order to accumulate a large reserve of oxygen for the muscle, which will not work well in an oxygen deficit. Even in jogging, one has to exhale twice profusely and inhale twice to make the lung capacity larger. Doing that means coordinating two running steps to each inhale and alternating with two running steps on exhale.

Each time I taught a class or a private student, I was careful to provide reminders about breathing in and out. Inhale when raising the arms and exhale when lowering the arms and bending the body forward, pressing the lungs to empty out further. I never heard the other instructors say "Breathe in" or "Breathe out" in any gym or dance class that I attended.

In a few weeks, I was fully booked with ten classes a day. Alex was so pleased he raised my hourly pay rate to $9.00, which at that time yielded a great payment of $90.00 a day. There were days I didn't go to the gym, especially in the summer when clients were away and the gym was empty.

However, I also had private clients. At the rate of $40.00 per hour, which doubled my salary, I mainly went to their apartments to get them in shape for their next vacation. I was very happy with my life in America. There were not enough words to express my gratitude. My poor family I had to leave in Romania was lifted up from poverty with the money I sent them.

***

One morning, Alex walked into my gym with an older lady and her chauffeur, who helped her by holding her bent arm while she used her cane with her other hand. Alex brought a chair for her to sit on, and the chauffeur left. "Lady Beatrice, this is Ion, my best instructor, who will help you get better." Dutifully, Alex smiled and helped her take off her mink overcoat.

My unusual client was probably 80 years old, very tall, and very frail. A pink training suit hung on her shapeless body. It took her quite an effort to use her cane to stand up. She smiled at me, slightly embarrassed. I helped her sit back down, and before I knew it, I began answering her questions about who I was. The way the sun was entering the studio through the windows, her pale complexion and white hair glowed. She spoke with a charming British accent.

Well, when it was time to do an exercise, to her amazement, I kept her seated on the chair. I asked her to hold her cane in front of her with both hands. Nice and easy, I asked her to inhale as she lifted the cane above her head and exhale as she returned the cane to her lap. Using the same breathing technique, I had her push the cane out from her chest and return it. After a few repetitions with her feet flat on the floor, I let her rest. Her rapid breathing became slower until she was comfortable. She was still seated when I asked her to lift one leg at a time and put it down again on the floor. I knelt down and held her foot, helping her bend and extend her leg with the same in-and-out breathing. Lady Beatrice said that it felt good.

After another rest period, I helped her stand and walk to the ballet bar in front of the mirror. I moved the chair next to her. She understood why and smiled. I had her hold the bar with both hands, slightly bend her knees and go up and down a few times, all while continuing to inhale and exhale. Then, I had her do the same exercise with her legs apart while still holding the bar.

Again, after a period of rest on the chair, I showed her how to gently move her head up and down, side to side, and circle it both ways. When Alex came to check on us, she held both thumbs up. Class time was over, so he went to call her chauffeur to pick her up. He assisted her with her coat, and she took out from her pocket a few expensive rings, which she put on her fingers. In a sweet voice, she told me how good she felt. I told her not to try to do anything we did at home. She understood my concern and asked Alex to schedule her in a permanent class at 10:00 each morning. She slowly walked to the elevator, helped by her chauffeur. [I must thank the (I.C.F) from which I graduated, which provided me with pre-med courses about anatomy and physiology. It taught me how to help athletes in rehabilitation and older people.]

Later, Alex told me she was a rich client who, in the past, owned a very fashionable magazine she sold when she learned she had cancer. After many months in the hospital, she was a cancer survivor and had decided to return to the gym. She showed up for her class religiously, and the following month, she walked independently, only using her cane.

***

I worked with Lady Beatrice for three months. When summer was over, she walked out of the elevator without a cane and sat down on the couch in the waiting room with the other ladies. With a large smile, she announced to me that she had done something spectacular. "Today, I walked alone without my cane or my chauffeur," she proudly exclaimed in her British accent.

"So what?" asked a lady next to her.

"It just so happens that I took a bus to the gym."

"Really? And?"

"I walked down the aisle between the seats to the end of the bus and sat down."

"Oh, ya, then what?" laughed another lady who was waiting for her class.

"The bus was moving."

"Big deal," said another lady, trying to be funny.

"It was a very big deal because I walked without touching the side seats like others were doing," she pointed to me and continued, "thanks to this young Romanian man."

A few hand claps followed. To complete the scene, I took a bow. Then, Lady Beatrice led me to the classroom.

$

10. PARTY CLUES

Lady Beatrice reached good levels of improvement and could go out shopping and watch Broadway shows. She would tell me all about her daily experiences. She was planning a big party before Thanksgiving, and she wanted me to attend as the main attraction for her friends and former business associates. For that reason, she bought me a beautiful tie she insisted I wear to her party, which was scheduled on a Saturday afternoon in late October at her lavish penthouse apartment on Park Avenue. She asked me to arrive around 5:00 PM.

At exactly that time, the doorman, dressed in an expensive uniform (I believed he was a general), called upstairs to announce my arrival. The elevator opened to a large living room full of guests who applauded me as I stepped into the room. Obviously, she'd told them about my role in her fitness rehabilitation. A few well-dressed gentlemen shook my hand, others patted my shoulders, and the ladies patted my cheeks as they congratulated me.

After this warm reception, Lady Beatrice introduced me to more guests in the dining room. I found myself drinking something red and very sweet from a large crystal punchbowl. It soon made me dizzy. The elegantly uniformed waitresses carried plates with various hors d'oeuvres, walking among some 50 to 60 people. Many were drinking champagne out on the apartment's large terrace. For the first time, I tasted shrimp, quiche, caviar, and other finger foods, which I did not mind, but I found my hunger increased.

While waiting for the real food, I mingled, still believing I was a big shot, only to realize that all those well-dressed older men and women standing around in groups, sipping from their crystal glasses, were paying no attention to my presence. The worst thing was when someone talking in a loud voice asked me something about Romania and Dracula, and I ended up offering uninvited information about how I lived on the West Side with furniture I had found on the street.

The rich crowd realized that aside from my being a good gym instructor, there was no conversation with them that I could handle. They were polite: they admired my tie and offered artificial, indulgent smiles. But they had better conversations to have with acquaintances at the party whom they had not seen for a long time. Lady Beatrice quickly judged my situation and tried to be with me. Together, we walked around the apartment. She described in detail the richly framed painted portraits, the Queen Anne furniture, and the contents of the curio cabinets.

***

She couldn't stay with me the entire time; her presence at the party was in demand. Learning I was hungry, Lady Beatrix took me to the large kitchen with a stove of a type I had never seen before, having six burners, a grill, a hotplate, two ovens, and a large hood above it to absorb the smells and smoke from what was cooking. On two burners, two large pans were filled with chicken parts turning brown in hot oil. On the hotplate were big mushrooms, small sausages, and colorful shish-kebob sticks, all smoking. On each side of the stove were two large sinks, and above them, lined up on the wall, were glass cupboards filled with colorful British china and glasses. Other electric kitchen gadgets

I had never seen before lined the reddish marble countertops. In the middle of the kitchen was a long, solid butcher block island. A Black woman was busy chopping something behind it.

After introducing me as a hungry guest, Lady Beatrice left, pushing a tea cart filled with various desserts on each of its many shelves. The older Black woman, wearing a big white apron and a white turban that went well with her red dress, pulled a chair up next to me and asked me what I would like to eat. Again, my English was so poor that I could not name one single food except "Bread." She understood my problem and opened the largest refrigerator I had ever seen, indicating I could choose anything from it. A few large, covered pots attracted my attention, and in one, I recognized a lamb stew. All were untouched as the guests preferred to drink, not eat.

She warmed up a large portion of stew for me and served it with big slices of brown bread, a few pickles, and a glass of red wine. She checked the chicken sizzling in the frying pans and the food on the hotplates. Then she sat across from me. She spoke in an accent I'd heard in my old Bridgeport neighborhood: "Honey, I never saw a Romanian in my life, and thank God you came. I thought I was going to lose Lady Beatrice!"

I was enjoying her excellent lamb stew, and I asked, "Isn't this an Irish meal?"

She laughed and said, "Honey, in that refrigerator is the United Nations of food. You name it, and I have it."

I replied, "You don't have any Romanian stuffed cabbage."

She said, "I have German stuffed cabbage and Hungarian goulash."

I asked, "What do you serve all those guests?"

She answered, "Those guests do not eat. They only sample food and drink, and they talk about golf, football, fishing and hunting."

I was curious, so I asked, "Who are they?"

She gave me a long answer, "Honey, what can I tell you? They are not Russians who arrive already drunk, not Latinos who talk at the same time, nor French or Italians who talk with their hands, not the Irish who sing together, or the Jews who sit to eat and drink. For sure, you do not see any *n-----s*—none have ever been in here besides me, who came along with the apartment."

I asked, "So who are the guests?"

She exclaimed, "Say whaaat?" and then explained: "Honey— they are the WASPs." Seeing the amazement on my face, she continued. "They are the remains of the British folks, now becoming White Anglo-Saxon Protestants, who drink standing up. When they begin to wobble, they will stop drinking and go home."

I kept eating. I was impressed by the logic and wisdom of the Black woman, who I believed to be well-educated besides being a good cook. She returned to her stove while I finished eating and drinking half a glass of the good, expensive wine to wash down the grease of the lamb stew. Seeing the cook was too busy to socialize with me further, I waved to her as I left the kitchen, and she waved back in a friendly manner.

***

I walked out on the big terrace. It had a four-foot wall not to allow anyone to fall from the 11th floor.

It was cold and already dark. So, only a few men were still drinking while watching the traffic below going back and forth on

Park Avenue, which ended with the huge Grand Central Station and the Pan Am Building tower.

One of the well-dressed gentlemen, looking rather like a football coach with his flat-top haircut, solid neck, turned-up nose, red face and strong body, approached me. "Shall I bring you a drink? What would you like?" he wondered. I politely refused his offer, which made him ask, "What is the Romanian drink?"

I answered, "We have tzuica."

"What is that?"

"It is a brandy made of distilled…"

"Like a bourbon?"

"No, it is made of fermented plums."

"That must taste awful and be an acquired taste," declared the gentleman, who changed the subject to a question closer to home.

"What do you think of our America?"

"Our America," I underlined with my voice, "is very good to me, but I know so little about it."

"Well, we are the superpower of the world, and I don't think Communist Soviet Russia or any other global power can change that. What do you think?"

I shrugged my shoulders. Looking down over the terrace wall at the bumper-to-bumper traffic below, I pointed to it and suggested, "Maybe that will change everything?"

"What is that?" he asked and looked at the line of slow-moving cars.

After a short pause, I answered, "All is fine in our America until those cars stop moving."

"Why would that happen?"

I explained, "It would happen if no gasoline supply were available."

"That would never happen here. Maybe in Romania, but not here in the land of plenty," exclaimed the man as he finished his drink.

He had nothing left to discuss with me, an ignorant immigrant from a third-world Communist country who did not understand the mighty American economy, so he left to refill his glass.

***

A short time later, a total oil embargo from the Arab States (except Iraq and Libya) meant oil exports stopped coming into the United States. In a matter of days, miles-long lines of American cars waited at gasoline stations without any gas left in the pumps. The car owners were reduced to duplicating the frustrated Romanians standing in endless lines to buy bread and other basic goods, which seldom arrived at the stores.

In no time, frustrated American drivers began to fight for position to be closer to the gas pumps. Soon, gunshots were heard being fired from inside the unmoving cars.

A lack of vital necessities has been proven to disturb any peaceful society at any time in history, and the United States was no exception. However, it successfully recovered from the crisis and went on to continue its extremely enviable, abundant lifestyle.

━ $ ━

11. NO SUCH LAW

One of my most memorable happenings in coming to America was opening a checking account and seeing my name printed on each check, which was illustrated with cowboy scenes. It made me feel important and powerful. I could write a check to buy anything. I had money in the bank. For the time, I only had $261.00, but there I was on my lunch break on a Friday afternoon, rushing across the street from the gym on the west side of the Avenue of the Americas to deposit my paycheck in full at my bank.

It was a terribly hot day in September in Manhattan, which was wisely built with straight streets and avenues perpendicular to each other, allowing the breeze from both rivers to crisscross their drafts right over the middle of 57th and 5th, which separates the great city into Uptown and downtown. It was too bad that by the time the fresh, cool air blowing from the East and West rivers arrived, it was hot and humid. This is due to the overheated steel and glass canyons as the skyscrapers reach for the clouds. Yet, imagine if Manhattan had the winding streets of Istanbul.

As I came out from my building's air conditioning, a wave of heat clouded my eyesight, but by running to the bank, I generated my own ventilation. It suddenly stopped when I saw a long line at the bank's entrance. Both doors were opened wide, as were all the windows. The bank's air conditioning was broken. I was the last one waiting in line on the hot street pavement, and I was eager to step inside the shade of the bank.

Finally, I slowly entered the building. Only two tellers were working, as it was lunch hour. Both had large fans blowing behind them. I began to perspire heavily. Breathing the hot air inside the building was worse than being out on the street.

I have to mention one thing about Americans, so wrongly judged abroad for nonchalant behaviors and disorderly conduct: they are most disciplined while standing in line whether waiting for a bus or for their turn to be seated in a restaurant. At the bank, they were lined up in one long line, even though there were two tellers. It reminded me of being in Romania when I stood in a long line for hours in front of the closed grocery shop, waiting for a truck to deliver some food. If someone tried to cut ahead in line, shouts and curses followed to discipline the intruder.

Making a small step forward after each customer finished with the teller, I counted how many people were still ahead of me: it was exactly twelve. I looked behind me at the line coming into the bank, and I felt better seeing ten people, some reading newspapers, some talking, an older man with white hair and a white beard resting his hands on the handles of his wheeled walker.

Instinctively, I felt compassion for the poor fellow bent over his walker. He kept wiping his face with a large handkerchief and was breathing hard. I'd made two more tiny steps forward when I heard a muffled noise. I looked back, and I saw the walker rolling away from the line. The old man was flat on his back on the floor. People were moving away from him. I immediately jumped to help, but I was pulled back by other men in line who told me not to touch the man who'd fainted.

A bank clerk called in the emergency, and the line continued to slowly advance toward the two tellers, everyone walking around and avoiding the man on the floor. I went back to my place in line, now number eight, and I kept looking at the old man lying unmoving on the floor.

Soon, I heard the sounds of ambulance sirens. An ambulance and a police car stopped in front of the bank. Two young paramedics and one policeman ran to attend to the old man. They put something under his head, opened his shirt, loosened his belt, and gave him something to smell which made him open his eyes. They listened to his heart, took his blood pressure, and gave him an injection in his arm. When the man began to whisper, they gave him something cold to drink and put an icy bandana around his head. They helped him up so he could rest his arms on his walker again. They asked him to take a few steps, and he said he was okay. The paramedics and the police officer left with the same deafeningly sharp sounds from their sirens blaring.

Like the brave Romanian I was, I walked over to the old man to have him take my place in front, but again, I was pushed back and warned not to touch him. I returned to my place, now number four in line, when I heard a thump and saw the walker rolling away from the line again. I went to help the man, who was now flat on his face with his arms underneath him, choking. Again, I was pushed away, this time by a bank clerk. Revolted by everyone's lack of concern for the man, I said, "For God's sake, someone help him!"

The ambulance came with a police car again, and they revived the elderly man, who again shuffled his walker to his place in line.

"Please, let him go to the teller or take my place in line," I shouted.

Everyone looked at me with stern eyes to mind my business.

I approached the teller. With a crooked smile, he registered my deposit, gave me my receipt, and called, "Next, please."

I walked around the paramedics, the policeman, and the old man, who succeeded in standing up and holding on to his walker. He was the seventh in a line that was moving at a snail's pace in the Saharan heat—it was probably over 125 degrees.

Once in the street, I felt a tap on my shoulder. A gentleman with an undone tie smiled and said, "I see you are not from around here. Never touch or try to help someone like the old man. He could die, and you could be held responsible for his death. We don't have a Good Samaritan Law here. If you touch a dying person, his family can sue you for everything you have."

He walked away in the opposite direction.

I rushed to reenter the air conditioning of my building, thinking, "Imagine—losing the $390.00 I have in the bank."

$$\blacksquare\!=\!\$\!=\!\blacksquare$$

12. ANOTHER STUDENT

For some reason, Alex never gave me a woman's class to teach, even though many switched to take the specialized private lessons I taught. Some of my students were famous, like Calvin Klein and a few of his important attorneys, who took my private classes. I led a men's class attended by some of Wall Street's important businessmen. I had another class of women and men, all personalities from the textile industry. For a while, I had Holston, his friend Elsa Parrety, and a few executives in the same private class.

One private student of mine was the actor Roy Sheider, who asked Alex not to give him any other instructor but me. At that time, Roy was middle-aged with a boxer's nose and a very dark suntan. He was a rather small but trim individual with a deep suntan who wanted to broaden his narrow shoulders. I advised him to wear a large towel around his shoulders when his naked upper body was filmed. However, the lightweight Roy was probably the best gymnast in the entire studio. He managed to do handstands on rings and high swings between the parallel bars. He was decent, never advertised his fame, and dressed so modestly that nobody on the street could guess who he was.

One day, Roy told me to book another private student in his class since he would be away for a few months filming in Nantucket or someplace like that; he was not sure where. Taking advantage of the fact that he liked me, I remembered that Sofrone, the man who saved my life, was a stuntman who'd gone to Hollywood, but he was only working in a pizza shop that he owned. Therefore, I asked Roy if he might find a way to help my friend, and he was glad to take Sofrone's name and number. Moreover, he said that the head of the stuntmen's union was his friend. He would certainly meet with Sofrone to see what could be done.

That night, I called my friend at his pizza place and told him the good news about Roy Sheider trying to help him. I advised him, "Be sure when he calls you to be nice to him." Sofrone was very pleased. I called him once in a while to ask if Roy got in touch with him, but it seemed the movie star was too busy.

A few months passed. Before winter, Roy returned to the studio to work out. He was out filming the future hit, *Jaws*. He said it was directed by a nice man named Stephen Spielberg. And the thriller movie was a great box office success! One day, Roy came with his hair and fake goatee colored red. Knowing that I was a good ballroom dancer, he laughed, saying that he auditioned to play the legendary choreographer and director Bob Fosse for the future movie *All That Jazz*.

Taking advantage of his good mood, I asked about Sofrone. Roy said his friend who was willing to hire him could not do it because Sofrone's name was not on the Hollywood stuntman list. I explained that Sofrone was a stuntman in Romania and France, and he'd moved to America just to work in Hollywood.

Roy made a puzzled face and asked if Sofrone was born in America. If not, he explained that Sofrone could not be a stuntman in Hollywood. All had to be born in the United States. It was a new rule made to keep foreign competition away.

I called Sofrone with the bad news, and as it turned out, the situation caused him to become a very successful businessman in his own right. He eventually owned ten Greco's New York

Pizzeria parlors in Los Angeles. One was next to Grauman's Chinese Theater on the famous Hollywood Boulevard. He never did any stunt work in Hollywood, but he was always in demand to deliver pizzas to the greatest studios in the world. He made it big in the largest city in America and enjoyed his own version of "God Bless America."

$$\blacksquare \$ \blacksquare$$

13. THE TEST RESULT

One day, my boss ran to the upstairs gym to inform me that I should take my lunch early because, at 1:00 PM, a very important client was coming for a private lesson. He advised me to be very professional because this client had not liked any of the instructors who worked with him previously.

At 1:00 sharp, a young, barefoot, unshaved man with a loose blue t-shirt and black shorts walked into my gym room. Shaking my hand, he asked me to evaluate his athletic abilities. He had a dark complexion with dark spots like freckles on his face and short black hair. He had short, hairy legs and appeared to have very little muscle.

I took him through a brief warm-up of easy calisthenics to loosen him up, gave him three-pound weights to steady his moves, asked him to hang on the trapeze, and then to try doing a chin-up. Hanging from the trapeze with his knees bent made him very nervous, and he asked to skip the dangerous apparatus. I moved him along to hang on the rings and asked him to gently swing back and forth. He didn't understand, so I demonstrated how to do it by making a step forward and a step backward. Next, I showed him how to hold tight to the rings and swing his body in a straight line with his legs and together up in an upside-down position. I tried to help him by holding his feet, but he was shaking and sweating profusely.

I sat him on a mat with his back against the wall so he could regain normal breathing and calm down. He told me that while he had been away for a few months, he had experienced much stress and fatigue, which was why he had failed each test so far. We continued with floor exercises that posed no danger of falling and getting hurt. I simply asked him to stand up straight, look straight ahead into the wall mirror, and copy my arm and leg movements. With both arms down, I lifted one leg straight forward, parallel to the floor. He did the same pretty well and repeated the movement with the other leg. I asked him to raise his arms above his head and, in parallel motion, to alternately lift his legs. He almost fell forward and had to hold on to the ballet bar in front of the mirror.

I asked him to hold the bar with both hands and swing each leg side to side, which he did well. Then, I asked him to kick back one leg at a time without bending his arms, which he also did well. Encouraged, I placed him in the middle of the mat and showed him how to balance on one leg with the other leg held straight out to the back, parallel to the floor. He had to look straight forward and keep his back straight. He tried it a few times with each leg but always had to jump to regain balance.

Just for fun, I showed him how to swing his back leg forward and jump 180 degrees to face the opposite direction while keeping the leg straight and his arms out to the side like the wings of an airplane. He tried hard but fell on the mat, only to try again and again, always messing up the half-turn. He laughed at himself and said that indeed, he had a problem with his balance, but he assured me of his discipline to practice and asked me to be his instructor in the future. Our half-hour lesson was up, and he shook my hand, trying to have a firm grip. He told me his name was Michael, but I could call him Mike.

***

Mike booked himself for a one-hour private lesson each day. He was never late. He worked hard learning to correctly do pushups and how to use small weights while properly breathing in and out, all the while making little progress on the apparatuses, including the parallel bars.

But soon, he could do the leg balance with a precise half-turn, switching from one leg to the other. He asked to learn front and backward somersaults and how to do the candlestick position on his shoulders, holding his hips with his hands and splitting his straightened legs in all positions without holding his breath. Still, he wanted to avoid the rings and trapeze since they move even more when one tries to control them.

Mike was polite and paid a lot of attention to detail so he could practice at home. He reached the level of being able to do a forward dive somersault and get up with his arms extended straight out in front of him. He learned to do a backward somersault straddle in the "V" position with his legs straight apart.

Almost a month passed when one evening, an older student named Paula, who could swing upside down on rings while almost touching the ceiling, was waiting to start her class. When she saw me at the water fountain, she jumped, shouting, "Why didn't you tell me Mike Bennett was your private student?"

I stopped drinking water from my paper cup and asked, "Who is Mike Bennett?"

The ladies waiting for the next class all laughed, and Paula continued in a raised voice, "You don't know who Mike Bennett is? He's only one of the best choreographers on Broadway, second only to Bob Fosse! You'd better introduce me to him because I want to audition for his shows. Why do you think I've taken dance classes and lessons in this gym for 20 years? Huh?"

I felt like somebody had hit me in the head. I helplessly looked around for sympathy but only got disapproving headshakes.

For almost a month, I had been training Mike Bennett on how to hold his balance on one leg and all the other gym crap, not realizing all of America was praising his choreography and directing of shows which earned many awards, like *A Chorus Line*.

I remained friends with Mike. He invited me to all his shows and gave me tickets to other Broadway and off-Broadway shows, even to shows that he could not attend. He listened attentively to the comments I offered him after each show or play that I saw. I taught Mike until I no longer worked at the studio, and I lost contact with him at that point. I was sad when I learned he died of AIDS in 1987.

— $ —

14. A MAN WITH TASTE

I had always looked up to my new friend Zamfir, who, like me, was a Romanian immigrant. He'd come to America much earlier than I had. He knew how to say in English, "Zangu [*Thank you*]," "D'un'stand [*Do you understand*]," "Kikirizi [*Take it easy*]," "Parno me [*Pardon me*]," "Gobigudiu [*God be with you*]," "Neremine [*Never mind*]," "Rumefer [*However*]," and the "F" word [*no explanation needed*]. He was a middle-aged, big man. Judging by his black leather jacket, which made him look even bigger, and the thick gold rope chain around his stocky neck, he had good taste. The look complemented his thick white hair, black mustache, and penetrating black eyes. In any restaurant he walked into, he was always given the best table and a drink on the house, for most believed he was a mafia boss.

I was lucky when he agreed to come with me one evening to buy a gentleman's brimmed hat with my first salary check of 95 dollars. I wanted to look presentable for any future job interviews and to make the girls turn their heads when I walked by.

We spoke in Romanian, but what was so good about Zamfir was that he also used many English words. I would pick up some and use them later with the same distinction. We walked down Broadway and entered the first hat shop we came to.

The only person there was the salesman, who was happy to see two potential clients. He smiled and rubbed his hands together, saying, "Greetings," to which Zamfir replied, "Cretins." He said to me, "I bet this is another one who doesn't speak Romanian."

Zamfir pointed to the hats on the shelves, rubbed his right

thumb against his index finger and asked, "Cow much?"

I understood the gesture, and I indicated a beautiful cowboy hat, to which the vendor said a number we did not understand.

Zamfir took a pen and a piece of paper from the counter and asked him to write down the price in Romanian. It was $73.99 plus tax, and I approved by nodding my head.

The salesman rushed to take down the hat.

But Zamfir jumped at me and whispered, "Are you a millionaire?" And he shouted to the eager salesman, "Non, non, non. Not money!"

I protested that I liked the hat, but Zamfir calmed my enthusiasm by asking if any of my relatives were cowboys. It was a good argument, and I looked for another hat. Quickly, the salesman, who understood our money problem, presented me with a similar style gambler's hat and wrote down $59.99.

The number greatly irritated Zamfir, who shook his head and hands to indicate a firm "No." He signaled to the salesman to lower the price, dropping in English a nervous "Kikirizi [*Take it easy*]."

Shaking his head in disappointment, the vendor came back with exactly the hat I wanted, a black felt Creek. He wrote down the price: $46.99. I liked it so much that I applauded and put the hat on my head, walking to look at myself in the large mirror by the desk.

Like a vulture, Zamfir jumped on me to say, "My man, are you insane to pay half your salary on a hat? Hey kid, did you steal your money?"

"But I really like it..."

"I'd like to have a yacht, but I know my limits. D'un'stand [*understand*]?"

"That is not exactly the case," I argued.

"By the way, where would you wear a hat like that except to a funeral? Do you have someone who will be buried soon?"

"I told you; I want this hat. If I buy one now, I will never buy one again!" I admired myself in the mirror.

Zamfir came behind me to explain: "Listen, my spugi [*spooky*] kid. You are crazy to pay a lot of money for something you cannot wear in summer when it is too hot and will lose its color in the sun, or in the fall because the rain will change it into a sopping wet washcloth, or in the winter because it will freeze on your head, or in spring when the winds will make it fly into the mud. Are you insane? Besides, you are not a professor any longer, and won't be for a long, long time. D'un'stand? Why not buy a cheaper hat that you can fold and carry in your pocket if you wish?"

"I can wear this one when I go to the theatre..."

"To do what, smart kid?! To leave it in the coat room?"

To make a long story short, after many mutual negotiations, I settled for an imitation vintage hat for $6.99 plus tax.

"Now, that is the hat you need: beautiful, good quality, and if you want, you can wear it with your short pants, you dandy kid."

I paid for it, and I have to admit, Zamfir was right: the hat was cheap, but I swear, it looked like a deluxe garment. It even had a lining and a colorful label. With the hat in my hand, we walked out of the store, and in the light outside, my hat looked even better. I placed it on my head, and proudly, I noticed the people in the street looking at me. I snuck a peek at my hat in all the shop windows we passed.

"Hey, kid. Are we going to celebrate it?" asked Zamfir.

"Celebrate what?"

"To honor your new hat purchase with a beer, some sausages and the like. Agree?"

"Of course, I agree. How often do I buy such a luxury?"

***

Before I knew it, I was with Zamfir wearing my new hat in the Queens subway, where everybody seemed to admire its maroon color. Soon, we entered the Romanian Oak restaurant where everybody cheered Zamfir, the man who knew all the deals, and according to his own prediction, would be the first Romanian congressman.

The rest of the patrons were older refugees, and only two of them had succeeded and had their own car repair shops. Of the rest, many had formerly been well-to-do in Romania and came to America with big dreams but were working in factories or as doormen in Manhattan, while their wives worked in hairdresser's shops, mostly as manicurists or in spas as skin specialists. Some had saved enough money for a down payment and had bought a small row house or a small apartment, and all were mortgaged.

They came to the Romanian Oak to socialize or to celebrate an event and hear only their mother tongue. It made them feel at home. Of course, the much older Romanian immigrants were in better social and financial situations, and many were doctors, or lawyers, or had small businesses, and they went to the Romanian Church.

The restaurant owner, who was old and bold, was once a virtuoso concert violinist. He often played Gypsy songs on his expensive violin to entertain the customers. Now, he carried a round table to the middle of the restaurant, and a waiter carried the two best chairs. Dressed in a Romanian embroidered floral shirt, the owner wiped the chairs and laid an immaculate white tablecloth over the table.

A waiter (who'd graduated in classical piano from the music Conservatory in Bucharest) brought out bread, a jar with dill pickles, mustard, salt, and sugar, a little jar with toothpicks, silverware wrapped in cloth napkins, and extra napkins for us. A beautiful waitress (a graduate of the philosophy college in Romania) skillfully pulled the cork out of a long bottle for Zamfir (who never graduated from any school). He pinched her butt, smelled the cork and approved his favorite wine.

In addition, the owner brought out the main treat of the restaurant, a bottle of tzuica, the yellowish-colored plum brandy, newly imported from Romania. He happily and noisily slammed it on the table as in the Old West, along with two oversized shot glasses.

With all in place, and my hat in full view on the table, Zamfir finished reading the menu and snapped his fingers at a waiter who ran over and politely bent over to listen to the order, his pen ready on the notepad. Zamfir sipped from his wine glass and asked me what I would like to eat.

"Maybe a soup and salad," I timidly said.

He asked the waiter what he recommended, but hearing phrases like "house bread," "boiled egg salad," and "eggplant salad," Zamfir stopped him. "Son, write it down: first, Beluga caviar and Romanian yellow smoked cheese and eight mititei [small, skinless, garlicky grilled sausages], to go with the tsuica. Then, two of the best steaks done medium to go with my red wine, French crepes filled with raspberries or peaches to go with two strong coffees and seltzer water. D'un'stand?"

"Yes, boss, Mister Zamfir!" exclaimed the waiter, running to place the order.

I told Zamfir that I was a good cook and an expert at making mititei, which was a favorite treat for any Romanian.

He smiled, patted my shoulder and said, "Kid, we are in business. I'll tell you later."

The rest happened like in a dream. As we ate what I believed was the best food in the world, Zamfir, who drank a few glasses of wine, told me about himself. He knew how to make money, he knew how to do business (since America is nothing but a big business), and he was the boss of making money. I drank a glass of wine and listened while admiring my hat.

The owner played his violin, and the former classical pianist played a potpourri of Romanian love songs and Argentinean tangos on the keyboard while many people danced around us. I did a tango with the beautiful waitress, my hat tilted toward my right eyebrow like a real hidalgo, and everybody applauded us. Feeling encouraged, I danced an even better tango.

I have to say, with the dancing and with Zamfir eating everything and telling me how big and rich he was going to be, we had the time of our lives.

All was well until the check came. The owner, smiling, presented it and explained that he had rounded the entire meal to seventy dollars—without the tip.

Zamfir dismissed him with a flick of his hand. Lighting a cigarette and blowing smoke in my face, he said to me: "Kid, usually I pay for everybody, but considering that it is your hat we're celebrating, and I do not want to hurt your feelings, I will let you pay the bill. It is $70.00 plus a $20.00-dollar tip, so it comes to only $90.00. D'un'stand? I'll see you later—and make sure you wear your hat."

Zamfir stood up, shook a few hands, pushed the owner away and walked outside the Romanian Oak Restaurant, smelling of garlic.

I sighed and held my hat in front of my face. There went the rest of my first paycheck... plus a little more.

$

15. DRACULA'S SAUSAGES

I realized that Zamfir, who once called me a "kid," liked me. It seemed obvious, especially the time he showed me an old yet still-running minivan. The US Postal Service had the vehicle at auction, and Zamfir paid just $60.00 for it. Using his influence, he took it to a Romanian repair garage, where the mechanics cut out a large window on the driver's side. Inside, they installed a butane stove with a wide grill, a water tank and a large sink, and a spacious refrigerator. Thus, the van became a working food truck, complete with a big round chimney to collect the smoke from the grill and expel it through the roof.

"Hey kid, you don't work Saturdays and Sundays. Why don't you work for me? We can cook *mititei* in this van and sell them at the biggest flea market in New Jersey. I'll give you ten percent of my profit—okay, 15—from what we sell if you'll prepare, cook and clean. I will call them 'Dracula's Sausages' since American suckers are crazy about our Prince Dracula."

I had nothing better to do on weekends, so I agreed on the spot.

***

I have no idea how Zamfir registered the van with the motor vehicle department, obtained a business license, passed inspection and received the health department's approval—or if he had done any of these things. But by the next Friday evening, we were in his van (now outfitted as a food truck) which had been freshly painted on both sides with large letters, "DRACULA'S

FAMOUS SAUSAGES," crossing the George Washington Bridge into New Jersey.

While driving, Zamfir shared his detest for hamburgers with no taste unless dunked into ketchup and claimed he was going to revolutionize America with the garlicky, skinless Romanian sausages. "Dracula's Sausages" promised to keep the vampires away. He assured me that this Saturday at the flea market, the appetizing smell of the sausages cooking on the grill would attract buyers like honey attracting flies. He predicted, "In two weeks, I will open a fast-food restaurant. In two more weeks, I will be a sensation on TV news programs. In one year, I will own a food factory, and in two years, I will conquer America with my garlicky, tasty smoked sausages. D'un'stand?!"

***

He kept driving and talking about achieving the American dream and being rich and famous. I learned later that he had only a hand brake in the van. After more than one hour of driving, we stopped at a supermarket to buy 20 pounds of fatty ground meat, all the spices for me to mix in and ten French baguettes. Our purchase included small bottles of mustard and 20 large heads of garlic to be peeled, crushed and mixed in with the meat to give the *mititei* its unique aroma and taste to be ready for sale the next day.

It took me almost all night to prepare the sausages in the small kitchen inside a two-room apartment Zamfir had rented for each weekend in a town famous for its largest flea market in New England.

We were among the first vendors to arrive, I drove Zamfir's rental car, and he drove the food truck to the flea market, where there were a few thousand tables covered with merchandise waiting for the owners to arrive. This was another fact that I knew was not possible in Romania, where thieves would empty the tables overnight.

We stopped the food truck right in the middle of the market, unlocked and opened the metallic cover over the large window, and attached a wooden counter, so we could serve customers. We set up two small tables with condiments, napkins and a few plastic chairs under beach umbrellas to make the area welcoming, along with a big plastic garbage bin to keep the area clean. The refrigerator was stocked with cans of Coke and Pepsi.

Zamfir mounted a red, yellow, and blue Romanian flag and a large poster of Vlad the Impaler in front of the food truck. There were shadowy lines on his face, caused by having rolled up the paper poster for transport. Inside the food truck, I lit the briquettes under the grill. In a short time, the smoke was so dense that I had to jump out.

I began rolling the little sausages by hand and lining them up on large plastic trays outside the van. A swarm of flies was attracted to the sausages, so Zamfir moved the trays inside the van where the smoke would kill anything. My boss, on his knees to avoid the densest smoke, began waving a plastic tray above the charcoal, till the coals produced flames. Minutes later, he jumped out of the van coughing, and missing a step, rolled onto the grass. His white hair had instantly turned black in the smoke. Tears streamed down his cheeks, leaving dark lines on his face. He looked like Dracula on the poster hung on the front of the van.

"Hey, boss! You lost your big gold chain," I announced.

"No. I have it, right there." He pointed to the van. I understood then that he'd bought it with money from the sale of his heavy gold necklace.

Ready to grill, I put on a red apron. I'd clumsily written on it with a black permanent marker: "SAY THANKS TO DRACULA." I began placing rows of mititei on the hot grill. Grease leaked down into the red embers and flames erupted. Outside, Zamfir used Scotch tape to post large signs on which he's written in red, "DRACULA'S DELICATESEN" and under that, in larger blue print, "ONLY $2 each," all over the van.

The flames roasted the casing-less little sausages, and a strong garlic odor, combined with the heavy smoke, surrounded the area around the van. Vendors and early buyers were now pouring into the vast open market, and Zamfir giggled, "Here comes money— money for us!" He placed a few sample mititei on a paper plate, to ply the first happy customer. Each sausage was placed on a small slice of the French bread, and a toothpick was stuck in it, just like Prince Dracula impaled his enemies.

***

The food truck was covered in smoke and smelled of garlic. Other vendors first looked with curiosity to see what had happened, and then they gave us encouraging smiles. One came to us to ask what was going on. With a lot of gesturing and pointing at the grill, to Dracula's picture, and to the price, Zamfir offered the man a little sausage on a toothpick. The man understood and went back to the other vendors, showing them the Dracula's Sausage and pointing to the cloud of spicy smoke.

Encouraged, Zamfir rushed out with a paper plates filled with the toothpicked-sausages placed on small slices of bread, treating his neighbors to free samples. Coming back, he rubbed his hands and ordered me to grill more mititei because of all the samples he'd given out. The next tray of mititei produced even more of the choking, black smoke.

To our disappointment, everyone came back, threw the famous Dracula's Sausages samples into the garbage bin and asked us to stop making the horrible smelling smoke, which was keeping buyers away from their tables. Yet, the same smoke attracted more curious people to come to the truck, and a few bought the problematic sausages. In just a few minutes, Zamfir made more than $50.00. He beamed with enthusiasm, "What did I tell you kid? Stick around me to make it big!"

However, the first buyer returned to ask for ketchup. He threw the sausage in the garbage when we had none to offer. A second one came, gasping for air. He threw the sausage in the garbage bin and asked for his money back. Because so many came to ask for ketchup, Zamfir jumped in his car to go buy the popular condiment.

He returned to find vendors assaulting me and the food truck over the terrible smoke which kept their customers away. Zamfir, using his best Mafioso look and cursing like only a descendent of Romanians and Dracula could (including in the same sentence saints, devils, mothers, and even holidays and animals), agreed to move the offensive food truck away.

***

By noon, the food truck was parked at the edge of the flea market and Zamfir offered his famous Dracula's Sausages at a reduced price of $1.50, including ketchup. The customers' reaction to the beloved Romanian snack was the same, and by 3:00 PM, Zamfir reduced them to $1.00, then to $0.50 and finally, free samples, which changed nothing about the resentful reactions of the sensitive American public. Some buyers who ate the sausages accused them of causing vomiting and diarrhea and for that reason, asked for their money back.

On top of everything, the health inspector from the state of New Jersey (probably tipped off by the flea market's organizers) came and closed the business down, demanding that Zamfir take the van back to New York immediately. But he could not, because the van's battery had died. The starter would not even click. The inspector fined Zamfir $500.00 for loitering and endangering public health. He allowed the van to remain parked in the flea market until morning.

***

We returned the next day with a new battery, but the van was gone! Cursing again in Romanian by inventorying all possible names to fit the situation, Zamfir declared he would never again try to change Americans' taste in food.

═ $ ═

16. THE INVENTION

There were not too many Romanian refugees in Manhattan. Many of them lived on the Upper West Side in an old hotel at 86th Street and Broadway, because welfare benefits covered their rent and left a small allowance for food; plus, their Medicare expenses were paid. It was only three blocks away from St. Dumitru, the Romanian Orthodox Church. The residents would walk to the church and then return feeling good about identifying themselves with such a respected landmark.

However, when a McDonald's restaurant was built at 71st Street and Broadway, some began to eat there, and it soon became the midpoint marker where they would turn around on their walks to return to their hotel. New Romanians arrived and walked together in compact groups as they traditionally had during their leisure walks in their home cities. Now, they traversed the distance of just 15 streets on their evening promenades. They spoke only in Romanian, told jokes, laughed, poked each other and once in a while, even sang together.

Between 86th and 71st, there was the Opera Hotel on the east sidewalk, probably named after the large theater at the ground level. One Romanian was proud to live there and pay the rent—the mysterious Mr. Grigore. He already had a green card and worked, as he claimed, as a chief engineer downtown. He was always dressed properly in a suit and tie and wore well-polished shoes. He avoided his noisy Romanian compatriots, to the point of walking on the other side of the street if he happened to see them coming. Apparently, he did not have a single friend. He was very private and secluded himself from others.

One day, he was in McDonald's to get change for the subway, when he was cornered by a group of Romanians. They asked him if he was ashamed to socialize with them.

Mr. Grigore answered: "I have no time to socialize with anybody because I am an engineer and an inventor. I came to America because I had an invention that would change the entire American plumbing and bathroom industry, and most likely the entire world. I will not be the first Romanian millionaire, but a billionaire in dollars—not Romanian money. First, I must complete this important project, which so far has taken all my money to experiment and redo the blueprints. Now, excuse me, but my time is very precious, and I cannot waste it with losers like you." And stiffly, he walked out of the restaurant.

Mr. Grigore's speech left the group of eight Romanians speechless, as they realized who the mysterious man really was.

***

A month later, Mr. Grigore was inside the United States Patent and Trademark Office in Washington D.C., and a clerk asked to look at his blueprints. After a long few seconds for Mr. Grigore, the clerk smiled and said, "I know about this device to flush the toilet: one was patented in the year 1911. Sorry, but a patent already exists. Among over 150 million patents, this one is among the most debated. Do you have any other inventions?"

Mr. Grigore could not answer. Speechless, he left the patent building and apparently moved out of the Opera Hotel in Manhattan. The Romanian group never saw him again. However, legend says that he became a billionaire and bought an island where he built a mansion, retired and lived happily ever after.

=$=

17. ALEX, THE EDUCATOR

My new Romanian friend Alex invited me to dinner. He had come to America much earlier than I had. He had one son named Johnny, who was five years old. I brought him a water pistol as a gift. But Alex quickly snatched it out of my hand, concerned that even a toy gun would teach little Johnny that playing with guns is fun when, in fact, it is very dangerous. Besides, he believed Johnny Boy needed to become a pacifist, not a gunslinger who would get into trouble with the law.

I respected Alex's opinion, and I listened to his ideas about raising his son not in the old-fashioned Romanian way based on authority and punishments. Those would hurt his son's feelings. Rather, he would be raised with understanding and love in the American way. Alex told me there was no room in his house for Spartan or other military-like education, which was based on strict discipline and tough love. He felt that would ruin a small child's personality and seriously affect him for the rest of his life.

There was a sudden noise in the kitchen. Alex called his wife and asked where Johnny was.

"Johnny is eating," she said after welcoming me with a wave.

Alex seemed puzzled and disturbed by the news. "Why is he eating at this hour before dinner?"

"I told him it was okay because he was crying for dessert!"

"Dear, I have told you so many times he must respect meal hours. Do you want him to live a chaotic life?" Alex rushed into the kitchen and came back, pulling the small boy with long hair by his hand. Johnny was licking a teaspoon he held in his other hand. They stopped in front of me. Johnny began to jump up and down, screaming and crying that he wanted to eat his cake. Alex tried to calm him down. Pointing to me, he asked the boy to tell me his name. The wife went back to the kitchen, slamming the door.

"I want my cake! I want my cake!" Johnny screamed and tried to throw himself on the floor, but Alex held him up by his arm. I tried to intervene by saying something to distract the boy, but Johnny threw the teaspoon against the wall and began to kick his father. His mother entered the room and began to cry, and Johnny, now in tears, kept shouting, "I want my cake!"

Alex leaned towards me and whispered, "Stubborn, yah? Just like me." Then he said to Johnny, "Maybe you'd like to play with my watch?" He handed his wristwatch to Johnny, who pulled the pin and began rotating the watch hands as fast as he could. Alex smiled and again leaned towards me with another whisper: "See how intelligent and inventive he is? Just like me!"

Johnny went into the kitchen and came back with a paring knife.

Again, Alex tried to explain, "He once saw me opening the back of the watch with a knife. What a memory he has, don't you think?"

"I think it is very dangerous. He might damage the watch or cut himself."

A sharp cry from Johnny announced that he was bleeding. He threw the watch against the wall. Alex rushed to rescue the watch. Johnny, furious, began stabbing an Art Deco-style vintage radio with the knife. Alex, while checking his expensive watch, jumped to hold his wife back, who came running to stop their son's stabbing of the radio.

"He is ruining my expensive radio!" she yelled.

Alex calmly said, "Let him do it, and after the radio is destroyed, he will see the consequences. It will improve his mind, and he won't do it again."

"The radio was a wedding present from my aunt!" The wife began to cry and ran back into the kitchen.

Alex commended Johnny's actions by admitting that, like father, like son, they both defused a crisis in the same way—by seeking revenge.

Next, he went to his son and began to negotiate: "If you give me the knife, I will let you have the cake."

As if nothing had happened, Johnny surrendered the knife and went back to the kitchen, sucking at the bleeding wound on his palm.

"See, my friend, there is an art to raising a child in America. Never brutalize him or restrain his will. Rather, let him learn valuable lessons for the rest of his life by giving him the freedom of choice. Agree?"

I wanted to tell him that the toy water pistol I'd brought as a gift would have eliminated the temper tantrums and damage, but instead, I just shrugged my shoulders.

— $ —

18. TWO OPINIONS

Each day at ten o'clock in the morning and five o'clock in the late afternoon, an octogenarian—impeccably dressed from his Fedora hat to his double-breasted navy blue suit and red bowtie, holding a colorful parasol—slowly walked along the edge of a Florida beach, doing his daily exercise. He ignored the beautiful women in their skimpy swimming suits. Large, expensive mansions with big windows and red-tiled roofs indicated that this was a private beach. The venerable gentleman was one of the wealthy owners.

He always saluted a handsome, well-built man in his twenties who had a perfect suntan and imported sunglasses. The man lay on a folding chair and treated himself to drinks from a large, white cooler. The older gentleman saluted him by touching the border of his hat with his shiny walking stick, and the man, by flicking his hand, acknowledged the polite gesture.

Day after day, they exchanged this ritual until one afternoon when the older gentleman walked up to the young man, politely saluted him, and asked:

"Excuse me for intruding, young man, but I wonder if you are a university student on summer vacation, and what school do you attend?"

"I do not go to school," answered the young sun worshipper.

"Are you taking a long break from your business?"

"I ain't got any stupid business."

"Are you independently rich?"

"I wish…"

"Don't you want to do something for yourself besides sitting on the beach?"

"Do what?"

"Well, work for somebody…"

"What for?"

"To make money and learn a skill."

"And then what?"

"And after a while, open your own business."

"And then what?"

"Expand the business and…"

"Why?"

"So you can sell it for a lot of money—what else?"

"What next?"

"Then, you'll still be young, but with your previous experience, you could build an even bigger business…"

"Why?"

"To sell it for even more money! And when you are my age, you can retire like I have and spend all day at the beach!" The old gentleman shouted victoriously, rolling his parasol.

"But I am already there!" exclaimed the young, satisfied, robust man, pulling another bottle from his cooler.

— $ —

19. WHEN SIZE DOESN'T MATTER

As the passenger plane flew over Texas, a small, nearly bald man with a big nose, slanted eyes and large ears, dressed in an expensive black suit and expensive shoes, sat squished in his seat between two large Texans. They had broad shoulders and wore blue shirts to match their blue jeans with wide, studded belts: one featured a horse on its buckle, and the other a wide-horned bull. Their large cowboy hats, one white with a reddish Mustang in front and one black with large yellow horns affixed in the same place, rested on their laps. The frail passenger in between, with his perfectly pressed white shirt and black tie, held his maroon briefcase between his legs.

The two cowboys carried on a loud conversation, ignoring the silent man between them. The flight attendant served whiskey, no ice, in large, wide glasses to the Texans and prune juice in a tall, narrow glass to the narrow-shouldered man they deemed to be an elegant city slicker.

One Texan looked at the prune juice and wondered aloud: "Hey, little man, isn't that Bloody Mary without a celery stick too strong for you?"

The man ignored the joke, and the Texans continued their loud conversation as they got better acquainted. They cheered, loudly clinking their glasses in front of the delicate man's nose, who moved his head back and then sipped his prune juice from its delicate glass.

The cowboys each proudly talked about the ranch he had, left by his respective great-grandfather, which continued to grow in acreage and herd count with each passing generation. One turned to the man in the middle and asked:

"How about you with the prune juice? What did your great-grandfather leave for you?"

Uncomfortable with the question, the man coughed politely in his fist and, with dignity, answered: "I am a first-generation American. My parents came here from Europe after World War II."

The Texans turned their attention back to each other. They drank their whiskey from their heavy glasses and continued to talk above the head of the man sinking in his seat between them. They complained about high taxes, the drought, and slow markets while proudly detailing their estates, which each generation of their families had contributed to, with their mansions with many added rooms, patios, and swimming pools.

The one from the window seat looked down at the land they were flying over. He pointed and nearly shouted, "Hey, look—there is my 3,000-acre ranch! You can see my 300 horses, their stables, the riding arenas and the small river running across it all."

The other cowboy leaned over the little man's legs to look out the window down to the ranch, where he saw the horses running free. He congratulated the other, who took the opportunity to describe his passion for horses in more detail.

"I call the ranch 'Fastest Hooves.'"

The airplane lowered in altitude, tilted its left wing, and took a large curve.

This gave the other Texan the opportunity to shout. He pointed down: "Holy cow, there are the two lakes from my 6,000-acre ranch with more than 2,000 head of cattle. Look at how many barns I have!"

Now, the first cowboy looked down at the grazing herds while the owner leaned over the little man and further described his ranch. "I named it 'Only Cows and Bulls.'"

When the airplane began circling a large city, the cowboys looked at the fragile man, and one, believing himself to be wise, asked: "Now, little friend, how many acres does *your* ranch have, huh?" He winked at the other cowboy.

"Four acres!" answered the well-dressed passenger immediately.

A burst of laughter erupted from the cowboys.

"*Ho, ho, ho…* four acres! Listen to him."

"*He, he, he…* only four acres? You call that a ranch?!"

"*Ha, ha, ha!* And what do you call your ranch?"

The dignified man pointed to the city below and said, "They call it Downtown, Texas!"

The cowboys looked at each other, stopped laughing, and sat silently, waiting for the airplane to land.

$

20. LET'S SHARE

Sandu had immigrated to America a year ago. He had all his ambitions to do well arranged in good order. The first thing was to buy a car and send a picture of it to those suckers in Romania who laughed at him, saying he would be better off if he'd never left his village. They would envy him since nobody in their village had a car. Sandu rented a room in a neighborhood, and the bathroom he had to use was across the street in a gas station. He got a job working at the gas station, cleaning the entire building, which included a repair shop. He ate the gas station's stale, outdated food that was to be discarded. One day while working at the gas station, he bought a 22-year-old Chrysler New Yorker. Its owner was so desperate for money to buy drugs that Sandu got the car for just $125.00 cash.

The car was old and had many problems: it burned too much oil, the brakes needed to be replaced, and the tires and wipers did not work. Sandu drove in the rain and snow with his head hanging out the window to see the road ahead. One door had to be tied with a wire so it wouldn't swing open on the highway, and the transmission leaked. But the radio was loud and clear, and that is what counted the most to Sandu.

He took his car to the beach, where a friendly Puerto Rican mechanic with a camera took beautiful pictures of Sandu in front of and alongside the oversized car. In one picture, Sandu was inside: he held the steering wheel with one hand, resting his elbow outside the open driver's window. In another, he climbed on top of the roof with its peeling paint. He was only five feet one inch tall, but he stood proudly on the car, holding both middle fingers as high as he could. With this picture, he would give his loser Romanian friends a triumphant message of what was so good about living in America—having a car.

Still, Sandu wanted to drive his car to Manhattan and take pictures with the car in front of the Empire State Building and Saint Patrick's Cathedral to teach those sore losers a lesson in respect once and for all. But, because of the car's condition, it could not be driven a hundred miles away and then make the return trip. It would take Sandu from May until September to fix his car so he could safely drive it anywhere he wanted.

In the meantime, he planned his ultimate revenge on the village bums. He let his hair grow long till it touched his shoulders, grew a mustache as if he were a member of a Harley-Davidson motorcycle gang, and bought a pair of aviator glasses to go with his studded blue jean jacket. A pack of Marlboro cigarettes stuck halfway out of the jack's chest pocket, even though he didn't smoke. He bought a cowboy hat with colorful rows of beads on its band and a miniature horseshoe on the front to convey the unmistakable message that he was a man's man to the white trash from his village: he had made it big, and life in America was good. However, he only took pictures from his knees up, so his dirty, broken sneakers wouldn't show.

After all these preparations, Sandu took an unpaid day off. With $23.00 in his pocket, he went to buy postcards to send along with his pictures in colorful "Via Air Mail" envelopes to deliver the final blow to those no-good nobodies from Romania.

***

Sandu was driving north on Highway 95 to the Big Apple on a beautiful morning after rush hour. He had the radio blasting so the girls in other cars would notice him. Because he was short, he added two pillows to the bench seat to lift him up behind the wheel and make him look taller. He also wanted to be able to see the road better over the hood. That improvement triggered an immediate, dangerous consequence—he could not reach the pedals with his short legs. He moved the bench seat closer to the steering wheel, blocking it with his legs and chest, so now he had to push himself into the back cushion to be able to steer to the left and right. But the blasting radio and the camera he borrowed from the Puerto Rican for a carton of Kent's canceled any inconveniences.

Mile after mile, Sandu felt blessed to live in America. He almost felt like he was flying along in the aerodynamic car, passing other cars, leaving behind one exit after another. Suddenly, right before a bridge, he hit a pothole. The car almost jumped in the air, and the engine stopped working. Sandu succeeded in safely pulling his dead car onto the highway's shoulder, right under the shadow of the bridge. He opened the hood, looked at the engine and left the hood up to signal for help. He got back in the car to wait for help. He was trying to tune the radio when he heard a loud voice.

"Hi, brother. You want the radio? You can have it. I'll take the carburetor and the starter. Let me get my tools," said a young black man with his sleeves rolled up."

"Zeng u," shouted Sandu, impressed that an American would help him.

Behind the Chrysler, a white guy stood with a long tire wrench. He began trying to undo the lug nuts. Waving to Sandu, he shouted, "I'll get the tires 'cause they're new! How is the battery?" He laid the long tool down and came to look under the hood. Sandu did what any responsible, proud owner who had put eight hundred dollars into fixing his car would do and stood alongside, admiring the engine. The guy continued, "What do you want to take?"

"I want my car good!" said Sandu in his poor English.

"This car ain't worth a shit! Hurry up and take the radio before the police get here."

"Take the radio?" Sandu asked. He wasn't sure how that would help.

Overhearing their dialog, the black guy, carrying a toolbox and looking confused, pointed first at the car and then at Sandu.

Something clicked for Sandu. His owner's instinct kicked in, and he jumped between the two thieves, yelling, "Zeh car is mine!" He embraced the Chrysler, saying, "Is briken… broken."

The two stood open-mouthed, and the white guy shook his head, saying, "Broken? Oh, man…," while the black guy threw the red toolbox to the ground and spit out a bitter "Shit man, why waste our time?" and he ordered Sandu, "Come here and watch!" He connected a loose battery cable, which had disconnected from the battery during the pothole jolt. "Now the car is good. Move out. Hasta la vista!" he waved to Sandu.

Sandu tried starting his car. It worked!

As he took off, he reflected on the unexpected help he'd had from the two Americans. He decided he'd better improve his English to avoid future misunderstandings.

═ $ ═

21. THE PARKING TICKET

I lived only 45 minutes from Yale University, where I had a friend. He called me last minute to come and see legendary xylophonist Lionel Hampton in concert, which would start in one hour at the renowned, ornately decorated in gold Yale concert theater. To make it in time, I drove 95 miles per hour in my old Chrysler New Yorker, whose slim, aerodynamic shape nearly began lifting off the pavement at that speed. It felt like the front wheels did not even touch down Highway 95. I was in such a hurry I forgot that the Yale exit was the only one on the left. Thank God nobody was driving near me. I took a sharp turn onto the bridge connector. My car hit the concrete sides, leaving behind a comet of flames and sparks. I was so scared that I promised God I would never drive faster than 85 miles per hour for the rest of my life, and I kept that divine promise.

There I was, cruising in front of the glorious rotunda building, with its ancient temple-like columns, which I once helped restore to look like new, along with all the outside doors and windows on the Yale campus. Hundreds of people were entering the rotunda where the theater is. My friend was inside waiting with my ticket, and I kept driving in circles. The street parking spaces were packed with visitors' cars. Suddenly, an open space, the only one available across the street from the rotunda, was available. I parked and ran inside.

My seat was in the first row of the balcony, and I had an excellent view. Lionel Hampton thrilled the audience with crystal-clear sounds from his oversized xylophone. He was an old, awkward, small man with a little belly. At one point, he called on a beautiful young woman from the backup singers and began to dance the salsa with her. Salsa is a version of the rumba. It was done with a rapid one-two-three steps forward and the same steps back, embellished with hip and body movements, underarm turns, and tight turns, which ended in cross body leads with sharp turns and stops that confused the rhythm of the applauding spectators. Maestro Lionel barely kept up with the female dancer in her high heels and colorful dress, but the spectators generously applauded because, at one time, he was a very fast and good salsa dancer.

***

The concert was extremely entertaining. Afterward, I offered to take my friend back to his dormitory in my car. There was one important and disturbing detail: my car was missing. The parking space where I'd left it was empty. Alarmed, I looked around. *I must have misplaced the car*, I thought, but then I believed it must have been stolen. Fortunately, a patrol car drove by, and I reported my stolen car. I showed the sergeant where I had parked.

"Ah, I know the car! It was a Chrysler New Yorker. I placed a parking ticket on its windshield."

I protested: "There wasn't any notice that I should not park here!"

He scratched behind his ear and agreed. "But there used to be a yellow fire hydrant here, which was cut off, and everybody knew not to park where the fire hydrant used to be."

I asked what happened to my car.

He informed me, "Well, after midnight, it was towed. You

can go to the city towing lot, pay the fine, and drive it home." He saluted and drove away.

I looked at my friend, and we both looked for a taxi, which cost me, with a tip, $20.00 just to go retrieve my car. The car was there, and I paid exactly $80.00 to repossess it. I noticed the tires' sidewalls had been scratched up a bit, probably when I drove through the Yale exit.

My friend saw how upset I was. Smiling, he tried to joke with me. "Well, you paid $100.00 for your own car, but at least you had a free concert ticket."

"No, I owe even more," I moaned, showing him the $40.00 parking ticket the sergeant had left on the window.

***

When I drove back to New Haven, by two o'clock in the afternoon, I stopped to pay my ticket in person and get done with that nightmarish nocturnal memory. I entered the large building and found the correct door. I stepped into a very large room with oversized windows and a glass door in the back. Six female clerks sat at large desks with food spread all over, paying no attention to me. I coughed politely, and the closest one, with braided hair, fake eyelashes and colorful nails, asked, "May I help you?"

"I would like to pay my parking ticket."

"Here is a note with the address where you must mail the ticket along with a check." She handed me a small paper and turned around to continue her discussion with the rest of the employees. Some had red, yellow or green hair, and all were overweight.

I looked at the paper and asked, "Isn't this the address where

I am right now?"

"It is, but you have to mail it."

"To this room, where I am right now?

"Exactly!" another clerk shouted.

"But I am here, ready to pay." I showed the ticket and the cash payment I had ready.

The third one informed me, "We do not handle any money."

"Why not? I want..."

The first one cut me off: "Because only our boss can do it."

"In what room is she?"

All pointed to the glass door in the back.

"Let me talk to her."

"She is on the phone in a conference call."

"Then I shall wait!" I said, and I sat on a bench next to a massive file cabinet.

Another robust woman with shiny necklaces and big round gold hoop earrings came to me and advised that I should mail my parking fine because there were instructions that must be followed. Each envelope received was to be witnessed by two other clerks, who would then register the ticket. The check would be sent to the bank to clear.

"Who does these things?" I asked.

"We do: it is our job."

"So, why don't you do it?

"Our boss opens the envelope, and she is very busy right now. After this telephone call, she has a break for lunch." She pointed to the unpacked food on each desk. "See? We are waiting for her. Do you still want to wait?"

I looked at my watch and remembered I had an appointment

in 20 minutes. I left the room, thinking that no great idea or decision has ever come from a desk job—or from people who work 9 to 5.

$— $ —$

22. ADVICE IN ENGLISH

The supermarket in my neighborhood has not been the same since COVID-19 became the main worry. With my mask on, I was alone in the bedding product aisle, looking to buy two pillowcases. I tried reading the small print on a flowery package of pillowcases to see if they were made from natural cotton. But without my reading glasses, I could not find the information I wanted. I looked around for help, but I was the only customer in the aisle. There were no employees around to read the small print for me. I began to call out, "Hello, helloo, hellooo?" to no avail.

Suddenly a family of five entered the aisle, and the man waved at me. I waved back. The man, wearing a colorful shirt, came to help. I asked him kindly, "Would you please read me the small print and see if these pillowcases are made of cotton or not?" I handed him the package.

The man took the package. Without reading anything, he smiled at me and then put his head on the package, saying, "Sleep." He closed his eyes to be more convincing.

His family came up from behind. The children were speaking a strange language. His wife was covered from head to toe with a black mantle. A black turban covered his head, and two large round gold earrings peeked out from underneath it. The wife and children looked at their head of family, who was patting my package tenderly, repeating, "Sleep, sleep, sleep."

For some reason, I found myself imitating the man pointing at the pillowcases and saying, "Cotton, cotton, cotton?"

The tall man smiled and answered, shaking his long index

finger: "No, no, no 'cotton.' *Sleep!*" He again put his head on the package and extended his explanation, saying, "You sleep!"

I took the package back and put my head on it. "Yes, I sleep on, but I want cotton."

The man was thrilled. He turned back to his family and laughing, explained something in what sounded to me like a "barabara" language to his family. He pointed at me, and I understood the word "American." All laughed at my ignorance.

An associate employee, attracted by the conversation, came to the aisle. She was dressed like the other woman, earrings included, and she began to "barabara" louder and louder with the family. She seemed to understand the situation. She took the package from me, put her head on it and said to me, "You sleep well!"

I was in shock, but I managed to ask her to read to me about the cotton content. I tapped with my finger on the label.

Smiling, the employee, whose name tag revealed an unpronounceable name, also tapped on the package and said, "Sleep night, ok?"

The man took the package from her and again put his head on it, happy to have had his initial explanation backed up by the employee. His family clapped in admiration.

Another associate showed up to see what all the commotion was about. I jumped to ask her to read me the label.

But putting her hand out as if to stop me, the young, tattooed woman said in a sweet, foreign accent, "I do not know anything about this. I work in the produce department." And she left in a hurry, like a model employee late for duty.

With no other option, I put the package back on the shelf and walked away.

Seconds later, the family was walking after me, and the man was waving the package and shouting, "Sir, you good sleep!"

I wished he were right so I could wake from this bad dream about me and my faulty English language encounter with the future Americans.

━ $ ━

23. A PUZZLED VISITOR

For years, I hadn't heard anything about my high school friend Lucian, when unexpectedly, my parents called me to say he was coming to America to visit me. Actually, the Romanian Communist Party sent him to participate in an international agricultural congress. He was the engineering director of a model state farm, had received many awards, was well paid, had a personal chauffeur, was a trusted Communist Party member who did not defect and ask for political asylum in America, and obviously, he was trusted to represent Socialist Romania at the congress.

Indeed, after Lucian participated in the congress, he called me. The next day, I picked him up at the train station, stunning him with my new Cadillac Fleetwood, champagne in color with a matching leather interior, an electronic dashboard and a fine stereo radio. In an instant, I felt the imposing attitude and look of my visitor, a Communist leader marked by his gray suit, dirty gray tie, and unpolished gray shoes. He carried a wrinkled vinyl briefcase and a burlap package. I knew the package was from my parents.

Otherwise, he was the same short, chubby fellow with puffy red cheeks that I remembered. His neck rolled over his shirt collar, and the shoulders of his suit jacket were covered in dandruff. All these details indicated his high position and the good living he made in food-deprived Romania.

As I drove him on Route 95, he kept wondering aloud about each car we passed, asking me how much it cost. When I shared that my car cost $48,000.00, Lucian's eyes opened wide, and he asked me if I was rich. He felt better when he learned I made monthly car payments.

He was genuinely amazed when he saw my big Tara-style red brick house with its four large white columns in front. Inside, he was impressed by the big chandelier in the round hallway and the wooden spiral staircase. I showed him my four television sets and five fireplaces. Lucian was looking for a fake fireplace and asked me to take him to a flea market so he could buy cheap gifts for his family and boss. He went inside each room to see how rich I was. He again calmed when he learned I paid a monthly mortgage.

I opened the package from my parents. I pulled out a green bottle of tzuica, which had been carefully wrapped in a beautiful tablecloth embroidered with red roses. There was an envelope containing a long letter, a few pictures, and a plastic bag that smelled of pine trees because of the round cheese (like Manchego) it held that was encased in thin pine bark. Also wrapped inside were three floral-embroidered shirts for my children.

We shared a good lamb stew dinner. Our conversation was enhanced with many funny memories from our younger years, washed down with shots of tzuica smelling of distilled prunes. The hot bath and ten hours of sleep after dinner made Lucian look good. He was quite energetic the next morning.

***

After a nice breakfast, we hopped into the Cadillac (after my visitor professionally kicked the tires). It was Saturday, and I headed north, where I knew there was a large flea market. The weather could not have been better, and a trip through the rural areas would show my buddy how beautiful America can be. My visitor noticed that even minor roads, including some forest paths, were asphalted. He wondered why cows, donkeys, pigs and poultry weren't on the roads and neither were there any children playing. As a matter of fact, except for the speeding cars, nobody was on any road. As he observed the large portions of grass between the paved places and on each side of the main road or along the highways, Lucian wondered why no horses, cows or sheep were grazing there.

I had to contradict him with arguments he never expected, and for a while, he just looked around, wondering why there were no fences between properties and no dogs or other animals around the houses. As for the houses, Lucian thought their windows were too large, and their chimneys, built three-quarters outside the house, let out all the heat to warm the universe. My responses left him open-mouthed in total disbelief. He decreed that Americans are wasteful, perhaps even stupid.

However, Lucian admired all the churches we passed and wondered how many kinds of Christians there were in America since each church seemed to be of a different denomination. He asked to see a Romanian Church, but the closest one was in Manhattan or Queens in New York City. Lamenting that fact, he continued looking at the large fields of corn, grains, and potatoes we drove past. Again, he wondered why nobody was out working the fields. Suddenly, he was startled. He pointed to the right and shouted, "There is an American farm, which is exactly what I want to see. Pull in front of the big barn!"

Slowly, I drove up the hill where there was a large barn and a country house with a covered porch all around it under the second floor. Everything was surrounded by a sea of tall cornstalks dancing in the wind. I stopped on the side of the barn, which was filled with cows lying down, and we looked around to see if there was someone to talk to. Nobody was to be seen, so I honked the horn a few times, yet only the wind was present, moving the tops of a few candelabra-like trees.

*****

Surrounded by the unmistakable smell of cow manure, we entered the barn. It was as large as one-third of a football field, with two sides open for cross-ventilation and natural light. We passed a spacious enclosure surrounded by a wooden fence filled with some 30 calves we could not see from the car. We entered the barn which housed many cows of the same black and white patterns as the young ones.

Inside was a wide path in the middle, and on each side were many individual stalls, each with enough room for a cow to rest with its head to the outside. In front was a chute supplying hay from the loft above and a large bucket with water triggered by the cow's chin. The back of the small platform was covered with hay and ended in a two-foot rolling gutter with running water to collect the urine and dung from the cow whose rear ended above the gutter.

Lucian analyzed the entire automatic feeding and self-cleaning installation. He discovered each cow's udder had a plastic device with sucking tubes attached to it that pumped the milk to a main pipe that exited to a tall collection barrel, one in each of the four corners of the barn. He could not believe his eyes. The automatic milk production machines worked for hours until they automatically stopped, leaving enough milk for the calves, which were housed in an equally large enclosure that led into their own barn, where they were sheltered.

Lucian kept pointing and exclaiming how the system functioned without requiring workers to milk the cows by hand. He counted 52 cows and told me that in his advanced state-owned farm, at least 25 workers were needed to milk the cows by hand and then clean the barn in two shifts. He took numerous pictures and asked me to take pictures of him and the cows so he could prove he saw this wonder of an American farm.

***

Suddenly, an older man with white hair, blue overalls and tall rubber boots approached us, inquisitively smiling. He was the owner of the entire farm.

I introduced myself and my visitor, mentioning his high position in the Romanian farming industry and his lack of English. The owner was glad to see us and was willing to answer questions. And there were many. Lucian first asked how many farmers attended to the cows. The man said it was a small farm, and he was the only one who worked the entire complex, but a high school kid helped each afternoon with some of the chores.

The second question Lucian asked was where the breeding bulls were since he did not see any. The farmer took us to the front of the barn to a large closet. On the numerous white shelves inside were tall glass containers of many colors, rows of long pumps, glass cylinders, pipettes, vials and jars. He said all the bulls he needed were in there: they could reproduce cows with longer or shorter legs, more or less meat, and designate the color of the hides. He explained that the quantity of milk from one milking was at least 8 gallons a day. Lucian had a Texan calculator and converted the figure to Romanian liters: that was an incredible 30 liters per cow versus only 3.5 liters of production per Romanian cow. He was visibly shocked and coughed to regain his voice.

Next the farmer explained what he fed the cows. He took us outside and moved his right arm from left to right above the huge field of corn. Lucien asked how many workers he needed to seed all that land. The owner took us to a shed where his farming equipment was protected from the rain and snow. Smiling, he pointed to a green tractor. "Only I and that incredible tractor, which has never broken down in ten years, do all the work." Lucian asked how much the tractor cost. The owner bought it by mail from Canada for less than half the price of any other tractor listed, the best bargain he ever found. He bragged that he only changed the oil for the motor and transmission when needed. He wanted to buy a few more and resell them here for a hefty profit, but the Canadian dealer was out of stock of the little Hungarian tractors, which sold out immediately.

Lucian walked to the tractor, read something on the side of the engine hood and called me to come over and read the same label written in steel letters, "The Red Flag Factory. Brasov. MADE IN ROMANIA." We looked at each other in disbelief. Lucian was from Brasov City in Transylvania.

We showed the owner our discovery. He asked where Romania was, where the Black Sea was, and finally, where the Danube River ran. He congratulated us for building the precious tractor and invited us to stay for lunch. We politely declined.

***

As we drove away, Lucian looked 20 years younger. He forgot about buying presents and was ready to rush to fly back to Romania, where he would proudly share all his wonderful news.

He'd discovered Americans were not as wasteful or stupid as he had believed. In a few hours, he'd learned more about modern farming than he had learned in years of studying to be the state farming director at Bucharest University.

━ $ ━

24. ZORRO

My three grade school-age children never understood why they were the only ones who did not have a pet to play with. All their classmates had pets. Their complaints sounded accusatory toward me: "Daddy, you do not understand that this is America, and you are *Rumelian*." They deformed the name of my birthplace, Romania, and spoke with disdain to make it sound as if it was synonymous with being anti-pet. They continued their complaint: "You hate animals, and we love them. Don't you love us and want us to be able to play at least with one dog, like all the other American children?!"

The pet they most wanted was a puppy.

I was wise enough to know that, in fact, children under the age of ten are abusive to pets. They push pets past their tolerance limits as they try to train them to do tricks. A cat would scratch and a dog would bite from abuse in the name of training or play. My second reason not to have a pet was that after a while, I knew I would be responsible for cleaning up after it, feeding it, taking it for a walk and to the veterinarian for the next 15 years. My life would be to comfort the dog first and then to decide what was good for me. The reason I didn't want a pet was not that I hated animals. I didn't want a needy, irritated, unhappy dog in the house. I wanted to avoid having a pet become a pest.

With each passing year, the same scenario repeated, and my children continued to make their accusatory allegations against me, citing the neighbors', their playmates' parents', teachers' and even the pediatrician's positive experiences with pets.

I stood firm in my position despite the situation reaching the level of them crying, screaming, refusing to eat, and trying to avoid me. They would longingly watch advertisements for dog food and dog shampoo, of course, the *Lassie* TV serial. As a father concerned about my children's attitude toward me and wanting to avoid the continual frowning looks from everybody I knew, I decided to buy a pet.

***

In the spring, I came home one afternoon with a small cage (it was covered to increase the surprise). I sat my children in front of me. "Guess what pet you are going to have?" I announced in a fatherly voice.

They looked at the small cage and whined, "Daddy, we do not want a rat or a bird, a turtle, or a snake…" The complaints began to pour forth, punctuated by sobs and rolling eyes. But I was not willing to negotiate.

In slow motion, I removed the cover and watched their eyes become wider and wider while they held their breath until they burst into a chorus of questions: "What is that? A porcupine? A skunk? A beaver? A …?"

Interrupting their guesses, I said in the most pleasant voice I could, "It is a hedgehog!"

The trio reached a new level of disappointment, asking in chorus, "It's a *what?*"

I rolled the small spikey-looking ball out of the cage onto the floor. The trio went silent.

Finally, my daughter, the youngest, said, "It does not have a head." My second son observed, "It does not have legs." My oldest son concluded as he touched it, "It is a ball of sharp pins!" Stupefied, all three asked, "How do we play with it, whatever this is?"

My answer was exactly what I had been thinking all the time: "Children, you do not play with it. It will play with you! I'll let you get acquainted." And I left the room.

***

A few days later, my daughter took me by the hand to the garage. She had named the hedgehog Zorro. In a corner, they had built it a house from a box. A little dish with milk and one with cat food were laid out neatly in front of the house. Zorro was investigating his new environment as the two boys followed him. The little spiny thing, its face covered with fine hair, seemed very active as it sniffed at everything with its sharp, pointed nose. Its two small round eyes, like two black beads, did not seem to blink, and its small, sharp ears did not end at a neck but seemed part of the shoulders that sustained its two short front legs with five toes each. The rest of its body was covered by sharp spines, though the chest and belly were covered by fine hair.

The children were gentle with their new pet. Otherwise, Zorro would curl into a ball, and then they could not touch him. In this way, he controlled playtime, and if he felt abused in any way, he would protest with angry squeaking sounds and roll himself up into a ball. Otherwise, he made pleasant little puffing sounds. When patted on the belly (only in one direction), Zorro would purr like a cat. If the children ran outside the garage where the basketball pole was, Zorro would run after them. He was surprisingly fast.

Zorro's most surprising feat was against the neighbor's three Dobermans. My children often played on a little paved basketball court outside the garage. The neighbor's dogs would run over the low stone fence between our yards, dashing to attack the children. The children would scream, run inside the garage, and lower the door for safety. But this time, little Zorro charged the three black dogs. They ran on top of him. In the resulting scuffle, one jumped up in the air as blood came from its mouth: it had tried to bite the little ball whose sharp needles penetrated its mouth. The wounded dog barked painfully and ran back over the stone fence, followed by the other two frightened Dobermans. They never attacked or scared my children after that.

Another of Zorro's heroic acts stemmed from the fact that he continued not to touch the milk or eat cat food. Instead, he ate the mice, and being immune to any venom, he also ate the little snakes and skinks living in the bushes around the foundation of the house. He also ate the slimy snails and worms that crawled all over the yard. When all those creepy creatures were out at night, the nocturnal Zorro refused to be trapped in the garage. When he was in the garage or basement, he got rid of all the insects that no spray could fully eliminate.

At night, he patrolled the entire property and went to the neighbors' yards to the left and right. The neighbors acknowledged his efforts and were quite pleased with Zorro the exterminator's free services. They wanted to compensate our little hero with milk in dishes they left out for him. But Zorro did not touch their offerings since hedgehogs are lactose intolerant. When Zorro slept, he rolled up into a ball, like a solitary knight in his fortified castle.

What was best about Zorro was that the children, who would have loved to sleep with him (like others do with their cats and dogs), could not do so because he would curl into a ball, and his sharp armor would be very harmful. In other words, there was no way for my children to abuse or mishandle their pet. However, Zorro loved to be picked up and gently scratched or pet on the fine fur on his chest and belly while he purred contentedly like a cat. That was a convenient time to puff some anti-flea or lice powder onto him to keep him clean and healthy.

The over-friendly Zorro became a problem whenever I had to back the car out from the garage since he always came to greet me. I often had to stop and look around and under the car to make sure I did not kill the little hedgehog. Because he was so active at night, in the evenings, I had to use a flashlight to search for him before I could move my car.

The relationship between the cute hedgehog and the children grew each day, and they became so close that Zorro would run from our property to the street corner, some 100 yards away, to greet them when they came home from school since he could detect the sound of the school bus. The children on the bus would scream with excitement at seeing Zorro, while my three children would run off the bus joyfully shouting, "Zorro, Zorro, Zorro," pick him up, cradle him in their hands and bring him home. The routine became dangerous as the little thing running in the middle of the road to meet the bus could easily be run over by a car. I put up HEDGEHOG CROSSING signs.

Zorro became quite popular. My children took him to their baseball and soccer games so he could see them playing. Everybody wanted to look at and hold the unusual animal. My children were invited to play dates with the mention of bringing Zorro along, and soon, they were nicknamed "the Zorro children." Their teachers asked them to bring Zorro for show and tell, and before I knew it, Zorro was sleeping in his wire cage inside the school. I had to go and rescue him. He obviously could not have realized the potential danger he might face there.

Our Zorro made my children, and even me, popular in our small town.

***

All was good and memorable until one day in October, Zorro vanished, never to return to our home. The children desperately searched for a mile around to find him—dead or alive. They cried because they wanted Zorro back so badly. I went to the pet shop to try to buy a similar-looking hedgehog, but none were available.

Then I announced to the tearful children that somebody had seen Zorro, who had found a Mrs. Zorro, and he had moved to her home to live happily ever after with her. They loved the story and told everybody that next year, Mr. and Mrs. Zorro would come with their children to visit us.

And that is the story of how I provided my children with a pet like none other, one they would never forget.

$

25. ONLY IN AMERICA

Sometimes, I wonder why some of the most famous American personalities are vigilante cowboys, bank robbers, criminals and gangsters who, from zero, dared to become heroes. I think of those like Carnegie and Vanderbilt, who built mighty industries; Ben Franklin, the founding father of early Americanism; Edison and Henry Ford, the giant industrialists; and the writer Mark Twain. All had no formal education, including Presidents Washington and Lincoln, and all are iconic. I think of the outstanding generals Ulysses S. Grant, who united all the American states by force of arms, and George Patton, the liberator of Europe. Both changed the world, and both died under the most dreadful circumstances. I consider those achievers American heroes.

All the above is said as a comparison in greatness. At a more ordinary level, things that no history books will ever mention happen, but it is all a part of the fiber that makes up American society. Most importantly, real happenings are better than any written fiction or moralizing movie made in Hollywood.

Here is a short story that I did not want to embellish with any of my usual appealing charm or wit. I title it "The Lost Earring."

***

Jane was driving from Florida to Kentucky. While approaching Louisville, she stopped at a rest area to stretch her legs and freshen up. When she walked into the restroom and looked in the mirror to brush her hair, she admired her beautiful gold earrings. Her fiancé had given them to her; they had belonged to his late mother. When Jane arrived in Louisville to meet John, she again stopped to comb her hair and discovered one earring was missing. Due to the sentimental significance and value of the precious gift, she panicked.

She immediately began searching inside her car—on the seat, under the seat, and all over the rest of the interior. She checked her purse, pockets, and luggage. She searched over and over again but with no luck. She called the Kentucky Highway Department's Information Center to find out the exit number of the rest stop she had used and their direct telephone number. Immediately, she called that rest area. She described the gold earring to the Lost and Found office employee. Happily, the answer was that, indeed, a traveler found it and turned it in. Jane promised to come the next morning and pick it up at that rest area.

***

Jane arrived at the rest area office. She was in shock when she learned that an employee had taken the earring home for safe-keeping. But the employee had not come to work that day. Jane asked the clerk to call the employee at home to return the earring.

Two days later, Jane and John drove one hour from Louisville to the rest area, where the lost and found employee handed Jane the much-missed golden earring.

Considering that hundreds of people must have walked by wherever that earring had fallen in the rest area (on the cement sidewalk or the floor of whatever room inside the building) and that one person picked up the golden treasure, the odds of it being returned to the rightful owner were astronomical. Yet, the one anonymous person who could have kept it did not.

In what other country could this anecdote happen with the same happy ending? It proves an undeniable reality: most Americans are honest and compassionate. They are ready to help others. In that manner, they formed a most civilized society, in spite of much criticism from the rest of the world.

$$\blacksquare \$ \blacksquare$$

THE END